DATE DUE

DEC 1 '00			

DEMCO 38-296

CONSUMER BEHAVIOR IN ASIA

Consumer Behavior in Asia

Hellmut Schütte
with
Deanna Ciarlante

NEW YORK UNIVERSITY PRESS
Washington Square, New York

or recycling and
1 forest sources.

Library of Congress Cataloging-in-Publication Data
Schütte, Hellmut.
Consumer behavior in Asia / Hellmut Schütte with Deanna Ciarlante.
p. cm.
Includes bibliographical references and index.
ISBN 0–8147–8114–4
1. Consumer behavior—Asia.   2. Market segmentation—Asia.
3. Market surveys—Asia.   4. Marketing—Asia.   5. Consumers—Asia–
–Attitudes.   I. Ciarlante, Deanna.   II. Title.
HF5415.33.A78S38   1998
658.8'342'095—dc21   98–18783
                                                                    CIP

Printed in Great Britain

Contents

List of Figures

List of Tables

List of Abbreviations and Acronyms

AFTA	ASEAN Free Trade Area
APEC	Asia Pacific Economic Cooperation
ASEAN	Association of South East Asian Nations
ASEANIEs	ASEAN and NIEs
CNN	Cable Network News
DC	developed country
FIFA	Federation of International Football Associations
GIA	Gemstone Industry Association
GM	gentil membre
GO	gentil organisateur
JFA	Football Association of Japan
JSL	Japan Soccer League
LDC	less developed country
LSRSL	Large Scale Retail Stores Law
MLS	Major League Soccer
NIE	newly industrialised economy
OL	office lady
R&D	research and development
WTO	World Trade Organisation

Acknowledgements

When I went from Europe to Indonesia in 1972 to work as a young executive for a large multinational company in the field of marketing, I found myself in a different world wondering whether the accepted ideas, concepts and practices in Western markets were also true to Asia.

Ever since, and even more so since I joined the academic world in 1981, I have probed the assumption underlying the belief in the existence of a global consumer. During all those years, half of them spent in Asia and half in Europe and the USA, I met with a large number of executives, academics, researchers, students and, of course, ordinary consumers and tried to explore with them the differences and similarities between Asian and Western consumers. I owe my gratitude to all those who gave me some insight.

It was in the 1990s that I began to research the issue of consumer behaviour in greater depth, launching a number of research projects. With Valerie Vanier, who had just returned from a posting as marketing executive in Hong Kong, I produced the first working paper. This was broadened considerably with the help of Renita Kalhorn, whose previous career included giving music lessons to the Japanese community in Tokyo. I then explored the variations of consumer behaviour in China with Poy-Seng Ching, a Malaysian who now lives in Beijing. With Peter Yoo, I looked at leisure behaviour in Asia, from the eyes of a Korean who had appreciated life in California before joining us, as the others had, here in Fontainebleau, France.

Subsequently, I began working with my co-author Deanna Ciarlante, who had been partly educated in Japan, had obtained her MBA from INSEAD, as had Renita and Peter, and who shared the same interest in probing the universality of existing theories and practices. It was her input and hard work which finally enabled us to put our ideas into a book format.

Jocelyn Probert, Research Analyst at INSEAD's Euro-Asia Centre, frequently acted as a sounding board and final controller. Her in-depth knowledge of Asia made her critical comments highly valuable. Mary Boldrini provided reliable back-up support from the library. Without Katie Taylor, my secretary, nothing would have worked. While I was constantly

travelling in Asia, she kept the project moving and ensured that no dead-
lines were missed.

To all of those named, I am deeply indebted. The financial support from
INSEAD's R&D funds is also acknowledged.

H. SCHÜTTE
FONTAINEBLEAU
Summer 1998

The author and publisher wish to thank the following for permission to
use copyright material: The World Resources Institute for Table 6.1; The
Free Press, a division of Simon & Schuster, for Figure 3.1 which is
reprinted from *Diffusion of Innovations*, 4th edn, Everett M. Rogers. Copyright © 1995 by Everett M. Rogers. Copyright © 1962, 1971, 1983 by
The Free Press.

Every effort has been made to contact all copyright holders but if any have
been inadvertently omitted the publisher will be pleased to make the necessary arrangement at the earliest opportunity.

An Alternative Consumer Behaviour Theory for Asia

Introduction and structure of the book

In recent decades, Asia has been home to many of the world's most dynamic markets. The region now represents 25 per cent of the world economy and about 50 per cent of the world's population. It is for this reason that few international companies can afford to ignore Asia as a market of primary importance, despite the crisis which hit parts of the region in 1997/98. Western firms without a presence in the region often fail to perceive the opportunities they miss in Asia to generate sales and profits or acquire experience, although their very absence represents the most substantial competitive threat to their future in the long run.

In light of the importance of Asia as a market, there is a surprising paucity of work that establishes a marketing theory specific to Asia. The vast majority of consumer behaviour, marketing and management texts are written by Westerners, with a distinctly Western (and primarily American) perspective. As the birthplace of modern management theory, the USA has been the world's largest producer and exporter of organisational theory in such areas as motivation, leadership and organisation. Certainly, such theory contains biases reflective of the culture and time from which it emerges.

In the case of consumer behaviour, few would argue with the view that Asian consumers do appear to be distinctively different from Western consumers. Thus far, however, very little thought has been given to rethinking the theories, underlying models, concepts and views of Asian consumer segmentation, the motives of Asian consumers and how they behave. Lee and Green note the need for cross-national validation studies of consumer behaviour theory and 'the tendency for consumer researchers to implicitly or explicitly assume that models of consumer behaviour developed on American consumers are universally applicable, without testing the underlying model assumptions or the model linkages'.[1] Additionally, Lee and Green point out that nearly all psychological theories are of Western derivation and that very few attempts have been made to validate any of them in non-Western cultures.

The cross-cultural transposability of consumer behaviour theories must therefore be questioned. It is not because these theories are cross-culturally invalid; indeed, there is much in common. However, if the objective is truly to understand consumers in order to maximise marketing success, it is imperative to ascertain whether concepts of consumer behaviour currently in use have relevance to the Asian consumer. Western firms attempting to market to Asian consumers must fundamentally re-evaluate their approaches if they are to ensure the suitability of their proposition in the context of the Asian consumer. This suggests that adapting a firm's marketing approach based on a thorough understanding of Asian consumer behaviour is more fundamental than simply developing tastes such as green tea ice cream (Häagen-Dazs) or mayonnaise and potato *mayo-jaga* pizza (Domino's) in Japan and seafood-flavoured Cheeto's in China.[2] While such modifications of products to the local context are to be applauded, we can go much further.

In conducting the research for this book, we have been faced with the reality that the literature we deemed accurate and relevant to the topic was far richer on Chinese and Japanese consumer behaviour than on that of other Asian consumers. We did not consider this a reason to prevent us from discussing an alternative consumer behaviour theory for Asian consumers, for it is not our intention to present a catalogue of consumer behaviour practices in all Asian countries. Instead, this book is intended to illustrate how, on many fundamental dimensions, Asian culture is different from Western culture, and it is this which makes the need to rethink consumer behaviour theory and models in an Asian context a necessity. We illustrate these differences with reference to many Asian cultures. The majority of our examples of cultural characteristics, value orientations and consumer behaviour are, however, drawn from the Japanese and Chinese cultural context.

We also faced the challenge of avoiding the stereotyping of cultures. When we discuss the behaviour and psychology of the individuals of a culture, we are aware that variations between individuals certainly exist and that cultures are rapidly changing. Individuals originating from the same societies and cultures do, however, have a tendency to exhibit similar behaviour and share similar ways of thinking. We take the position of Befu, who explained:

> It may be impossible to eliminate stereotyping altogether even from scientific discourse. The question is, therefore, how to use stereotypes and how to inter-pret them when used by others. That Americans believe in free will, for example, does not mean that they will exercise it all the time or that their actions are based exclusively on it. Similarly, the truism that the Japanese are group

oriented does not mean that all Japanese are; or that group orientation is the only form of relating Japanese recognise.[3]

In this first chapter, we state and support our basic argument that Asian consumer behaviour is distinctively different from non-Asian, specifically Western, consumer behaviour. This is followed in Chapter 2 by a look at Asian culture. We outline the differences between Asian and Western cultures along the underlying cultural dimensions such as religion, tradition and philosophy, and explain the effect of such differences on aspects relevant to consumer behaviour, for example the concept of self and interpersonal relationships. In Chapter 3, the impact of culture on the individual consumer in Asia is explored in terms of communication styles, and perceptions of and attitudes towards products offered. In Chapter 4, the applicability of existing consumer behaviour models and theory is evaluated in the Asian cultural context, and we suggest modifications to many well-known consumer behaviour concepts.

In Chapter 5, the leisure industry offers an active example of the concepts we develop. Chapter 6 provides a practitioner's guide to marketing in Asia and outlines the implications of Asian consumer behaviour on segmentation, positioning and branding, while shedding some light on the implications for marketing research in Asia. Chapter 7 further elaborates the need for adjustment or the development of an alternative marketing mix for Asia.

In Chapter 8, we discuss the current move towards globalisation and its implications for consumer behaviour. We conclude that we are moving towards a more modern, but not necessarily a more Western, world. A world of more modern cultures does not necessarily mean a more homogenous world. Cultures will respond differently to the process of modernisation and will remain unique. Consumption even of identical products in different parts of the world does not indicate a sameness of cultures. Consumers will continue to be influenced by their unique cultures and thus consumer behaviour will continue to vary cross-culturally.

Consumer behaviour in Asia: premises

Cross-cultural perspectives in consumer behaviour theory

Our first task is to make the case that a separate consumer behaviour theory is necessary accurately to describe the behaviour of Asian consumers. To do so, we must first establish the following two premises:

1. Consumer behaviour is strongly influenced by culture.
2. Asian culture is distinctly different from Western culture.

We can then conclude that a consumer behaviour theory specific to Asian consumers is a necessity for any firm seeking to market products successfully to Asian consumers.

To argue for a distinct consumer behaviour theory to explain the behaviour of Asian consumers puts us in the camp of the 'cultural meaning' theorists. There are, in fact, a variety of perspectives concerning cross-cultural consumer behaviour theory. Currently, the four main approaches to cross-cultural consumer behaviour theory are: (1) the global perspective, (2) the 'imported' perspective, (3) the ethnic consumption perspective, and (4) the cultural meaning perspective (Table 1.1).[4]

Table 1.1   Cross-cultural perspectives in consumer behaviour theory

Consumers	Consumer Behaviour Theories	
	Universal	Specific
UNIVERSAL	1. GLOBAL PERSPECTIVE • Consumers are global in preferences and behaviour → CB theories are globally applicable	3. ETHNIC CONSUMPTION PERSPECTIVE • Although consumers are global in preferences for certain products, they differ in behaviour → CB theories are not globally applicable
SPECIFIC	2. 'IMPORTED' PERSPECTIVE • Consumers differ in preferences but are global in behaviour → CB theories are globally applicable	4. CULTURAL MEANING PERSPECTIVE • Consumers differ in preferences and behaviour → CB theories are not globally applicable

Note: CB = consumer behaviour.

The *global perspective* is rarely used today in its purest form. It continues to be applied in situations where consumers are considered actually to be 'global' (for example, international business people) but is most appropriate in the case of high-technology products that tend to lack a predefined culturally based meaning for consumers (for example, fax machines). As many companies face pressure to rationalise costs, they seek to standardise processes such as manufacturing, marketing and distribution. There has thus been renewed interest in creating 'global' products. Ford's introduction of the Mondeo in European markets, the platform of which is identical to the Contour and Mystique, is one such example. There is wide agreement, however, that for many product/service categories consumption is distinctly 'culture bound', thus preventing the existence of a 'global' consumer. As Usunier notes, 'The globalisation process is pushed on consumers rather than pulled by them.'[5]

In the *'imported' perspective*, consumers are considered to vary in the types of product that they prefer but to conform generally to the same patterns of behaviour. Thus consumer behaviour theories that have been developed and established in the West are considered applicable to other markets, but products are modified to suit the local marketing context. As Van Raaij notes, while such an approach may accommodate some differences in consumer behaviour, a far superior approach would be for 'researchers in other cultures to study their own reality rather than to replicate American studies'.[6]

The *ethnic consumption perspective* takes into account the effect of culture on consumer behaviour. Consumers of different cultures are considered to behave differently. However, there are certain products that are global in their appeal. Consumers can, therefore, be global in their preferences. At the same time, their national consumer behaviour can be influenced by the importation and diffusion of immigrants' culturally based values, behaviours and products. One example would be the influence of Latin culture on the consumption patterns of the average resident of South Florida. Surrounding communities pick up elements of the immigrant culture so that many products eventually have wider appeal than merely among the importing cultural group.

The *cultural meaning perspective* holds that consumers are cross-culturally different in both their preferences for products and their behaviour. An individual's motivation to consume is due not merely to the product's specific attributes, but also to the culturally based meanings that are embodied in the product and the consumption act. Although a product may sell in the USA as well as in Japan, the reasons for the product's popularity may be completely different because of the difference in cultural context. A Prada handbag may be bought to set the American individual apart as wealthy and successful. The same handbag may be bought by the Japanese consumer to conform with her peer group rather than to set herself apart. Understanding such meanings in each cultural context can greatly aid marketers in communicating appropriate messages to the consumer in an effective manner.

In this book, we will adopt the cultural meaning perspective. Since this theoretical approach rests on the importance of culture, we must first establish the influence of culture on consumer behaviour. The concept of 'culture' is vast and therefore difficult to define concretely. Of the many possibilities, two definitions are particularly suited to the meaning of 'culture' in the context of this book:

> [Culture is] the configuration of learned behaviour and results of behaviour whose component elements are shared and transmitted by the members of a particular society. (Linton, 1945)[7]

> [Culture is] transmitted and created content and patterns of values, ideas, and other symbolic-meaningful systems as factors in the shaping of human behaviour and the artefacts produced through behaviour. (Kroeber and Parsons, 1958)[8]

Together these definitions stress two important aspects of culture: (1) culture is *shared* by the members of a given society, and (2) culture is, by its very nature, dynamic and transmissible. Usunier emphasises this dynamic aspect of culture as well as the problem-solving aspect: 'It is almost unthinkable that a culture could stand perfectly still... Other sources of culture intervene, as a result of which new solutions are used for tackling existing issues or for solving entirely new problems.'[9] Nationality is one source of culture but often not the main one. Other sources of culture include language, political system, education, profession, group (ethnicity), religion, family, gender, social class and corporate or organisational culture.[10]

There is wide agreement among consumer behaviour scholars that culture creates behavioural norms and that therefore a very significant link exists between culture and consumer behaviour. Knowledge of cultural context allows one to predict, to some extent, the actions of those people in that culture.[11] Without cultural understanding, marketing managers cannot correctly anticipate consumers' reactions to decisions regarding every element of the marketing mix, including, for example, advertising, positioning and product features. Sheth and Sethi further add, 'an understanding of the process and conditions by which different cultures move on the continuum can help in understanding and predicting the circumstances under which a given product or idea tends to be accepted in society'.[12] Thus, we make our first premise:

PREMISE 1:   *Consumer behaviour is strongly influenced by culture.*

Culture is the sum of learned beliefs, values and customs that create behavioural norms for a given society.[13] Beliefs refer to the accumulated feelings and priorities that individuals have about 'things' and possessions. Values are situation non-specific, serving as guides for culturally appropriate behaviour widely accepted by the members of a particular society. Customs, on the other hand, are overt modes of behaviour that constitute culturally approved ways of behaving in specific situations.[14] These elements of culture can be organised into three levels: (1) behavioural practices, (2) values, beliefs, preferences and norms, and (3) basic assumptions (Figure 1.1).

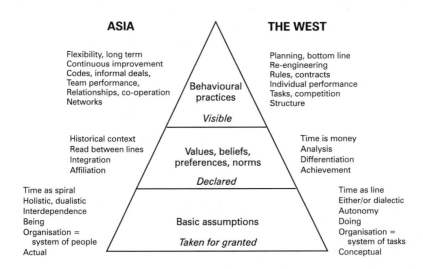

Figure 1.1   Three levels of culture

This structure implies that behavioural practices – the most visible aspect of culture – are only the tip of the iceberg. To gain a firm understanding of the source of cross-cultural differences in consumer behaviour, one must venture below the surface to examine not only a society's declared values and beliefs, but also the basic assumptions taken for granted by that society's members.

Dimensions of cultural values

Hofstede identified four underlying dimensions of cultural values: (1) power distance, (2) uncertainty avoidance, (3) individualism/collectivism, and (4) masculinity/femininity (Table 1.2).[15] The position of a certain culture along these four dimensions determines what are considered to be culturally appropriate interaction models in particular societies. Although these dimensions were originally measured for management and organisation practices, they are also applicable to marketing and sales, and have been used extensively in cross-cultural studies in international marketing.

Table 1.2   Hofstede's underlying dimensions of cultural values

Cultural Dimension	Basic Issue	Contrasts Across Cultures	Examples
1. Power distance	Does society value equality or inequality in interpersonal interactions?	⇨ LOW POWER DISTANCE ⇨ Power is relatively equally distributed	West
		⇨ HIGH POWER DISTANCE ⇨ Hierarchy is strong and power is centralised at the top	Asia
2. Uncertainty avoidance	What is the attitude towards risk in society?	⇨ LOW UNCERTAINTY AVOIDANCE ⇨ Calculated risk is seen as necessary in order to seize opportunity	Singapore/ Hong Kong/ Sweden/USA
		⇨ HIGH UNCERTAINTY AVOIDANCE ⇨ Risk is regarded as threatening and to be avoided	Portugal/ Japan/ France/ South Korea
3. Individualism/ collectivism	Do people rely on themselves or others (that is the group)?	⇨ INDIVIDUALIST ⇨ Self-reliance is valued, as is the need for the individual to satisfy his own needs within the group	West
		⇨ COLLECTIVISTIC ⇨ Dependence is valued and society expects the individual to subordinate his own needs to those of the group	Asia
4. Masculinity/ femininity	To what extent and at whose expense should the weaker members of society be cared for?	⇨ FEMININE ⇨ Caring for others and nurturing roles and attitudes are favoured	Scandinavia/ Thailand/ Netherlands
		⇨ MASCULINE ⇨ Personal achievement and assertiveness are favoured	Japan/ Switzerland/ Great Britain

Power distance measures the extent to which a society tolerates inequality of power in organisations and in society. In a high power distance society, hierarchy is strong and power is centralised at the top. Individuals are very conscious of their rank, and superiors and subordinates feel separate from one another. Korea is an example of a high power distance society. In a low power distance society, members of an organisation feel relatively close to one another and have a sense of equality as human beings. Sweden is an example of a low power distance society.

Uncertainty avoidance reflects a culture's tolerance or intolerance of uncertainty. In a high uncertainty avoidance culture, uncertain, ambiguous, risky or undefined situations are viewed as threatening and to be avoided at all costs. In order to avoid uncertainty, rules and procedures are clearly established. In a low uncertainty avoidance culture, risk is regarded as a natural component of life that can often produce opportunity. Because individuals are the engines of change, they must take risks, the downside of which can be evaluated and managed. France and Japan rank high on uncertainty avoidance, whereas Singapore and Denmark rank low on this dimension.

The *individualism/collectivism* dimension encompasses the way in which the self and others are regarded as well as the interaction between them. It reflects the extent to which a society regards the individual as its most fundamental component and the degree of acceptance of an individual's satisfaction of his or her own needs within collective groups. Collectivist societies consider not the individual, but the group, to be the most fundamental component of society. In such societies, the individual's rights are secondary to those of the group. China is an example of a collectivist society, while the USA epitomises a society strongly characterised by individualism.

The *masculinity/femininity* dimension of Hofstede's framework reflects the extent to which the society is dominated by 'masculine' characteristics (for example, assertiveness, performance, ostentation and self-concern) or 'feminine' characteristics (for example, nurturing, interdependence between people and caring for others). The masculinity dimension has been named this way since tests revealed that men tended to score highly on one extreme and women on the other, no matter which society they came from. The basic difference between feminine and masculine cultures is their response to the question 'To what extent and at whose expense should the weaker people of a society be helped?' Using this definition, northern European countries could be regarded as typically 'feminine' societies, while Japan and the USA could be termed typically 'masculine' societies.

There is great variation between both Western and Asian cultures along two of Hofstede's cultural dimensions: uncertainty avoidance and masculinity/femininity. However, as the later chapters of this book will

illustrate, along the dimensions of power distance and individualism/
collectivism, Asian cultures tend to lie at one end of the spectrum, while
Western cultures are gathered at the other. While there is certainly great
variation between the individual Asian cultures themselves, the similarities
between Asian cultures along these dimensions and their contrast with
Western cultures lead us to conclude that 'Asian' culture is indeed fundamentally different from 'Western' culture.

PREMISE 2: *Asian culture is different from Western culture.*

Trompenaars further affirms this interpretation through his five value
orientations of how we relate to other people (Table 1.3). These are: (1)
universalism versus particularism, (2) individualism versus collectivism,
(3) neutral versus affective, (4) diffuse versus specific, and (5) achievement
versus ascription.[16] A given culture will tend to lie along one direction of
each of these dimensions. In a similar way to Hofstede's underlying
dimensions of cultural values, the relative position of individuals along
Trompenaars' dimensions indicates the beliefs and behaviour that guide
those individuals through life.

Table 1.3   Trompenaars' five value orientations

Value Orientation		Example
1. *Universalism*	: Rules-based behaviour	Germanic countries
versus		
Particularism	: Relationship-based behaviour	Asian countries
2. *Individualism*	: Individual's rights are supreme	Western countries
versus		
Collectivism	: Group's rights are supreme	Asian countries
3. *Neutral*	: Emotions are subdued and expressed indirectly	Asian countries
versus		
Affective	: Emotions are expressed freely and directly	Western countries
4. *Diffuse*	: Focus is on the context of the situation	Asian countries
versus		
Specific	: Focus is on specific issues	Germanic countries
5. *Achievement*	: Status and respect are achieved by 'doing'	Western countries
versus		
Ascription	: Status and respect are ascribed by 'being'	Asian countries

The *universalism/particularism* dimension refers to the extent to which behaviour in a society is largely rules based or, alternatively, relationship based. In other words, a universalist society focuses on the need to apply established rules to all persons equally and resists making exceptions to the rules. A particularist society, meanwhile, will focus on the exceptional nature of the present circumstance and the need to value human relationships above the requirement to obey established rules. Switzerland and Germany are examples of universalist societies, while many Latin American societies would be particularist societies. It is important to note that a society may be universalist in some respects and particularist in others depending on the rules in question.

Trompenaars' *individualism/collectivism* dimension is similar to that of Hofstede's. However, his *neutral/affective* dimension introduces an additional component to the framework of value orientation, the level of emotional expressiveness. In a neutral society, feelings are carefully controlled and subdued, and responses are generally directed in an *indirect* way. Japan is an example of a neutral culture in which the language itself allows for extreme ambiguity and the avoidance of direct responses. In an affective society, a far fuller range of emotions may be expressed. A *direct* response is expected and appreciated, and any attempt to respond indirectly is regarded with suspicion. The Italians and French are examples of affective societies characterised by a high level of emotional expression.

Cultures along the *diffuse/specific* dimension have also been termed low context/high context societies. In low context cultures, people tend to focus on the specific issues at hand and regard their counterparts as having a specific role in a given situation. A person coming from a low context culture will feel the necessity to 'get down to business' and 'focus on the issues'. In high context cultures, people generally address broader issues and regard their counterparts in a more diffuse context than that of the specific situation. In such societies, relationship-building is of prime importance. Time spent getting to know counterparts is not considered 'wasted', as it would be by someone from a low context culture, but as an integral issue in fulfilling long-term objectives. Knowing one's counterpart fully from the start will avoid the risk of unfortunate surprises later on. Middle-Eastern and Asian societies are typically characterised as diffuse cultures, while American and Scandinavian cultures for the most part focus on the specifics.

In low context cultures, title and rank are regarded as specific to the situation. Thus your boss may be your superior in the office but you may be his superior on the golf course. In such cultures, relationships between superiors and subordinates tend to be more casual than in a diffuse culture where your boss is your superior in the office and on the golf course, no matter how much better you are at golf.

Another feature of this diffuse/specific dimension is the difference in the types and levels of depth of friendships in each society. Americans are often criticised by others as being 'superficial' and perhaps 'insincere' because they are often immediately friendly even to those they do not know well but then do not develop such friendships beyond a certain level. As Trompenaars points out, this is due to the fact that members of specific cultures like Americans have relatively small areas of private space and large areas of public space (Figure 1.2).

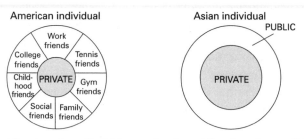

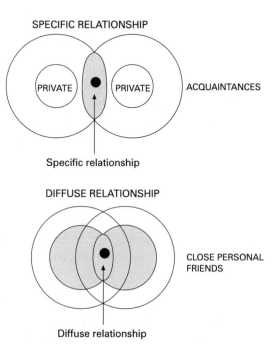

Figure 1.2   Relationship models[17]

However, this public space is divided into different domains. For example, a friend may be a 'golf friend' or a 'work friend', but that does not mean that the friendship will carry into the other domains of the individual's life. In a diffuse culture, the private area is relatively large, while the public area is small. This limited amount of public space means that relatively superficial friendships are not readily formed. Instead, friendships take a long time to develop and occur less frequently. Once firmly established, however, a diffuse culture friend can freely enter all domains of one's private space.

The *achievement/ascription* dimension refers to how status is accorded in a society. Societies in which members gain status through what has been individually achieved are achievement orientated. Those societies in which status is gained through the individual's family status, gender, age, education, social status and so on are ascription orientated. This dimension has much in common with the classification of 'doing' and 'being' cultures, and is closely linked to religious belief. For example, the Protestant religion puts great emphasis on the power of the individual to achieve and thus pushes the individual towards doing, acting and being efficient in order to achieve self-respect and the respect of others. Many Asian cultures, on the other hand, are greatly influenced by Buddhism, which regards life as more of a cyclical phenomenon than a 'one-shot' deal. Emphasis is placed more on 'being' virtuous rather than, on 'doing' things in order to achieve virtue.

The later chapters of this book will illustrate the extent to which, in terms of power distance and individualism/collectivism, the cultures of Asia tend to lie at opposite ends of the spectrum from the cultures of the West – the very cultures which form the basis for most of the existing body of consumer behaviour literature and theory. We will also look at how the uncertainty avoidance and masculinity/femininity dimensions are characterised among Asian cultures and their subsequent impact on Asian consumer behaviour. If consumer behaviour is indeed influenced by culture and Asian culture is fundamentally different from Western culture, then it follows that:

CONCLUSION: *Asian consumer behaviour is different.*

If we assume that a sound understanding of the consumer behaviour of a specific market is necessary to develop a successful marketing mix, the necessity of an alternative theory of consumer behaviour for Asia should be obvious. No longer should it be the case that, as has been noted else-where, 'Consumer behaviour is largely "made in the USA" with all the risks that Western, American or middle-class biases pervade this type of research in the questions we address, the concepts and theories we use and inter-pretations we give.'[18] This book is but one step in the process of develop-ing that alternative theory.

'Asian' culture and values and 'Asian' consumer behaviour

In discussing Asian culture and its subsequent effect on consumer behav-iour, we make two assumptions. First, we argue that, despite the multi-plicity of cultures in Asia, there are many characteristics that are more or less common across many Asian cultures. Examples are the importance of the family, group orientation and the issue of face, all of which have an impact on consumer behaviour. Second, we argue that the cultures found in Asia are to some extent specific to the region and are therefore different from those in the rest of the world, particularly the West.

These two assumptions of similarities within Asia and differences from others justify the use of the terms 'Asian culture' and 'Asian consumer behaviour'. They in no way deny the existence of cultural heterogeneity in the region, but they do imply that the differences within Asia are less significant than the differences from the world outside Asia.

Two contradictory trends underline our assumptions. On the one hand, the rapid economic growth of the region's economies over the past few years has led to significant changes in values and social structures. These have in turn led to greater diversification of consumer behaviour *within* each individual country. At the same time, growing similarities of lifestyles and tastes *across* borders among certain segments of the population result in almost identical conspicuous consumption habits across the region. The immense popularity of Western luxury goods among high-income earners and teenagers in Asia is, however, not proof that they have joined the global bandwagon. They may try the same goods but for different reasons. For example, brand-name goods may be bought more for 'face' reasons and the importance of the regard of others rather than because of an indi-vidual preference for the product.

The term 'Asian values' has been popularised by Singapore's articulate former prime minister, Lee Kuan Yew, who is fond of attributing the economic success of his country and the other tigers of Asia to 'Asian values' such as 'learning and scholarship and hard work and thrift and deferment of present enjoyment for future gain'.[19] This definition is not what we mean in the context of this book when we discuss Asian culture and values, for these may not be orientations exclusive to Asian cultures. Instead, the attributes to which Mr Lee refers are features of many traditional societies. As such societies progressively feel the impact of economic growth, technological change and social transformation, these values will also undergo change. No culture is static. As Oliver Goldsmith wrote in 1770, 'Wealth accumulates and men decay.'

This is not to say that tomorrow's Asia will resemble today's West. Indeed, many of what we term 'Asian' cultural characteristics and values are based on a system of clear and consistent rules and procedures that have endured for many generations. The foundations of Asian cultures such as Confucianism, Buddhism and Islam have developed over thousands of years and will not be discarded easily in favour of Ronald McDonald and Mickey Mouse.

Notes

1. Lee, C. and Green, R.T. (1991) 'Cross-cultural examination of the Fishbein behavioural intentions model', *Journal of International Business Studies,* **22**(2): 290.
2. 'Custom-made', *Asian Wall Street Journal,* 30 September 1996: 24.
3. Cited in Johnson, F.A. (1993) *Dependency and Japanese Socialization,* New York: New York University Press, p. 215.
4. Usunier, J. (1996) *Marketing Across Cultures,* Hertfordshire: Prentice-Hall, p. 107.
5. Usunier, J. (1996) *Marketing Across Cultures,* Hertfordshire: Prentice-Hall, p. 182.
6. Van Raaij, W.F. (1978) 'Cross-cultural methodology as a case of construct validity', in Hunt M.K. (ed.) *Advances in Consumer Research,* V, Ann Arbor: Association for Consumer Research, p. 699.
7. Linton, R. (1945) *The Cultural Background of Personality,* New York: Appleton-Century-Crofts, p. 32.
8. Kroeber, A.L. and Parsons, T. (1958) 'The concept of culture and social system', *American Psychological Review,* **23**: 582–3.
9. Usunier, J. (1996) *Marketing Across Cultures,* Hertfordshire: Prentice-Hall, p. 28.
10. Usunier, J. (1996) *Marketing Across Cultures,* Hertfordshire: Prentice-Hall, p. 12.
11. Markin, J. Jr (1974) *Consumer Behaviour: A Cognitive Orientation,* New York: Macmillan, p. 469.
12. Sheth, J.N. and Sethi, S.P. (1977) 'A theory of cross-cultural buyer behaviour', in Woodise, A.G., Sheth, J.N., and Bennett, P.D. (eds) *Consumer and Industrial Buyer Behaviour,* New York: North-Holland, pp. 369–86.
13. Yau, O.H.M. (1994) *Consumer Behaviour in China,* London: Routledge, p. 49.
14. Kotler, P. (1994) *Marketing Management,* 8th edn, Englewood Cliffs, NJ: Prentice-Hall, p. 174.
15. Hofstede, G. (1984) *Culture's Consequences: International Differences in Work-related Values,* Beverly Hills, CA: Sage.
16. Trompenaars, F. (1993) *Riding the Waves of Culture,* London: Economist Books, p. 29.

17. Adapted from Trompenaars, F. (1993) *Riding the Waves of Culture*, London: Economist Books, p. 81.
18. Van Raaij, W.F. (1978) 'Cross-cultural methodology as a case of construct validity', in Hunt, M.K. (ed.) *Advances in Consumer Research*, V, Ann Arbor: Association for Consumer Research, p. 699.
19. Zakaria, F. (1994) 'Culture is destiny: a conversation with Lee Kuan Yew', *Foreign Affairs*, 73(2): 116–17.

2 Distinguishing Features of Asian Culture

Before proceeding with a discussion of Asian consumer behaviour, it is necessary to have a basic understanding of those cultural characteristics which are specific to Asia and which result in a pattern of consumer behaviour fundamentally different from that found in the West. In this chapter, we will look at Asian religions, concept of self, others and the collective group, roles and status, and family dynamics in order to understand how Asian culture differs from that of the West, particularly along Hofstede's cultural dimensions and Trompenaars' value orientations.

Religious traditions and philosophies

Religion influences how an individual conceives his purpose in life and what he regards as his responsibilities to himself, others and his god. Religion can form the basis of how an individual chooses to lead his life. As such, religion has a profound impact on culture, particularly in traditional societies. In this section, we will look at the influence that some of the major religions in Asia have on Asian culture.

Confucianism

A traditional starting point for understanding Asian culture is the work of the philosopher Confucius, who lived about 2,500 years ago. His teachings form the fundamental cultural underpinnings of many Asian societies, East Asian societies in particular. Born in feudal China, Confucius witnessed anarchic feudal wars destroying what had been a peaceful land in his youth. He concluded that stability was the most important goal for society and taught how it could be achieved through the correct management of interpersonal relationships and the relationship between individuals and society.

In order to rule a state, Confucius preached, one first needed to have one's house (family) in order. And in order to manage a household correctly, one needed to look continuously within oneself in search of faults that could be improved, if not corrected, through learning. One of Confucius' followers, Hsun-tzu (298-238BC), saw that conflict arising from innate bad human nature could be avoided only through education via learning the *li* (rituals and ceremonies to emphasise proper conduct according to status).[1] Confucius did not believe that man's passions and impulses must be wholly suppressed but that they should be regulated in order to achieve personal harmony. His guidelines for how to achieve such balance contribute even today to the high degree of moral self-control or self-regulation exhibited, at least in public, by the individual Chinese person.[2]

According to Confucianism, the most important virtues include: loyalty to the state or emperor, respect for elders, filial piety, faith in friendship, reciprocity in human relations, and education and cultivation. These virtues are reflected in the five cardinal relationships identified by Confucius: (1) ruler and subject, (2) father and son, (3) older brother and younger brother, (4) husband and wife, and (5) older friend and younger friend. Correct observance of these human relationships and close following of the norms prescribed for each instance of interpersonal relationships are regarded as being integral to the proper functioning of society. Some of Confucius' disciples later elevated the relationship between father and son (child) to a position above all of the others, hence the pervasiveness of the principle of filial piety in Asia today. As the old Chinese saying 'Rejoicing the hearts of parents with beans and water' illustrates, one must do one's best to please and support one's parents, even in the face of abject poverty.[3]

Regarding relationships outside the family, Confucius preached that social harmony must be maintained above all and that, to maintain harmony, the community's well-being must supersede that of the individual should the two come into conflict. When the community is a state, Confucius prescribed that the people respect and obey the ruler, who should in turn be benevolent to his subjects.

Overall, the Confucian philosophy is one of great conservatism in which emphasis is placed on maintaining the *status quo* and harmony. Confucius did not address questions of life after death or religious dogmas. Instead, he concentrated on creating a set of guidelines for living properly and harmoniously.[4] One of the consequences of Confucian dogma in China is that 'the highest value... is to live properly, which particularly concerns being polite and obeying the rules'.[5] As this philosophy encourages accepting one's position in life and not questioning authority, it sets the basis for the high power distance characteristic of Chinese culture. Additionally, the emphasis on maintaining the harmony of the group forms the foundation of the collectivism of Chinese society.

In China, Confucianism underwent great disruption during the Cultural Revolution. Communism was to form the bedrock of Chinese society, and Mao sought systematically to destroy the core of Confucianism – the family. Confucianism was severely criticised, and deeds according to the doctrine were strictly forbidden.[6] Scholars, who had traditionally enjoyed the highest status in China, were reviled as betrayers of the masses. The fact that, today in China, Confucianism is alive and well and even enjoying a newfound popularity is testimony to the durability of its principles.

First exposed to Confucianism in the 2nd century BC, the Koreans' selection for domestic use of elements from the vast repertoire of Chinese Confucianism depended on their changing perceptions of what Confucianism was and what role it should play. Koreans gradually came to view Confucianism as the fount of truth from which all civilised peoples should draw sustenance, and by about the 18th century, Korea had become a normative Confucian society. Today, Koreans are considered to be more faithful to the Confucian tradition than are the Chinese.

Confucian Asia includes primarily the Chinese world consisting of post-Maoist China, Hong Kong, Singapore and Taiwan as well as Korea and Japan. Buddhist Thailand and today's Vietnam are not part of this world, although they are strongly influenced by it through the presence of ethnic Chinese in their populations. This influence also holds true for Indonesia, Malaysia and the Philippines, although in their case Islamic or Christian values are dominant. However, an examination of these countries with non-Confucian origins reveals that they also emphasise the importance of family and exhibit strong group orientation, both cultural characteristics fundamental to Confucianism. The fact that many cultural characteristics are shared between the Asian cultures gives credence to our discussion of an 'Asian' culture.

Buddhism

Begun in north-eastern India in about 500 BC by a man who became known as the Buddha, or 'the Enlightened One', Buddhist teachings accept the impermanent nature of life and its movement according to regular patterns of cause and effect perceivable by the human mind. In the Buddha's day, Indians believed (and still do) that all animals and humans live many lifetimes, the form of each life being shaped by how one lived in the last. Buddha accepted this idea, and made it part of his *karma* system of cause and effect.[7]

Buddhism was brought to China from India some time in the 1st century AD. Although Buddhist thought was quite different from Chinese philosophy – more individualistic and psychological than the family-centred Chinese tradition, with its emphasis on agriculture, government and a long, happy life in the midst of the world – by the end of the 2nd century there were several centres of Buddhism in China, and it spread rapidly from then on.[8]

In Korea, Buddhism and various folk religions remained major forces along with Confucian philosophy, especially among women and the lower classes. Buddhism is thought to have been introduced to Japan from Korea in 552 AD, when the King of Paekche sent a mission bearing presents to the Japanese emperor. There was debate among the Japanese over whether to accept Buddhism as a religion, some arguing that the native gods of Shintoism and others would be offended by the respect shown to a foreign deity. Prince Shotoku of the imperial family, however, came up with a way to reconcile the different religions. He compared the religions of Japan to a cooking pot on a tripod, the legs of which are Confucianism, Shintoism and Buddhism: 'Let Shintoism be the trunk from which Buddhism spreads its branches, luxuriant with the etiquette of Confucianism to achieve a flourishing in the real world.'

The Japanese people thus came to follow existing Shinto rituals and to believe in Buddhism at the same time: Shintoism focused on rituals of fertility, purification, rites of passage and growth, while Buddhism concerned itself with illness, death, enlightenment and education. Even today, Japan, with a population of 125 million, is said to have 125 million Shintoists and 125 million Buddhists. Religions and ideologies are not regarded as precluding or counteracting one another; nothing is eliminated. Instead, all function together and supplement each other.

Islam in Asia

Born in Mecca in 570 AD, the prophet Mohammed founded the religion of Islam. Mohammed believed that God had revealed himself to both Christians and Jews, but they could not agree to follow God's commands or to live in unity among themselves. He asserted the necessity of going back to the original principles and the teachings of Abraham. Thus emerged Islam, a word that appears to mean resignation or submission to God. Accordingly, Islam is based upon the belief in one God whose power and knowledge are infinite. Although a beautiful paradise awaits believers and God will forgive man's lesser crimes, serious sins will meet with retribution to be feared. The believer must endure the difficulties of life in the knowledge that putting his trust in God will provide him with eventual reward.

The Koran, considered by believers to be the literal word of God, forms the basis of Islamic belief and is believed to be a transcript of a tablet preserved in heaven, in which is written all that has happened and all that will happen.[9] From the Koran arises a system of Muslim law that encompasses every aspect of life, be it ritual, personal, family, criminal or commercial. The five 'Pillars of Faith' include: (1) prayer, (2) alms-giving, (3) fasting, (4) pilgrimage, and (5) the profession of faith in God and his apostle. Although the Koran appears to require prayer only three times a day, tradition insists upon five. The amount of alms-giving, although once formalised, is now left to the conscience of the Muslim. The most significant fasting occurs at Ramadan, during which no-one may eat, drink or smoke between sunrise and sunset. As for pilgrimage, every Muslim ought to make the journey to Mecca once in his lifetime. Prohibitions include wine and pork, and idolatry is an unforgivable sin.

It is impossible to describe a coherent process of diffusion of the Islamic faith in Southeast Asia as it was 'a process that waxed and waned, that took its strength from an irregular series of pulses over centuries'.[10] Islam was introduced into Southeast Asia from the 7th century onwards, primarily by Muslim traders. A significant diffusion of Islam along the port towns began from the 11th century via Indian and Arab merchants, and proceeded into the rural periphery via the local rulers. By the 16th century, the faith had spread to such an extent that it had come to change significantly the character of Malay and Indonesian societies.[11]

Collectively, the countries of Southeast Asia make up the largest concentration of Muslims in the world,[12] with an approximate total population of more than 200 million. While Muslims form the majority in Indonesia (90 per cent of the population), Brunei (100 per cent) and Malaysia (52 per cent), they are a minority in Thailand (5 per cent), the Philippines (10 per cent) and Singapore (17 per cent).[13] In each of these countries, Islamic law forms the basis of regulation in family matters such as marriage, divorce and inheritance. However, the governments of these countries remain strongly secular (with the exception of Brunei) and, in general, the practice of Islam in Southeast Asia reveals little similarity to the far more austere Moslem regimes of the Middle East.

There has been an intensification in recent years of the practice of Islam among many Southeast Asian Muslims. As traditional village values erode through rapid urbanisation, media influence and consumerism, Islam is increasingly sought to provide order and meaning to modern life.[14] In Malaysia, the north-eastern state of Kelantan is now the first state to be controlled by Malaysia's opposition party, Parti Islam se Malaysia, the leaders of which believe that the customs of Islam and the words of the Koran are not open to modern interpretations. With this leadership, the Islamic *sharia* penal system has been introduced, under which thieves could have their right hands amputated, drinkers of alcohol could receive 60 lashes and adulterers could be stoned to death.[15] However, both governments and citizens of Muslim Southeast Asia broadly prefer the secular and tolerant Islam that can be witnessed in urban Malaysia and Indonesia today.

By and large, the Muslim societies of Southeast Asia serve as an example of how Islam can flexibly fit into modern life. In Asia, particularly in Malaysia, technological development, mass education and modernisation flourish side by side with a flowering of Islamic belief.[16] Innovative ideas have allowed strict adherence to Koranic code within the context of modernity. Banks, for example, have introduced new products to get around the Koranic prohibition on charging or receiving interest and have created 'Islamic indices' that include companies thought to be free of *haram* (un-Islamic) business practices. The Arab Malaysian Bank is marketing an Islamic credit card designed to reject charges for nightclubs, massage parlours and other proscribed activities. Should these nations prove successful in aligning modern life with the practice of the Islamic faith, they may prove a model for other Muslim nations whose development has been stunted in the name of religious adherence. Consequently, Asia could become the modern centre of Islam rather than remaining, as it has historically been, on the fringe of the Muslim world.

Folk religions in Asia

Confucianism offers a specific approach to life rather than a 'religion'. Thus it does not preclude formal religions from existing side by side with it. Folk religions existed in China, for example, and a variety of religious activities – including ancestor worship, sacrifices to spirits, belief in ghosts and demons, exorcism, divination and the use of spirit mediums – were practised by all except the strictest scholars, priests and monks.

In Japan, Shintoism is an indigenous animistic belief that forms the indirect but culturally pervasive source of many attitudes and customs that distinguish the Japanese from other peoples. Essentially a form of nature worship, Shintoism is based on cosmic harmony between the gods, the spirits, people and the physical world of nature. The Shinto concept of innumerable gods is an overlapping of a reverence for natural manifestations such as thunder, typhoons, mountains, waterfalls and large rocks with ancestor worship. There is a great emphasis in Shintoism on beginnings, growth, fertility and celebration. The New Year's festival, for example, with its themes of regeneration, purification and renewal, is celebrated in the Shinto tradition.[17]

Belief in fate

Among Asian cultures, there is a much stronger belief in fate, external forces and predetermined events compared with Western cultures. Greatly varied in origin and the means with which they are manifested across Asia, such beliefs have a profound influence on consumer behaviour.

The extent to which it is believed that man controls his own destiny is distinctly culturally determined and can be described in terms of the concept of *locus of control*. This concept refers to man's relationship with nature and fate, and is either internally or externally directed. Those individuals orientated towards an *internal locus of control* regard themselves as having control over their lives and destinies. Where man is believed to possess this potential to master his environment, success or failure in life is considered to be directly attributable to the individual. The American emphasis on individuality arises largely from the tradition of the Protestant ethic, which emphasises a personal responsibility for one's fate that can be assured only through hard work. Such faith in the power of the individual is characteristic of what Trompenaars would term an 'achievement' (versus 'ascription') value orientation.

The majority of Asian cultures can be characterised by an *external locus of control* and 'ascription' orientation. In other words, they regard man as a part of nature and believe that man should not try to overcome or master nature but should learn to adapt to it harmoniously. In the context of Chinese tradition, one should fight neither nature nor one's fate because nature has the Way (Tao) 'by which all things become what they are'.[18] In life, one will experience both the good and the bad, which must be accepted since they are entangled with one another and are also the cause of one another.

The Confucian emphasis on harmony requires the desires of the individual to be suppressed in favour of the requirements of the group. A person must accept his or her fate in life. Buddhism, with its belief in rein-

carnation and the cyclical nature of life, teaches of the brevity and imper-
manence of all things in life. Since there is more than one chance at life,
there is less pressure on people to be 'doing' orientated. One cannot *achieve*
one's way into favour with the gods. One must be concerned with the
status of future reincarnations and seek to *be* blameless and virtuous.
Action involves risk, while 'inaction is one of the surest ways to lead a
blameless life'.[19]

The concept of *yuarn* is culturally distinctive to China. *Yuarn* refers to
predetermined relationships with other things or individuals, which are
beyond one's control. It is believed that the existence or absence of relationships such as friendship and marriage is predetermined or governed by
a powerful external force. Thus interrelationships between people are
always passive. One may try to seek out such interrelationships to discover
whether or not there is *yuarn*. However, if *yuarn* does not exist or ceases
to exist (even in a marriage), there is nothing that can be done. The
concept of *yuarn* is thus consistent with and complementary to the orientations of external locus of control and ascription. It is a means of ascrib-
ing failure to external forces and stands as a ready explanation for both
propitious and calamitous events, acting as a buffer against intense feelings
of elation or regret. A 1995 nationwide Gallup poll revealed that almost
two-thirds of mainland Chinese surveyed believed that what happens to
them is not of their own doing.[20]

In Japan, the individual places faith in fate, destiny and *innen*. *Innen* is
a combination of *in*, the inner, direct cause, and *en*, the outer, indirect
facilitating cause, that produces an effect.[21] Although the typical Japanese does not consciously make this association with his belief in fate,
innen is imbedded in the Buddhist belief system. *En* has a particular
impact on social relations. As in the case with *yuarn*, without *en*, human
relationships such as friendship and marriage cannot occur between two
people. A marriage proposal is an *endan* ('*en*' talk) and marriage is
engumi ('*en*' match).

This belief in fate serves a similar purpose to *yuarn* in the Chinese
context in that it encourages individuals to be resigned to their fate when
things do not happen as hoped. One cannot change one's *innen* since it
comes from one's previous life. The Japanese refer to fate as *un* and
attribute a large part of success or failure to having good or bad *un*. A
person who is unsuccessful is consoled by the thought that he simply did
not have good *un* and there is nothing that can be done. One can influence
one's *un* by planning carefully and taking precautions, but there is no use
in having regrets as things, once done, are regarded as irreversible. Once
something has happened, fate will take its course. This may explain to

some extent the Japanese desire to plan to the minutest detail, thus scoring high on Hofstede's uncertainty avoidance dimension; through planning, risk can be minimised.

As would be expected in an ascription culture, the ideas of *un* and *en* facilitate resignation as they serve to remove self-blame and to avoid a feeling of failure or inadequacy on the part of the individual. Indeed, the fact that one often hears the phrase *shikata ga nai* ('There's nothing one can do about it') and the fact that a person's ability to *akirame* ('resign oneself') is considered a sign of maturity indicate the readiness of Japanese individuals to accept their situation in life.

Thais, as Buddhists, are also believers in the philosophy of *karma*, that is, that good and bad things happen as a consequence of one's actions in present and past lives. There exists the belief, however, that the gods and spirits can be induced to offer superhuman assistance to help someone succeed in an examination, win a bet or do anything that involves an element of chance.

Concept of self, others and the collective group

Concept of self and others

Culture has a profound impact on how individuals perceive who they are, what they are allowed to do and what their role is as a member of society. These perceptions are often so thoroughly internalised that they are difficult to express explicitly, but they are revealed through behaviour such as consumption. This is one means by which an individual expresses who he perceives himself to be and who he aspires to be. Thus, an understanding of the concept of self is important in forming an understanding of consumer behaviour, and the contrast along this dimension between Western and Asian cultures illuminates further the impact of culture on consumer behaviour.

Usunier divides the area of concept of self and others into four major categories: (1) concept of human nature: good or bad?, (2) appraising others, (3) appraising oneself, and (4) one's relationship with the group (Table 2.1). We shall discuss these categories in the context of Asia and also see how they help to delineate at which end of the spectrum Asian societies fall on Hofstede's and Trompenaars' dimensions.

Table 2.1 Concept of self and others[22]

Cultural Orientation towards:	Basic Issue	Contrasts Across Cultures	Examples	Corresponding Behaviour
1. Concept of human nature	Is human nature basically good or bad?	Good versus bad versus somewhere in between	USA: Good ⇨ China: Bad ⇨	• Unknown people are regarded favourably and friendships form quickly and easily • Unknown people are regarded with suspicion and friendships form slowly but are deeply rooted
2. Appraising others	When appraising others, what criteria are important?	Criteria such as (1) age, (2) gender, and (3) social class are given greater or lesser emphasis	West ⇨ Asia ⇨	• Lesser importance attached to age in determining respect • Greater importance attached to age in determining respect
3. Appraising oneself	On what criteria does one evaluate oneself, and which orientation is culturally appropriate?	Criteria such as (1) self-esteem and (2) perceived potency can be either high or low	West ⇨ Asia ⇨	• High self-esteem ⇨ assertiveness and self-assuredness • High perceived potency ⇨ individualistic and achievement orientated • Low self-esteem ⇨ modesty and self-effacement • Low perceived potency ⇨ collectivist and ascription orientated
4. One's relationship with the group	Is it the individual who is the fundamental component of society or is it the group? Whose rights are most important?	Individualistic versus collectivist	West ⇨ Asia ⇨	• Individualistic ⇨ protection of the rights of the individual, such as personal freedom, human rights and so on • Collectivist ⇨ group values favoured, such as loyalty, belonging, personal sacrifice and so on

Human nature

Although most people are largely unaware of it, we all hold a view on the nature of innate human behaviour. We may see it as basically good, basically bad or neutral (that is, subject to both positive and negative influences). Our view of innate human nature is clearly reflected in the dynamics of friendship. If we believe that human nature is basically good, we may be more open and friendly to those whom we do not yet know well. We are able to form friendships quickly, but since friendships are easily formed, only a very few of them will have depth. If we believe that human nature is innately bad, we will be more wary and guarded when meeting strangers. Only through repeated contact will friendships form. Since true friends are hard to find, those friendships that do form will be characterised by a certain depth of relationship. The ease with which Americans meet strangers and feel comfortable and familiar with them reflects a belief in human nature as innately good. The Chinese, in contrast, are extremely hesitant to trust or depend upon anyone outside their kin group, revealing a less positive view of human nature.

Appraising others

We are constantly appraising others during our daily interactions, whether in friendships, business dealings or other situations. The extent to which we use certain criteria, such as age, gender and social class, and the way in which we interpret them are extremely culture bound. The importance placed upon age by a society is associated with a high power distance cultural orientation. The importance that most Asian cultures attribute to age as a criterion for appraising others reflects the emphasis that Confucius placed on respecting and caring for one's elders. Gender is an important evaluative criterion in all societies, particularly so in Asia where gender indicates highly specified roles and norms of behaviour. Finally, the degree of social stratification as well as the criteria upon which social class is attributed vary across societies. Chinese regard social class as belonging not to an individual but to the family or kin group. It may come from professional standing, education, power and so on. In the USA, social class is largely a reflection of income level, whereas in European societies it may take several generations to attain a certain social standing.

Appraising oneself

We all hold a certain view of ourselves that is typically in line with what will be perceived as acceptable by our family and peers. Cultural differences in self-appraisal can be found in the areas of *self-esteem and potency*.[23] Self-esteem refers to whether one regards oneself as good or not that good, and can be correspondingly high or low. American education tries to instil in students a sense of high self-esteem in order to motivate them to achievement and self-confidence. Children are encouraged to be assertive and self-assured. Asian children, on the other hand, are taught the values of modesty and self-effacement, which are considered to be conducive to cultivation of the mind. This is not to say that Asians lack self-respect; instead, they do not assume that they automatically deserve to regard themselves with esteem. Social research on the Chinese sense of self reveals that Chinese describe themselves in less positive terms than Americans but more positively than the Japanese.[24] Indeed, much emphasis is placed upon modesty in Japan, where a common response to being paid a compliment is *'Iie, sono koto wa nai desu'* ('No, that is not so').

Potency refers to the extent to which a person views himself as powerful in being able, as an individual, to accomplish objectives or manage situations. A high potency view corresponds to individualist and achievement orientations. Believing that doing more will achieve results, a high potency orientation can lead to high levels of activity in the form of overwork, overexercise and so on. With their faith in the importance of the collective group, their tendency towards a Buddhist 'being' orientation and their view of the cyclical nature of life, many Asian societies exhibit a low potency orientation. The Japanese, on the other hand, tend to de-emphasise capability and instead hold the view that it is single-minded effort that determines success. As discussed previously, if something does not turn out to be possible, resignation may be justified, but until that point one must *gambaru* ('strive') with all one's might. Japanese view the process of striving and struggling as character-building and can exhibit 'perseverance and endurance to the point of masochism'.[25] Many Japanese sports and religious practices focus on the concentration of mental and physical energy. The underlying belief is that, through concentration, anything is achievable. As the Japanese proverb states, 'A shaft can pierce a rock if pushed by a concentrated mind.'

One's relationship with the group

We will discuss the individualism/collectivism orientation as a model of interaction *between* people in later sections. This orientation is, however, also pertinent to a discussion of the concept of self and others, for it defines what we view as the 'borders' of our self. Individualist cultures allow a clearly defined border where the self ends and others begin. Collectivist cultures lack such obvious borders, preferring ambiguity between the self and others.

Whether a culture is individualist or collectivist depends on the society's fundamental assumption about whether an individual's rights are supreme and must be protected because it is at the *individual* level that progress can best be made. The alternative view is that the rights of the individual should be subjugated to that of the group and should not be allowed to disturb group coherence and social harmony because it is at the *group* level that progress can best be achieved. The thoroughly collectivist orientation of the Chinese is reflected in the way in which they describe themselves by using group-related traits and roles. Their ideal 'self' is closely involved in social relationships. As Bond comments, 'The dimensions they use to describe themselves and others are likewise focused on interpersonal concerns, not on mastery of the external world or absorption with narrowly personal processes.'[26]

The Japanese, too, tend to see themselves in terms of others. Japanese tend to identify themselves in terms of their *ba* ('social frame') rather than in terms of personal attributes. While strongly collectivist, they nevertheless place great importance on the self separate from the group and feel that it is important to *jibun ga aru* ('have oneself'). When describing themselves, many terms would be about the individual 'self' rather than just the group 'self'. Individuality can be found through introspection, leading the individual into his inner world and enabling him to examine his *kokoro* ('heart').[27] Since the Japanese do not feel that what is in one's heart (*honne* or 'true feelings') must necessarily correspond with what one projects outwardly (*tatemae* or 'outward appearance'), it may be easier to conform to the pressures of the group on the outside without sacrificing one's personal view.

Traditionally, all societies were more collectivist than individualist because of the interdependence characteristic of agrarian communities. Individualism as such is a rather modern phenomenon, which began in 16th-century England through the work of such philosophers as Moore, Bacon, Hume and Locke. Individualism has come to be considered a natural component of a 'modern' society. However, Asian cultures are now challenging this assumption. Japan, a 'modern', first-world nation by any standard, is still strongly collectivist. South Korea, Hong Kong and Taiwan, too, are all thoroughly modern societies that continue to have firmly entrenched collectivist orientations. Of course, as in any rapidly modernising society, there exists much concern that Asia's young people are becoming 'too' individualistic and losing traditional morals and virtues. It remains to be seen whether this is the case or whether the values of Asia's teenagers are 'rock solid' as described in a recent article in *Far Eastern Economic Review*: 'Their elders complain that they are acquisitive, fickle and faddish, steeped in Western fashions and shallow consumer values. On the inside, though, most cling to the family as the bedrock of life; they are fiercely proud of their own countries and cultures and often reject what they see as the "individualism" of the West.'[28]

Interpersonal relationships

Interpersonal relationships in Asia are strongly influenced by the typically collectivist orientation of these cultures. The corresponding high degree of social cohesion, social harmony and social sensitisation among these societies creates a distinct divergence with the behaviour of the more individualistic consumers of Western cultures.

Social harmony

In China, a number of cultural norms have been established to achieve social harmony and guide day-to-day behaviour. The principles of *li* ('rite') is one of these norms. Confucius first prescribed practising *li* as a means of achieving *jen* ('man'). *Jen*, explains Hsu, 'is the central substance of man as a social and cultural being',[29] and it cannot be achieved without applying *li* in one's interactions with fellow human beings. *Jen* is an essential element of Confucianism and represents an ideal state in which an individual maintains harmonious social relationships with his fellow man. Thus the Chinese individual thinks foremost of himself in relation to other people and the way in which they are connected.

The principles of *li* guide the individual in his interactions with others by spelling out the proper way to behave in various social situations and towards various individuals with whom he has interpersonal relationships. Thus *li* guides one to achieve the ideal state of *jen*. The principles of *li* require an individual to behave not according to his desires or for self-centred reasons but to follow what is prescribed by ritual, constantly monitoring his own behaviour to ensure that it is socially acceptable on any occasion.

The effect of *li* has been highlighted in studies by Yang concerning Chinese achievement motivation.[30] Yang found that Chinese achievement goals are often presented as being for the benefit of the group, for example the family or the state, rather than of the individual. Moreover, standards against which achievement is to be measured are defined by other people rather than the individual concerned. In his experiments, Madsen[31] designed a boardgame to assess competitive and co-operative responses in children. When he changed the reward structure, he found that children in the USA would quickly shift from co-operation to competition. He could not, however, effect such a switch with Taiwanese or Hong Kong children. They continued to co-operate even when it was not in their individual interest to do so. Madsen concluded that the desire for interpersonal harmony is too strong to be overcome by temporary economic loss of advantage.

The Japanese and Koreans, too, place great importance on interpersonal harmony. The Japanese are extremely sensitive to and concerned with social interaction and relationships, perhaps even more so than the Chinese.[32] This is mainly due to the fact that Japanese more readily form and place more emphasis on relationships outside their kin group and thus form more and wider-reaching reference groups such as the company, home town, neighbourhood, hobby group or even the nation.[33]

In general, the Japanese invest more sensitivity, compulsiveness, circumspection and refinement in the creation or maintenance of smooth and pleasant social relationships than do either the Chinese or Koreans. The Koreans are likely to focus on the family more than any other group,[34] while the Chinese tend to feel less affinity with anyone outside the kin group. Chinese society exhibits a unique mix of collective and individualistic values. While the Chinese forego individualistic self-interest in the context of the inner circle consisting of family and close friends, Chinese society outside this group can be a 'vicious dog-eat-dog environment'.[35] This difference from the Japanese may be attributed in part to the fact that Korea and China have experienced invasion and occupation, and have thus had to be more concerned than the Japanese with survival needs. As a result, it may be more difficult for Koreans and Chinese to establish solidarity and mutual trust in any relationship not founded upon kinship. Additionally, Koreans and Chinese may have internalised Confucian teachings more intensely than the Japanese so that the system of Confucianism directs their behaviour, thus making unnecessary the greater social sensitisation characteristic of the Japanese.

Empathy

For the Japanese, *omoiyari* ('empathy') is a virtue of such importance that it is 'considered indispensable for one to be really human, morally mature, and deserving of respect'.[36] *Omoiyari* reveals the importance given to sensitivity towards others. It is the ability to put oneself in the place of the other and feel vicariously his pain or pleasure. Listening to a Japanese conversation, one hears a high degree of empathetic agreement as the speaker seeks agreement with *'Neh?'* ('Isn't that so?'), and the listener provides agreement with phrases such as *'Soo, desu neh?'* ('Yes, it is, isn't it?') or *'Eh'* ('Yes'). The ability of the Japanese to empathise is a great facilitator in consensus-building, for each is able to easily see the other's point of view.

In the Japanese context, empathy is shown by anticipating and accommodating the needs and wishes of the other. Thus the Japanese concept of hospitality is to make arrangements for everything ahead of time. One can see this in the way that Japanese tour groups have every detail planned so that, for example, lunch is served at 12:07 p.m. and a visit to a site might last for 12 minutes. The Western idea of hospitality in which a guest is presented with a variety of choices reflects the emphasis on individual choice in Western societies. The collectivist Japanese feel most comfortable relying on the empathy of others.

Belongingness

As most Asian cultures are strongly collectivist in orientation, societies place much emphasis on the concept of belonging. It is important for marketers to understand the dynamics of and importance placed upon reference groups that indicate belongingness.

Concern for belonging leads to a tendency towards collectivism that is expressed by an individual's identification with the collective goal of his group. Priority is given to the success of the group as a whole. Among Chinese, the kin group is the most important and longlasting of any membership group. Hsu comments that 'the primary concern of the majority of Chinese was how to protect and enhance their private kinship interests'.[37] For a Chinese, the kin group is the basis of human ties that are continuous and have only the vaguest of boundaries. Individual sacrifices may be required in order to gain the benefits that accrue to the group. Achieving family goals is more important than individualised self-fulfilment.

The Chinese child learns early in life that his individual desires are secondary to those of the family group. Thus, as Bond comments, 'Many

Chinese learn to "swallow anger" and to tolerate the intolerable because they do not see how they can live outside their family of origin or marriage. Chinese culture is no place to be alone.'[38] In the course of rearing their children, parents will not tolerate behaviour that disrupts the family and will punish it with reprimands, isolation or striking. In studies of Taiwanese children, shaming and isolation from the group were observed to be the dominant disciplinary techniques.[39] Such disciplinary techniques teach a child that isolation from the group is the ultimate punishment and is greatly to be feared. Thus a strong need for belonging-ness is developed from an early age.

Similar to the Chinese, ties to the family in Japan include both present members and those of past and future generations. Thus, the term *ie* ('house') refers to the family as a whole, including ancestors and future descendants. The *ie* is given a substantial and distinctive character by the fact that its unity is understood in historical terms. As a result, each house-hold member is not merely a parent or child, husband or wife, but a descendant of his ancestors and an ancestor of those who are to come.[40]

As noted previously, Japanese tend to identify themselves by the *ba* ('social frame') to which they belong. It can be a current frame, such as the company they work for, or it can be a frame from their past, such as a home town or even the era when they were born. Thus we hear Japan-ese referring to themselves as belonging to the post-war era or the *Showa* era. Within Japanese society, it is very important to have a clearly estab-lished identity, which is often the *ba* from which you come. This is exem-plified through the high reliance on introductory name cards (*meishi*) that clearly identify the company you belong to and your title. An under-standing of such details will facilitate smooth social relations since each person will know what style of language to use, depending on whether the counterpart is of higher, lower or equal rank. Japanese do not like ambiguity in belongingness and will generally regard someone of ambiguous or obscure belonging with mistrust. Thus Japanese place the highest importance on belonging.

Just as with the Chinese, the Japanese child is taught early in life the dread of being left alone and the misery of loneliness. Traditionally, Japan-ese mothers spent almost no time separated from their babies. The baby would share the mother's bed and would often be strapped to the mother's back while she worked rather than being left alone in a crib. Japanese mothers tend to worry less than Western ones about 'spoiling' a child and readily appease their babies when they cry. The constant physical contact with the mother sensitises the child to the feeling of *ittaikan* ('oneness')[41] that adult Japanese seek through belongingness in groups.

For Japanese, sense of identity is deeply anchored in group belonging-ness. Thus there is a strong concern for acceptance by peers, anxiety about exclusion and a near compulsion for always being among the in-group. There is great emphasis on co-operation, solidarity and shared goals. Thus individual desires are secondary to those of the group, for belonging is the ultimate satisfaction. Via this group identification – particularly character-istic of Japanese society, but also to a great extent of Korean society – even the personal experiences of an individual are shared by the group. In turn, the group's pride and shame are shared individually by its members. If an individual happens to make a mistake at work, the other group members would probably protect him, even though punishment, like reward, is meted out on a group basis. Even in a very serious case, where no reason-able excuse would justify an individual's actions, they would protect him with the group power and fabricate some irrational and emotional justifi-cation. Even in the knowledge that the person has done wrong, the group would retain their tolerance and sympathy for him.[42] The Chinese exhibit similar loyalty to group and share both in the pride of success of members of their inner circle and in the shame of failure.[43]

The security and good feeling of *ittaikan* that arise from the sense of belonging fosters a taste for togetherness. Witness the tendency of Japan-ese to form crowds, wanting instinctively not to be left out of whatever group activity is taking place. The Japanese individual feels most comfort-able within the security of his group and wants to go wherever others are. Rather than avoiding the crowded restaurant, shop or tourist attraction, the Japanese purposely avoids uncrowded places, choosing instead to be where others are.

This emphasis on physical togetherness tends to de-emphasise the need for verbal communication between members of the same group, and a high degree of homogeneity coupled with a group orientation allows an empathetic form of communication via indirect, implicit and subtle messages. Because of their emphasis on empathy, the Japanese feel that speech is a poor substitute for an intuitive understanding of what is going on in other people's minds. The Japanese version of a 'heart-to-heart talk' is actually a non-verbal exchange of emotional feelings. The desirability of non-verbal interaction is coupled with the moral belief that silence is a sign of honesty and trustworthiness, thus the phrase *kuchi ga umai* ('skilled mouth') is not a compliment!

Southeast Asian cultures also emphasise the importance of personal rela-tionships and belonging. Indonesians, for example, consider themselves members of the community first, and independent individual's second. Even the modern Indonesian living in an urban centre stays in close contact with his home town or village and returns there and to his family as often as possible. In general, Indonesians are not comfortable being alone and prefer the companionship of a family member or friend.[44] In contrast to Philippinos, Indonesians therefore do not like to emigrate to foreign countries where they would suffer from the feeling of loneliness and unfamiliarity. Being close to each other is even demonstrated physically. As any visitor to Indonesia will quickly observe, touch is a means of expressing affection in personal relationships. In Japan, as in the majority of other Asian cultures, such physical behaviour would be unacceptable despite the overall longing to be with or among others.

Commitment to group

Throughout Asia, the strong sense of belongingness is an anchor for self-identity. Reinforced by collectivism and conformism, it calls for the individual's strong commitment and loyalty to his group. Although primary loyalty tends to rest with only one group, the individual may readily become a member of many secondary groups. The Japanese man's primary group tends to be the company to which he belongs, while that of the Chinese is his kin group. However, Japanese and Chinese individuals are typically different in their readiness to join new groups and thus form multiple reference groups. Japanese readily join new groups such as hobby groups with enthusiasm and commitment. The Chinese, on the other hand, tend to belong to a smaller number of reference groups because of their relative reluctance to trust those outside the kin group. An enormous amount of time, energy and commitment goes into fortifying relationships within the kin group rather than forming numerous attachments of lesser depth. As Bond notes, 'In Chinese culture one's inner circle provides care and protection, over time, so that one can afford to expend less energy building a "safety net" elsewhere.'[45] Thus, although Chinese are highly collectivist in orientation within their primary groups, they are not group orientated towards groups in which bonds do not run deep.

Chinese and Japanese also differ in the longevity of relationships. For the Japanese, ties of kinship, friendship or group membership all tend to weaken through physical separation. This may be partly because of the Japanese reliance on physical contact and non-verbal communication. Chinese relationships, in contrast, remain constant despite long periods of separation. No matter where they live or work, Chinese members of a group formed on the basis of specific attributes maintain ties with other members through the group network and thus overcome separation in terms of both space and time. Because of this extensive network, Chinese are content to live and work abroad, secure in the knowledge that they are still a part of the group and can easily return at any time. Because the *ba* ('frame') can also continue from the past, a returning Japanese would also be welcomed back, but only if he had not changed so much as to lose his old group identity. If gone too long, he may be regarded with suspicion.[46] This explains the hesitancy of Japanese to remain abroad for too many consecutive years. The strong fear that too much time abroad will cause others to regard him as no longer a 'normal Japanese' limits a Japanese individual's opportunity for personal enrichment through integration into the new foreign environment.

Dependency

In Western culture, much value is placed on teaching one's children to be independent and self-sufficient. At the point at which the child can live autonomously, he is considered to have reached adulthood. In Asia, autonomy is not the goal. In China, for example, maturity is regarded as 'a movement towards an integration into the social fabric of the family, the clan or the village'.[47] It is the family and kin group, rather than financial independence, freedom and self-reliance, that is essential to a sense of security and belonging. Without one's relationships (*guanxi*), one is nothing at all. Among Chinese families, there is a strong sense of mutual dependence, which means that a Chinese is expected to assist family and friends and can expect the same in return.

Dependence is also a feature of Japanese interpersonal relationships. Dependence does not mean unilateral passive reliance on others but a mutual dependence that arises out of trust and reciprocal exchange. One must earn the right to be dependent by fulfilling obligations or by making concessions.[48] The existence of the word *amaeru* ('to depend and presume upon another's benevolence') is difficult to translate since the concept is relatively unknown in the West. Children in all cultures experience *amaeru* from their mothers as infants. The fact that this pattern never really breaks between a Japanese adult and his mother is what makes *amaeru* a cultural characteristic of significance. There is none of the stigma attached to dependence that exists in Western culture with its individualist orientation. Such dependent relationships exist in Japan within but also outside the family, typically taking the form of a quasi-familial parent–child relationship such as *sensei–deshi* ('teacher–disciple') or *sempai–kohai* ('superior–subordinate'). The parental sentiment (*oyagokoro*) exhibited in such relationships is characterised by warmth, benevolence and nurturing. Compared with Westerners, Japanese show much less reluctance to be in a dependent position (often preferring it) or even to beg for help.

In summary, the emphasis placed among Asian cultures on social harmony, empathy, belongingness, commitment to group and dependency illustrates the importance of interpersonal relationships and the orientation towards the cultural dimensions of collectivism among Asian cultures compared with Western cultures.

Complementarity of relations

Reciprocity is a universal norm that, in most cultures, has been accepted as a basic moral rule of social cohesion.[49] The rules concerning reciprocity and the ways in which reciprocity is conceived in Asia reveal distinct differences from Western cultures. Norms of reciprocity in Asian cultures tend to be far more formalised and binding than those in the West. The reasons for the greater emphasis placed on reciprocity among Asian cultures reflect differences along the individualism/collectivism, specific/diffuse and uncertainty avoidance orientations.

As we have noted elsewhere, Asian cultures are largely collectivist orientated. Unlike in Western cultures, it is not assumed that man can master his environment and control his own destiny. Instead, Asians are aware that, in an unpredictable world, you will need to be able to depend on others for help. If you are to survive, it is essential to be allied with those who will provide support and protection in times of adversity. Typical of the more diffuse orientation of Asian cultures is that time is taken to build relationships that may be helpful in the future. Reciprocity is an essential means of building such relationships, vital to survival in a collectivist culture. Understanding the norms of reciprocity in Asian cultures and the thinking behind them will, for example, provide a better grasp of gift-giving behaviour in Asia.

In the Chinese context, norms of reciprocity developed according to social and economic structural factors. Historically, the hierarchy present in encapsulated communities and the dependence upon resources controlled by a few power figures made it imperative for every person to know his social position and to remain aware of the obligation to give up resources should those in power demand it. An elaborate system for addressing interpersonal obligations and the mechanism by which such obligations could be won and lost were developed in response.[50]

From this situation arises the Chinese preoccupation with managing interpersonal relationships. The principle of *pao* ('doing favours') signifies one's honour to another. Every Chinese is brought up to be highly aware of this principle, for its application has a tremendous influence on social and business relationships. The application of *pao* signifies a sort of social investment for which the donor expects repayment. As Yau explains, 'The Chinese believe that the reciprocity of favours between two people should be as certain as a cause-and-effect relationship. It should also be continuous so that affinity for each other is well established.'[51]

Because of the collectivist and diffuse orientation of Chinese society, norms of reciprocity are broadly applied. Thus the return of a favour does not have to be directed towards the original giver him or herself but can be directed towards members of the same family or even close friends.[52] Even within the family itself, the norm of reciprocity is observed in the form of filial piety. The expectations of parents that their children will honour their filial duty is expressed in the proverb 'Foster your children to prevent misery in old age and hoard grain to prevent dearth.'[53]

In the business context, *pao* is used to foster *guanxi* ('connections') in order to build one's network of business relationships that are imperative for success in China. Based on clan and family affiliations, *guanxi* networks provide a degree of stability – or at least trust and reliability – in what is otherwise an uncertain business environment. Although these relationships are warm and personal, they also involve a reciprocal obligation, which is the essential feature of *guanxi*. China is a culture in which what counts is not only whom one knows, but also who owes whom a favour.[54]

Guanxi is similar to the concept of 'fraternity' in the Western world whereby two or more persons join together to attain common objectives. Over time, such close association serves to foster respect between members for one another, and each is expected to act in the best interests of the fraternal members. The heightened awareness of reciprocal obligation among members is, however, distinctly Chinese and not present in Western fraternal relationships.

The cultivation of *guanxi* often involves the exchange of gifts. The intended recipient of the gift is expected to accept the gift, and thereby accept the obligation to reciprocate. Failure to reciprocate involves a loss of face and signals an inability to repay the giver. The exchange of gifts thus creates an inner debt that must be discharged at some point. In a business relationship, if one wishes to continue a *guanxi* relationship, reciprocation will normally take the form of a more expensive gift in order to maintain the moral superiority and indebtedness of the other person. Reciprocation should not be immediate, however, so that an unpaid debt may be used to cultivate the relationship.[55] In the context of friendship, gift-giving is also a means of building up friendships. Gifts presented should be expensive enough to match the income of the givers so that they are giving face to those who receive their gifts and so that the giver gains face at the same time because they are thought of as being sincere. For friends, reciprocation should take the form of a gift of comparable or even higher value given as soon as possible.[56]

In Japan, *on* represents the concept of reciprocity. *On* has been described as 'a relational concept combining a benefit or benevolence given with a debt or obligation thus incurred'.[57] *On* represents both the 'social credit' that is conferred upon the donor and the 'social debt' accepted by the receiver. Similar to Chinese *pao*, the recipient is obligated to repay *on* in order to restore balance to the relationship.

The concept of *on* differs from that of *pao*, however, as it is focused less on actual repayment than on the sentiment of the recipient. The most important component of *on* is the gratitude, deep sense of obligation and guilt that an act of *on* confers upon the recipient. It is as important, if not more so, to be continually aware of the *on* received as it is to repay it. To be *on-shirazu* ('unaware of *on*') would call into question one's fundamental moral character.

The giver of an act of *on* must in no way imply expectation of repayment. This is in contrast to the pragmatic Chinese who pay strict attention to the balance between debts and credits. In the Japanese context, the desire is to appear purely altruistic with no expectation of repayment. Buddha is the embodiment of unlimited benevolence and to be *shinsetsu* ('kind') and have a warm heart are greatly valued among Japanese.

Reciprocity may take the form of immediate and symmetrical repayment, as is the case on prescribed occasions for giving such as life-cycle ceremonies (for example, birth, marriage and death), seasonal gifts (*chuugen* and *seibo*) or a visit to someone's home. The value of gifts is carefully noted so that, when the proper time comes, a gift of equal value may be returned. *On* is, however, not created merely through gift-giving, but also through acts of kindness and generosity. As such, *on* cannot be economically calculated or repaid. Instead, its significance lies in the creation or maintenance of a social relationship. In fact, one should ideally never be without *on*, for it is a sign of one's ties with society. The Japanese individual's self-image is strongly tied to his vision of himself as a social being.

The intense feelings of obligation involved in receiving an act of *on* can create a desire to be freed from this heavy burden as soon as possible in order to restore autonomy free of *on*. The burdensome aspect of *on* is called *giri* and reflects the sense of constraint placed upon the *on* recipient. Eager efforts to repay *on* are therefore more often a reflection of an individual's desire to unload a burden than a generous outpouring of gratitude. It is possible to avoid receiving *on* and undertaking *giri* by proclaiming that one is obligated by the virtues of reserve and modesty to practise *enryo* ('restraint'). As many of today's younger generation of Japanese regard *giri*-based gift-giving as a nuisance, the appropriateness of the content of the gift often goes largely unconsidered.

As in China, the importance placed upon the norms of reciprocity and gift-giving reflects the importance placed upon relationships and social ties in a collectivist and diffuse culture. Such norms acknowledge the embeddedness of individuals in groups and the importance of social hierarchy. Gift-giving is regarded as the most immediate and tangible means of fulfilling *on* or discharging *giri*. Whether and how well a person observes the intricate rules and etiquette governing gift-giving are essential to assessing his social character.

Group conformity

Because of the importance of the group in collectivist societies, there is a stronger pressure placed upon the individual to conform to group norms than in individualistic societies. The desire to conform translates into very distinct patterns of consumer behaviour and thus forms an important basis of our understanding of Asian consumer behaviour.

In China, quiet and tractable children are prized. While infants are shown considerable warmth, especially by the mother, the social training of the child involves restrictions in every sense with the objective of teaching obedience, control and restraint. Control is initially exercised physically rather than verbally. For example, babies are often swaddled in restrictive clothing and held or placed in a chair. It has been observed that Chinese parents tend to regard their children as extensions of themselves rather than as separate individuals and thus place low emphasis on speaking to their infants and small children. Parental restrictiveness, coupled with a relative lack of encouragement for self-expression, tends to create an extreme dependency on the mother as well as less extroversion, vocal expression and activity on the part of the infant. The greater priority given to non-verbal communication over verbal communication during the early years of life may be part of the reason for the verbal inhibition of Chinese adults when interacting with those outside their kin group.[58]

While there is no single Chinese pattern of disciplining children, verbal and physical reprimands as well as isolation from the group are common means of enforcing discipline both in school and in the home. The typical Chinese kindergarten features toddlers, sometimes as young as 18 months, sitting quietly at their desks following rote methods of learning numbers, letters and characters. Both child-rearing and educational practices produce children who are pliant, able to learn without questioning and fearful of isolation from the group. The child is thus more likely to conform, that is, to adopt group values, suppress his aggression and comply with the will of authorities.

The importance placed upon doing what is prescribed by society in a given situation translates into strong social pressure to comply with group norms regardless of the individual's own private views. If a Chinese is found to deviate from the group norm, he may be treated as an outsider who does not know how to adjust to the group, and his social acceptability will be at stake. Such isolation from the group is highly traumatic for the Chinese individual, and he may feel doubt over his ability to lead a normal, adult life. A Chinese individual therefore feels extremely uncomfortable being different from other people and doing things differently from the way they do.

There are few situations in Chinese society in which an individual is allowed to behave according to his private feelings and moods. Typically, feelings are only expressed openly with family members. There exist more rules surrounding the display of emotions in Chinese (and Japanese) culture than in Western culture. The indoctrination of these rules is so strong during socialisation that, even as adults, the Chinese react with less visible emotion than do Westerners to provocative events.[59] While Westerners may be confused by the relative lack of emotion shown by the Chinese, such reserve is a natural result of being part of a culture that values hierarchy, harmony and moderation in all things. An individual's uninhibited display of emotion cannot be tolerated in a conformist culture.

Japanese child-rearing is similar to Chinese methods in that non-verbal communication is emphasised and a high level of dependency on the mother is fostered. In comparison to American infants, Japanese infants are less vocal, restless or active. Rather than using physical and verbal reprimands, the Japanese mother teaches discipline by appealing to the child's sense of guilt or shame with comments such as 'If you do that people will laugh at you.' Thus the fear of standing out as an object of ridicule is fostered early in the Japanese child. From the beginning, the child is taught the importance of belonging and the corresponding need for interpersonal harmony and restraint in order to avoid conflict.

The emphasis on role propriety is an additional conforming influence encountered early in life and continued throughout adulthood. Japanese children and adults are encouraged to be 'like' (*rashii*) their prescribed role, whether it is older brother, girl, student and so on. It is definitely considered negative to be told that you are not being *onna-rashii* ('ladylike') if you are, in fact, a woman. Thus one is constantly aware of what it is to be 'like' one's status and of the corresponding proper behaviour, dress, possessions and appearance. For example, a male university professor would be expected to carry a briefcase with a label and appearance suitable for his status. The failure to conform to an appearance, behaviour or performance suitable to one's status generates dreaded feelings of shame. The pressure to conform under such circumstances cannot be overestimated.

The Japanese educational system, too, plays a role in encouraging uniformity and rigidity. Japanese educational authorities proudly assert that, on any given day, fourth-graders from Hokkaido to Kyushu will all be on the same page of the same book in every course. The downside is that the rigidity of the system dampens independent judgement and creativity, and positively discourages the expression of individuality. Instead, the emphasis is on how to work in teams. There are many exercises that aim to develop co-operation over competition.

Another conforming influence is the infamous 'examination hell' institutionalised by the Japanese school system. The relative lack of mobility within Japanese society means that to get into a good company a student must graduate from a good university, which means that he must have attended a good high-school, which means that he must have gone to a good middle school and so on. Combined with a sense of fatalistic irreversibility, Japanese parents, teachers and students place enormous emphasis on studying and the rote memorisation learning required for success in such exams. Students are taught to digest and retain enormous amounts of information with no time or encouragement for individual creative thought or expression.

It is not only the school system itself, with its many rules governing dress codes and behaviour during and after school hours, and the rigid structure of exams, but also the influence of peers that creates enormous pressure on the Japanese student to conform. Peer pressure exists in all cultures, but in Japan, where group belongingness forms the very essence of self-identity, peer pressure is distinctly more powerful. The much discussed problem of 'bullying' in Japanese schools, which has led several children to commit suicide, illustrates this issue.

In adult life, since a person's identity is anchored in group belongingness, acceptance by peers is of prime importance, and the desire to conform to the norms of the group is very strong. Dissension and idiosyncratic behaviour are discouraged and acquiescence is regarded as a necessary mechanism for consensual decision-making. In Japanese society, the pressure to conform often results in a kind of self-restraint called *enryo*, which means to refrain from expressing disagreement with whatever appears to be the majority opinion. In situations of formal decision-making, consensual decisions are typically reached not through expressions of agreement but through absence of objection. Those who disrupt the process through a lack of conforming behaviour will be looked upon with disfavour and regarded as sacrificing the strength and sense of uniform purpose of the group for the sake of their own individualistic, self-centred viewpoint.

While conformity is a requirement in terms of *tatemae* ('outward appearance'), one's *honne* ('true feeling') is permitted a kind of inner autonomy. As described earlier, within a particularist society such as Japan, divergence between one's publicly expressed and personal opinions is quite acceptable. An individual may have an opinion contrary to that of the group but must not allow it to stand in the way of group solidarity. There are alternative opportunities for expressing non-conforming opinions, such as nights out drinking with colleagues. Only under the influence of alcohol can an employee express a dissenting opinion to his boss.

The vast majority of Japanese tell pollsters that they value the approval of their peers over fame in their fields, either domestically or internationally. The belief is that life will be easier and more enjoyable if they suppress individuality and opinions in favour of inoffensive people-pleasing, whether in the corporate, government, scholarly, literary or artistic community. In fact, many Japanese scholars and artists reach the pinnacle of their worlds without ever producing a significant work of scholarship or artistic achievement. Although they may receive great acclaim within Japan, international credibility is lacking.[60]

Southeast Asian cultures are also highly conformist. The typical Indonesian, for example, tries to conform to the norms and values of his community rather than finding his own way of doing things. Decisions are made by a process of discussion and consensus, with major emphasis falling on the maintenance of group harmony.

Roles and corresponding status

The majority of Asian cultures are characterised by rigid hierarchical structures arising from the Confucian emphasis on social order and harmony. In Japan, social relations are facilitated by vertical relationships that help to avoid uncertainty and riskiness in dealing with others.[61] This preference for vertical relationships can be seen in the Japanese tendency towards the infinitesimal differentiation of ranks rather than the grouping together of two nearly equal ranks. Inequality provides guidelines for social interaction, making behaviour more predictable, and helps to avoid competition for status elevation. Such preference is in accordance with a society whose orientation is towards high power distance and high uncertainty avoidance.

A rigid hierarchical social structure leads naturally to a heightened sensitivity towards status. Individuals are always conscious of their place in a social group, institution or society as a whole, and of the proper behaviour, dress and speech corresponding to status propriety. They are also extremely aware of the need to maintain the dignity, or face, of others. Strong status orientation leads to a motivation for status display involving competition and one-upmanship. In this section, we shall discuss how the concept of face and the orientation towards status form the roots of Asian conspicuous consumption.

The concept of face

The concept of face represents the dignity based on a correct relationship between a person and the groups to which that person belongs.[62] This concept has profound implications for Asian interpersonal relationships. While the concept of face is not an Asian monopoly, Asians have developed a sensitivity to face and use it as a reference point in their behaviour in a much more complex and sophisticated way than is found in virtually all other cultures.[63] Across Asian cultures, the terms used to describe face and the exact way in which it operates vary somewhat from society to society, but the underlying dimensions are consistent.

The Chinese distinguish between two types of face: *lien* and *mien-tsu*. *Lien* refers to the moral integrity of an individual's character. Every individual is entitled to *lien* by virtue of being a member of society. Thus one thinks in terms of losing *lien* rather than gaining it. Should a person's behaviour cause him to be cast out of society, he has lost his right to *lien*.[64] *Lien* implies the presence of *ch'ih* ('shame'), which is one of the fundamental requirements of being human.

Mien-tsu, on the other hand, represents a form of face involving prestige or reputation based on personal effort.[65] It can be obtained through personal qualities or derived from non-personal characteristics such as wealth, social status, level of education, occupation or authority. *Mien-tsu* may be lost or gained when the quantity or quality of such characteristics decreases or increases. Since the standards and requirements are set by the social expectations of the group, one is highly dependent on the evaluation of others for enhancing one's *mien-tsu*.

Lien and *mien-tsu* are intertwined with one another. *Mien-tsu* cannot exist without *lien*, but also *lien* cannot exist without *mien-tsu*. In other words, when we talk of loss of face, it means losing not only *mien-tsu* but also *lien*.[66] Thus a person has no option but to meet the social requirements to gather status to his name and maintain *mien-tsu*. Failure to do so would jeopardise his standing in society, cause him to lose *mien-tsu* and cast into doubt his moral integrity in the eyes of society (*lien*). The importance of face cannot be overestimated; it determines the difference between being considered human and a member of society, and being nothing.

Thus Chinese individuals are very conscious of showing due regard for the *mien-tsu* of others. They are careful not to cause others to lose face and expect the same regard in return. To cause a person to lose face is regarded as an act of aggression, while to protect another person's face is seen as an act of consideration.[67] Compromise is a means of allowing all parties in a situation to save face. Indirect language is also employed to avoid confrontation, embarrassing situations and direct rejections. The Chinese try to avoid saying 'No' when asked to express an opinion in order not to embarrass or offend others. Other common strategies used to save face for others include avoidance of criticism of anyone, but especially superiors, and the use of circumlocution and equivocation when criticism of another's performance is unavoidable. Those skilled at preserving face for others are greatly respected.

Chinese individuals are conscious of the need to maintain a high degree of moral control, at least publicly, and carefully assess the possible effects of their actions on others before embarking upon a course of action. They are particularly mindful not to lose face for their family but instead strive to gain face for the family through the accumulation of wealth, prestige, status, power and so on. In a business or social context, the elaborate norms involved in gift-giving provide a crucial opportunity to gain – or lose – face. Inappropriate gifts, in terms of content or cost, can cause an embarrassing loss of face for both the donor and the recipient.

In the Japanese context, face is the individual's badge of respectability and the source of his self-confidence. A spotless face allows the individual to be viewed by his peers, superiors and subordinates as a person who is vitally integrated and in tune with society. Thus for an individual to keep his name and reputation unsullied is, in a sense, a duty and one type of *giri*.[68]

The Japanese child learns early about the importance of conventional manners and etiquette. He is taught to bow, to sit properly, to express thanks for favours and apology for wrong-doing. From the very beginning, the Japanese child is sensitised to the need for interpersonal harmony and restraint in order to avoid conflict. This extreme sensitivity for and concern about social interaction and relationships is intertwined with the notion of shame and the *giri* to name and family.

The concept of face is also present in Southeast Asian cultures. In the Philippines, the parallel social force is called *pakikisama*, or the ethic of smooth interpersonal relations. Combined with a well-developed sense of *amor proprio*, or personal pride, and a high sensitivity to shame instilled from childhood, these traits produce behaviour that is conciliatory, docile and free from open conflict. In Indonesia and Thailand, dignity and smoothness of behaviour are highly valued and form one of the key sources of respect. It is considered a deep insult to be made *malu*, or to lose face, in front of others – and more damaging than material loss.[69]

Although similar concepts of shame exist in all Asian cultures, what constitutes cause for loss of face in one culture may be perfectly acceptable in another. One example is counting one's change. Japanese will virtually never count the change received from a store clerk, as it would not only imply overconcern in pecuniary matters in a culture in which to be thought stingy is a highly negative stigma, but also imply mistrust and cause lack of face for the sales clerk. The Chinese, however, take pride in being sharp in money matters and carefully count their change. Should there be any discrepancy, they will demand redress. The cashier, far from being offended, takes it for granted that this will be done.

Status propriety and consumption

Asian conspicuous consumption will be elaborated upon in detail in Chapter 4. However, to lay the foundation for this discussion, we must first emphasise the importance of status propriety in Asian cultures. Confucian teachings emphasise the importance of obeying rules and living properly in order to maintain harmony within oneself and within society. Similarly, Buddhist teachings emphasise the need to harmonise with nature and not to fight one's fate. As discussed earlier, such teachings lead to the typically Asian orientations of external locus of control and 'being'. Within the context of typically highly hierarchical Asian societies, a person is to accept his place in society and behave and appear in a manner appropriate to that status.

The Japanese use the word *bun* to indicate an individual's place in society. The importance of knowing one's place in society and acting accordingly is revealed in such idiomatic expressions as 'to know one's *bun*', 'to adhere to one's *bun*', 'not to disgrace one's *bun*' and 'to fulfil one's *bun*'. Literally, *bun* means 'portion' or 'share' and signifies the fact that individuals are just fractions of the whole which is society. Regarding individuals in such a manner emphasises the sense of interdependency of individuals. If each individual is only a fraction, then all individuals must depend on one another to give life wholeness and meaning.[70] This may explain to some extent why Japanese find meaning in life and much of their self-identity in being socially useful.

In order to conform to one's *bun*, careful attention is given to purchasing products whose price, brand and packaging match a person's social standing. In the case of personal appearance, the colour, material and style of clothing should match an individual's status, which is defined by age, gender, occupation and so on. In Japan, for example, bright colours are considered distinctly feminine and youthful. *Kimono* are age-graded by colour and pattern so that a *kimono* worn by a married woman would be much more subdued in colour than one worn by a single woman. The way in which a woman's *obi* sash is tied must also be appropriate to her marital status. Even Japan's gangsters, the *yakuza*, adhere to status-corresponding codes of appearance and behaviour with their pin-striped suits, black shirts with gaudy designs, expensive jewellery and flat-top crew cuts or perms.[71]

The pressure for conformity leads to a high rate of diffusion of material culture and an incredible incidence of faddism in many Asian cultures. Particularly in Japan, everyone seems to be reading, watching, talking about or doing the same thing at any one time. Beyond the pressure to conform, however, is the cultural orientation towards hierarchy and status. Status orientation motivates those holding high status to a motivation for status display, which can often become considerably competitive once momentum is generated. Although the elements that connote status vary between the Asian countries, Western luxury products are currently the items that those who can afford them must have for status display. This is a very fortunate situation for the Louis Vuittons, Cartiers, Pradas and Fendis of the world!

Family orientation

In previous sections, we have highlighted the strong collectivist orientation of Asian cultures and the subsequent emphasis placed on maintaining harmony within the group through close adherence to group norms of behaviour and patterns of obligation. The family unit provides the individual's first experience in learning the importance of group belongingness. In all Asian cultures, the family is regarded as the most fundamental group in life. Particularly for those Asian cultures based on Confucian tradition, harmonious families are the building blocks of a harmonious society.

Family dynamics

Confucianism places extreme importance on familial relationships and their implicit responsibilities and rewards. Ideally, the Chinese family acts as the refuge for the individual 'against the indifference, the rigours, and the arbitrariness of life outside'.[72] The Chinese individual is ready and willing to make sacrifices for his family and, in exchange, expects his family to be there as his support, comfort and safety net. During the process of socialisation, the Chinese individual is taught to put other family members before himself, to share their pride and accomplishments, their shame and their failure, their sadness and their joy as if they were his own. Chinese children develop this heightened sense of connectedness with their families through a stream of daily interaction; circular tables, shared bedrooms, late night family outings, supervision of homework by elder siblings – all form the details of daily life that bind the individuals of the household together and teach them that their fate is a shared one.

A Chinese person never grows out of this intense relationship with the family; it is a lifelong affair. The goal of the child is not to grow up and move out and onwards as it is in the West. The familial relationship of mutual aid and dependence is a permanent one and also extends to aunts, uncles, grandparents, cousins and so on. As one Chinese proverb notes, within the family 'You and I are one.' Parents, in particular, remain an ongoing influence, whether through their selection or rejection of a potential spouse or the pressure they place on their grown children to fulfil their filial duty through financial support. The importance put upon filial piety is reflected in Article 15 of China's family law, which asserts that: 'Children have the duty to support and assist their parents. When children fail to perform the duty of supporting their parents, their parents have the right to demand that their children pay for their support.' A similar law is under consideration in Singapore.

The themes of mutual support and filial piety are echoed in Japanese society, where the family plays a key role in maintaining social stability. The family is also the most basic unit facilitating Japan's economic success. While the role of the mother is to channel all of her energy into the education of her children as well as the maintenance of the home and caretaking of her husband and parents, the father is free to focus all of his energy on work and the children to focus all of their energy on study. This division of labour has allowed Japan's economic miracle to take place. Perhaps the price of such focused energy and clear role division is that, among members of the modern Japanese family, relationships are somewhat less intense and intimate than those of a Chinese family.

In Japan, the mother–child relationship is one of the most important in an individual's life. This dependency continues to manifest itself in later life through a deep sense of obligation. Even an adult can never repay the *on* that he feels for the care, worry and suffering that his mother has borne during his lifetime.[73] Whereas the American adolescent struggles to acquire independence from his parents, a Japanese child never renounces his deep attachment to his mother. The rebellion common among Western adolescent boys to break the maternal bonds of childhood and move on to manhood has no parallel in Japanese culture.[74]

Although fathers in the younger generation express a desire to be more involved with their wives and children, a 1994 survey revealed that roughly half of the Japanese men surveyed spend fewer than 10 hours at home per day even when work is not busy, 15.8 per cent have *never* taken time off from work to be with their family, and nearly half have almost never done so.[75] Statistics such as these reveal that the structure of the Japanese family remains a central core comprising mother and children to which the father attaches.

Just as with the Chinese, the Japanese family is characterised by dependence and mutual support. In Japan, dependence and mutual support are fundamental components in the relationship between husband and wife, and mother and children. Within the home, the husband is utterly dependent on the wife for everything from house cleaning, cooking and childrearing, to fulfilling familial social obligations and for his own personal needs such as packing his suitcase, polishing his shoes and so on. Lebra notes that the pattern is often for wives to assume a maternal role *vis-à-vis* their husbands for it allows them to 'attain spiritual serenity... thus freeing themselves from sexual jealousy'.[76] The wife often also has fiscal responsibility within the family. She receives her husband's pay cheque and maintains the family budget, pays the bills and manages savings. Outside the home, however, the wife typically assumes the traditional role of dependence, not expressing any opinion contrary to that of her husband and allowing him to lead.

Today, the Japanese family is undergoing a period of transformation. Although traditional gender roles continue to be strong, Japanese women have more economic and social freedom and independence than ever before. Many put off marriage until their late twenties in order to enjoy their single years with high disposable incomes (since they live with their parents), which facilitates international travel and shopping sprees. Most, however, do eventually assume the traditional roles of home-making and child-rearing, and regard their twenties as a temporary, self-centred phase in their lives before the permanent phase as wives and mothers.

The Western dress and consumerism favoured among Asia's youth has led to a concern about a breakdown of Asian family values. However, although appearing superficially thoroughly Western, the devotion of Asia's youth to the family seems extremely solid. A 1996 survey of Hong Kong youngsters revealed that 74.5 per cent felt that parents should have a say in what friends they choose, 91 per cent that parents should have a say in how hard they study and 86.9 per cent that parents should have a say in how they treat family members. Research conducted by Leo Burnett in Kuala Lumpur reveals that while young Malaysians mimic American trends in music and fashion, for example, they remain quite conservative and value family life and parental consent. Young Thais also put supreme importance on traditional values such as respect for elders, respect for family and collective over individual action.[77]

Korea is in many ways the most Confucian of all Asian cultures. Thus it is no surprise that the bonds of filial piety and family loyalty are extremely powerful. Even among Korean Americans, there is general acceptance that a youngster must choose a spouse who will be approved by his parents, namely a Korean spouse. Although rapid urbanisation has meant the isolation of the nuclear family from the extended family because of small, single-family apartments, the solidarity of the nuclear family remains strong. According to a 1988 opinion survey of the Seoul National University freshman class, 42.1 per cent say they most want 'a harmonious family', compared with 'good friends' (41.1 per cent) and 'contributing to nation-building' (14.9 per cent).[78]

Role of the extended family

While the literature on Western families notes the growing centrality of the husband–wife bond as opposed to the parent–child bond, the economic and social changes accompanying industrialisation in Asia have not, to any great degree, had a similar effect there. Despite the growing popularity of 'love marriages' in Japan, as opposed, for example, to arranged marriages or marriages of practicality, the parent–child bond and bonds among the extended family members remain extremely important in the Asian family. Most parents continue to live with adult sons, and financial flows follow the pattern of traditional filial piety in an upward direction from adult children to parents.[79]

Despite the growth in the number of nuclear families and one-person households, and the declining proportion of three-generation family households, Japan, along with China, Taiwan and South Korea, continues to exhibit a high incidence of cohabitation of parents with adult children. In Japan, approximately half of the elderly live together with their married children. The tendency is to live with married sons, whereas in Thailand the norm is cohabitation with unmarried children. With the rising number of working mothers in Japan, grandparents are a vital source of child care.[80]

Role of the family in decision-making

As in the West, the husband–wife relationship is central to family decision-making in Asian cultures. It is thus appropriate to consider here the four husband–wife role typologies as documented in consumer behaviour literature: husband-dominated decisions, wife-dominated decisions, autonomous decisions (in which either the husband or wife, but not both, is the primary decision-maker) and joint decisions (in which husbands and wives collaborate in decision–making).

The distinct role division characteristic of Asian households is key to understanding the nature of decision-making. 'A husband sings, the wife hums along', notes one Chinese saying, while the Japanese phrase *fushoo-fuzui* ('The husband initiates, the wife follows')[81] describes the traditional Japanese ideal. Although there is variation between Asian cultures, many feature the husband as the authoritative head of the household and the wife as the manager of household affairs and of the education of the children. The influence of the West and the effects of modernisation have to some extent loosened the rigidity of these roles, but the general guidelines continue to be followed.

The effect of such distinct role division is that there is more autonomous decision-making among Asian couples than among Western couples. In the case of Singaporean Chinese couples, one survey indicated a lesser extent of joint, or syncratic, decision-making than among American couples. Autocratic decisions are the norm, wives being responsible for such family purchases as food and beverages, household appliances, children's courses and private tuition, while husbands have the final authority on car, television and insurance purchases.[82] In Japan, there is a similar vertical division of labour in the management of household finances. The wife assumes a large role in the management of routine household spending. Over 60 per cent of housewives control the family budget. They have a major influence in decisions about clothing and goods related to the home and education. For larger, more expensive consumer durables such as cars, stereo systems or videocassette recorders, however, the husband will either influence the decision-making or decide by himself.

Variation of these patterns in Japan depends greatly on whether the wife also works or devotes herself full time to the home. In cases where the husband is the sole breadwinner, about 20 per cent of families use the allowance system in which the husband gives part of his income to his wife and keeps the rest. The other 80 per cent of households use the delegation system in which the husband turns over all of his income to his wife for management and he is then given an allowance. Among families where both the husband and wife work, family income is managed by the wife among 43 per cent of those surveyed.[83] Obviously, the relative influence concerning purchases of the husband and wife varies, depending on which system is adhered to.

As families have fewer children, children play an increasing role in family decision-making. In China, the one-child policy has resulted in the recent phenomenon of 'little emperors'. Particularly in Chinese urban centres, where the one-child policy is strictly adhered to, the only child is the object of lavishing of money and gifts by both parents and grandparents. One survey of 425 urban families with single children between the ages of 7 and 12 found that children influenced 40 per cent of all household purchase decisions.[84] These children are becoming highly skilled in consumerism at a young age; 21.2 per cent of children surveyed shopped every day of the week, while 45.7 per cent regarded shopping as one of their favourite activities. Spending on children also serves as a vehicle to display a family's increasing status and wealth.

Growing influence of women

The advent of the Asian career woman is and will continue to be one of the principal influences on consumer trends in Asia. In 1995, women held almost a quarter (23 per cent) of the senior corporate positions in Hong Kong, Singapore, Kuala Lumpur, Taipei, Manila, Bangkok and Jakarta. Three years earlier, the figure was 19 per cent. Wide regional variations continue to exist, however. In Manila, 29 per cent of influential positions are held by women, and in Taipei 35 per cent. In Hong Kong and Singapore, however, fewer than 20 per cent are held by women.[85]

In Japan, women have become the most active initiators of change in contemporary Japanese society. They comprise more than 40 per cent of the total labour force: more than 70 per cent of women between the ages of 20 and 24 work, as do 54 per cent between the ages of 25 and 30, and 50 per cent between the ages of 30 and 34. Although many of the positions occupied by women are either part time or those of 'office ladies' (OLs), in which there is no real career path, women today are entering a far wider range of careers, including politics. In recent years, the increasing number of women opting to delay marriage and motherhood in favour of their careers has had a noticeable effect on the birth rate in Japan, which is now at an all-time low.

Even assuming that women continue to become more career orientated, the rigid social structure and pressure to adhere to social norms will make change slow. During the recent years of recession, for example, women were encouraged to stop working or were let go in order to free up jobs for men. The social pressure put upon mothers not to have a full-time career is also extremely strong. With a Japanese woman's identity so thoroughly wrapped up in her identity as a mother and her ultimate responsibility for her children's education, the awareness that her in-laws and neighbours may be doubting her dedication is extremely uncomfortable. Should a child fail his entrance examinations, all eyes will turn to the mother.

Women in Southeast Asian countries are also experiencing growing economic and social freedom and independence. In Vietnam, for example, the removal of state subsidies and the growing openness to the outside world have given many women in metropolitan areas an opportunity for wealth and independence unimaginable under socialism. In Hanoi, streets are crowded with home-based businesses – tailors shops, cafés, beauty parlours and so on – mostly run by women. Many of these women chose early 'retirement' from state factory jobs in order to take advantage of the freedom of the new market economy. In some cases, their business initiatives have made them the main income earners in their families, while their husbands continue to contribute small-bureaucrat salaries or state pensions.

The growth of opportunities for urban women in Southeast Asia has encouraged more 'modern' attitudes towards marriage, family and future prospects. Today's urban families in Southeast Asia are eager to send their daughters as well as their sons to university. Foreign language degrees are currently the most popular courses among college-bound girls, with economics and law rapidly gaining ground. Women increasingly regard a later marriage and fewer children as a means to a brighter future.

Notes

1. Kindel, T.I. (1983) 'A partial theory of Chinese consumer behavior: marketing strategy implications', *Hong Kong Journal of Business Management,* 1: 98–9.
2. Yau, O.H.M (1994) *Consumer Behaviour in China,* London: Routledge, p. 81.
3. Lai, T.C. (1960) *Selected Chinese Sayings,* Hong Kong: Wing Tai Cheung, p. 114.
4. Kindel, T.I. (1983) 'A partial theory of Chinese consumer behavior: marketing strategy implication', *Hong Kong Journal of Business Management,* 1: 98–9.
5. Jarvie, I.C. and Agassi, J. (1969) *Hong Kong: A Society in Transition,* London: Routledge & Kegan Paul, p. 151.
6. Yau, O.H.M. (1994) *Consumer Behaviour in China,* London: Routledge, p. 63.
7. Overmyer, D. (1986) *Religions of China,* New York: Harper & Row, pp. 40–3.
8. Overmyer, D. (1986) *Religions of China,* New York: Harper & Row, pp. 40–3.
9. Guillaume, A. (1956) *Islam,* London: Penguin, pp. 55–77.
10. Johns, A.H. (1984) 'Islam in the Malay World', in Israeli, R. and Johns, A.H. (eds) *Islam in Asia,* Vol. II: *Southeast and East Asia,* Jerusalem: Magnes Press, pp. 115–21.
11. Alatas, S.H. (1972) *Modernization and Social Change,* Sydney: Angus & Robertson, pp. 16–28.
12. Mutalib, H. (1990) 'Islamic revivalism in ASEAN states', *Asian Survey,* **30**(9): 877–91.
13. Mutalib, H. (1990) 'Islamic revivalism in ASEAN states', *Asian Survey,* **30**(9): 880.
14. 'Between God and Mammon', *Far Eastern Economic Review,* 9 May 1996: 58–60.
15. 'For God and growth in Malaysia', *Economist,* 27 November 1993: 67.
16. 'The very model of a modern Moslem state', *Financial Times,* 26–27 April 1997: 10.
17. Reader, I. (1991) *Religion in Contemporary Japan,* Honolulu: University of Hawaii Press, pp. 60–73.
18. Yau, O.H.M. (1994) *Consumer Behaviour in China,* London: Routledge, p. 69.
19. Usunier, J. (1996) *Marketing Across Cultures,* Hertfordshire: Prentice-Hall, p. 83.
20. Levy, G.R. (1996) *Consumer Marketing in China: Chasing Billions, Catching Millions,* Hong Kong: Economist Intelligence Unit, p. 51.
21. Lebra, T.S. (1976) *Japanese Patterns of Behavior,* Honolulu: University of Hawaii Press, p. 165.

22. Adapted from Usunier, J. (1996) *Marketing Across Cultures,* Hertfordshire: Prentice-Hall, p. 66.
23. Usunier, J. (1996) *Marketing Across Cultures,* Hertfordshire: Prentice-Hall, p. 70.
24. Bond, M.H. (1991) *Beyond the Chinese Face,* Oxford: Oxford University Press, p. 34.
25. Lebra, T.S. (1976) *Japanese Patterns of Behavior,* Honolulu: University of Hawaii Press, p. 163.
26. Bond, M.H. (1991) *Beyond the Chinese Face,* Oxford: Oxford University Press, p. 34.
27. Lebra, T.S. (1976) *Japanese Patterns of Behavior,* Honolulu: University of Hawaii Press, p. 159.
28. 'Rock solid', *Far Eastern Economic Review,* 5 December 1996: 50–2.
29. Hsu, F.L.K. (1971) 'Psychosocial homeostasis and *jen*: conceptual tools for advancing psychological anthropology', *American Anthropologist,* **73**: 23–44.
30. Yang, K.S. (1986) *The Psychology of the Chinese People,* Hong Kong: Oxford University Press, pp. 106–70.
31. Cited in Bond, M.H. (1991) *Beyond the Chinese Face,* Oxford: Oxford University Press, p. 65.
32. Lebra, T.S. (1976) *Japanese Patterns of Behavior,* Honolulu: University of Hawaii Press, p. 8.
33. Lebra, T.S. (1976) *Japanese Patterns of Behavior,* Honolulu: University of Hawaii Press, p. 22.
34. 'Improving your business in Korea', *Tokyo Business,* February 1994: 38–41.
35. Levy, G.R. (1996) *Consumer Marketing in China: Chasing Billions, Catching Millions,* Hong Kong: Economist Intelligence Unit, pp. 31–52.
36. Lebra, T.S. (1976) *Japanese Patterns of Behavior,* Honolulu: University of Hawaii Press, p. 38.
37. Cited in Yau, O.H.M. (1994) *Consumer Behaviour in China,* London: Routledge, p. 75.
38. Bond, M.H. (1991) *Beyond the Chinese Face,* Oxford: Oxford University Press, pp. 6–7.
39. Cited in Bond, M.H. (1991) *Beyond the Chinese Face,* Oxford: Oxford University Press, p. 13.
40. Watsuji, T. (1961) *Climate and Culture: A Philosophical Study,* Tokyo: Hokuseido Press, pp. 4–6.
41. Lebra, T.S. (1976) *Japanese Patterns of Behavior,* Honolulu: University of Hawaii Press, p. 142.
42. Nakane, C. (1970) *Japanese Society,* Berkeley: University of California Press, p. 122.
43. Bond, M.H. (1991) *Beyond the Chinese Face,* Oxford: Oxford University Press, p. 36.
44. Schütte, H. (1974) *Marketing in Indonesia,* Jakarta: Intermasa Publishing, p. 63.

45. Bond, M.H. (1991) *Beyond the Chinese Face,* Oxford: Oxford University Press, pp. 36–8.
46. Nakane, C. (1970) *Japanese Society,* Berkeley: University of California Press, p. 137.
47. Kindel, T.I. (1983) 'A partial theory of Chinese consumer behavior: marketing strategy implications', *Hong Kong Journal of Business Management,* 1: 99.
48. Lebra, T.S. (1976) *Japanese Patterns of Behavior,* Honolulu: University of Hawaii Press, pp. 50–7.
49. Hwang, K.H. (1987) 'Face and favor: the Chinese power game', *American Journal of Sociology,* 92(4): 944–74.
50. Hwang, K.H. (1987) 'Face and favor: the Chinese power game', *American Journal of Sociology,* 92(4): 944–74.
51. Yau, O.H.M. (1994) *Consumer Behaviour in China,* London: Routledge, p. 73.
52. Yang, L.S. (1957) 'The concept of *pao* as a basis for relations in China', in Fairbank, J.K. (ed.) *Chinese Thought and Institutions,* Chicago: University of Chicago Press.
53. Hwang, K.H. (1987) 'Face and favor: the Chinese power game', *American Journal of Sociology,* 92(4): 944–74.
54. Brunner, J.A., Chen, J., Sun, C. and Zhou, N. (1989) 'The role of *guanxi* in negotiations in the Pacific Basin', *Journal of Global Marketing,* 3(2): 7–23.
55. Arunthanes, W., Tansuhaj, P. and Lemak, D.J. (1994) 'Cross-cultural business gift-giving', *International Marketing Review,* 11(4): 44–55.
56. Yau, O.H.M. (1994) *Consumer Behaviour in China,* London: Routledge, p. 77.
57. Lebra, T.S. (1976) *Japanese Patterns of Behavior,* Honolulu: University of Hawaii Press, pp. 91–102.
58. Bond, M.H. (1991) *Beyond the Chinese Face,* Oxford: Oxford University Press, p. 11.
59. Bond, M.H. (1991) *Beyond the Chinese Face,* Oxford: Oxford University Press, p. 41.
60. Sakaiya, T. (1993) *What is Japan?,* Tokyo: Kodansha, p. 52.
61. Lebra, T.S. (1976) *Japanese Patterns of Behavior,* Honolulu: University of Hawaii Press, pp. 73–7.
62. Hofstede, G. (1984) 'Cultural dimensions in management and planning', *Asia Pacific Journal of Management,* 1(2): 81–99.
63. Redding, S.G. (1982) 'Cultural effects on the marketing process in Southeast Asia', *Journal of the Market Research Society,* 24(2): 98–114.
64. Yau, O.H.M. (1994) *Consumer Behaviour in China,* London: Routledge, pp. 71–5.
65. Kindel, T.I. (1983) 'A partial theory of Chinese consumer behavior: marketing strategy implications', *Hong Kong Journal of Business Management,* 1: 99.
66. Lee, C. (1990) 'Modifying an American consumer behavior model for consumers in Confucian culture: the case of Fishbein behavioral intention model', *Journal of International Consumer Marketing,* 3(1): 27–50.

67. Yau, O.H.M. (1988) 'Chinese cultural values: their dimensions and marketing applications', *European Journal of Marketing,* **22**(5): 44–57.
68. Zimmerman, M. (1985) *Dealing with the Japanese,* London: George Allen & Unwin, pp. 65–6.
69. Schütte, H. (1974) *Marketing in Indonesia,* Jakarta: Intermasa Publishing, p. 62.
70. Lebra, T.S. (1976) *Japanese Patterns of Behavior,* Honolulu: University of Hawaii Press, pp. 67–9.
71. De Mente, B. Lafayette (1993) *Behind the Japanese Bow,* Chicago: NTC Publishing Group, p. 44.
72. Bond, M.H. (1991) *Beyond the Chinese Face,* Oxford: Oxford University Press, p. 6.
73. Lebra, T.S. (1976) *Japanese Patterns of Behavior,* Honolulu: University of Hawaii Press, p. 102.
74. Lebra, T.S. (1976) *Japanese Patterns of Behavior,* Honolulu: University of Hawaii Press, pp. 58–9.
75. 'Families in Japan's company-centered society: survey of salarymen and families' (1994) *NLI Research,* **72**: 3–31.
76. Lebra, T.S. (1976) *Japanese Patterns of Behavior*, Honolulu: University of Hawaii Press, pp. 60–1.
77. 'Rock solid', *Far Eastern Economic Review,* 5 December 1996: 50–2.
78. Dong, W. (1993) 'Generational differences and political development in South Korea', *Korea Studies,* 17: 1–4.
79. 'Fings ain't wot they used to be', *Economist,* 18 May 1994: 59–62.
80. 'Families in Japan's company-centered society: survey of salarymen and families' (1994), *NLI Research,* **72**: 3–31.
81. Lebra, T.S. (1976) *Japanese Patterns of Behavior,* Honolulu: University of Hawaii Press, p. 60.
82. Hwang, K.H. (1987) 'Face and favor: the Chinese power game', *American Journal of Sociology,* **92**(4): 944–74.
83. Asia Letter Group (1991) *Insider's Guide to the Japanese Market*, Hong Kong: Asia Letter Group, p. 44.
84. 'Kids hold important vote in family spending decision', *Business Beijing,* November 1996: 42–4.
85. 'Women rise to the top', *SRG News,* January 1992: 1.

The Mind-set of the Individual Consumer

Thinking, learning and communicating

Child-rearing and educational practices largely determine how an individual's patterns of learning, problem-solving, information-processing and memory are formed. Whether an individual comes from a low or a high context culture and also a universalist or particularist culture will affect the development of his perceptual and cognitive skills. Those from a high context culture may more readily learn and remember the totality of images and messages, while those from low context cultures may tend to break down the whole to remember the elements. In terms of communication styles, a high context/low context orientation is typically reflected in the level of explicitness of the language. Thus learning, memory and communication styles are additional distinctly culture-bound aspects of consumer behaviour.

Problem-solving

Many authors have noted that Asians have a cognitive style that differs from the linear, analytical and abstract style of the Westerner. They describe Asians as having a 'more synthetic, concrete and contextual orientation in their thought patterns'.[1] There are many sources for this different cognitive style, which include a particularist orientation and non-specific language as well as the effect of child-rearing. We have discussed the specifics of Asian child-rearing practices in the previous chapter. What needs to be added to the discussion is the effect that child-rearing has on the individual's manner of approaching problems and processing information.

In China, where children are raised within the context of the extended family, they are exposed to a variety of viewpoints from their parents, grandparents, uncles, aunts and other adults in the family. Subsequently, they learn that circumstances have an important bearing upon what is right or wrong, and that compromise is in most cases inevitable. Thus, early on,

Chinese children become orientated towards what Trompenaars terms a 'particularist' (versus 'universalist') value orientation. Usunier terms this 'pragmatism', which he describes as follows:

> The pragmatist attitude first considers the extreme diversity of real world situations, and then derives its principles inductively. Reality will be seen as a series of rather independent and concrete problems to be solved ('issues'). These issues will make complete sense when related to practical, precise and even down-to-earth decisions.[2]

Thus Chinese tend to be comparatively less dogmatic and more flexible in following a learned principle. Comparative research has indicated that the Chinese are more concrete and practical than Americans in the objects that they choose to draw, and more pragmatic in their tendency to evaluate ideas in terms of their immediate application. Similarly, the Chinese have a tendency towards non-abstract thought. They tend to view events within a specific context and to discard the application of universal principles in favour of situational analysis.

As for Japan, the fact that children are brought up with simultaneous multiple belief systems (that is, Shinto, Buddhism and Confucianism) means that Japanese people do not refer to a single set of absolute divine teachings or an inflexible set of commandments. Their morality is based on social relativism, or a situation ethic. They rely on consensual decision-making, and even if they do not agree personally with the decision of the group, they see no conflict with their personal principles to go along with it. Thus they learn to believe that a decision is not intrinsically 'right' or 'wrong' but is suited to the situation. The 'correct' decision is the one selected by the group. If everyone's way of thinking changes, the Japanese sense of right and wrong can also change.[3] Thus we see that, in both Chinese and Japanese cultures, the manner of child-rearing allows children to develop a contextual way of viewing situations. Rather than judging things as 'right' or 'wrong' and 'good' or 'bad,' they develop a more 'particularist' or 'pragmatic' orientation in problem-solving and decision-making.

In contrast, Western children are usually brought up in the nuclear family, are less exposed to various points of view, are kept in a more closed relationship to life's events and grow up with the belief that there exists one 'right' way to do things. Christian ethics teach that there are absolutes: an individual has only one religion, there is only one God, a person is either guilty or innocent, something is either right or wrong and so on. Asian ethics focus on situational context.[4] Where the Western sense of conscience is based on guilt caused by knowing what is right and wrong, the Asian sense of conscience is largely based on shame aroused by the awareness of others. Shame is thus determined according to the situation.

What has been identified as the 'Confucian dynamism' dimension addresses the difference in cognitive styles between Asian and Western cultures by further illuminating the Asian orientation towards pragmatism. This dimension had never before been revealed by value surveys until Michael Bond worked with social scientists in Hong Kong and Taiwan to develop the Chinese Value Survey (CVS). The CVS revealed the presence of a dimension identified as long-term/short-term orientation. Bond subsequently termed this dimension 'Confucian dynamism' owing to the fact that both opposing poles of the dimension contain Confucian values.

Importantly, the CVS failed to reveal the uncertainty avoidance dimension readily found in survey results of Western cultures and instead revealed a long-term/short-term orientation absent in survey results of Western cultures. Hofstede holds that this presence of a Confucian dynamism dimension and the absence of an uncertainty avoidance dimension are fundamentally related to a society's orientation towards absolute truth or, alternatively, pragmatic solutions. Confucius did not teach of *Truth*, but of *Virtue*. Confucius taught of practical ethics rather than absolute truths. Uncertainty-accepting cultures (for example, Southeast Asia, India and Scandinavia) are less concerned with absolutes and take a more relativistic stance, whereas cultures that are high on the uncertainty avoidance dimension (for example, Latin American and Mediterranean) tend to foster a belief in an absolute Truth. Japan and South Korea, being high uncertainty-avoiding cultures on most dimensions, are the exceptions but are low uncertainty orientated on this dimension of belief systems.[5]

Further explaining the Asian pragmatic, particularist, cognitive orientation is the fact that Eastern religions such as Hinduism, Buddhism, Shintoism and Taoism do not offer any written document explaining the Truth for the human community to embrace. These religions do not consist of *believing* in absolute truth but of ritual, meditation and ways of living. Thus, when asked what he *believes in*, devoid of a context in which to pragmatically evaluate this situation, the Asian individual is puzzled. As Hofstede notes, 'This is an irrelevant question in the East.'[6]

The orientation of Western societies towards absolute truth can be directly attributed to the existence of scripture that delineates Truth in Judaism, Christianity and Islam. This focus leads to an analytical way of thinking that proved an advantage in discovering scientific laws and creating the engine of change in the form of the Industrial Revolution. In Asia, what is true and who is right is far less important than what works and how human efforts can be co-ordinated in order to reach a common goal.

This pragmatism, combined with the Asian orientation towards synthetic thinking, helped Asian societies to apply scientific concepts and technological advances to business and contributed to the economic success stories across Asia, East Asia in particular.

Learning and memory

Although education systems vary across Asian cultures, learning in Asia takes place predominantly through rote memorisation. In the Japanese educational system, examinations primarily test the student's capacity for memorisation rather than analytical or creative thinking. The Chinese system has a similar emphasis on memorisation, and both Japanese and Chinese students show markedly superior capacities in absorbing information and memorising facts compared with their Western counterparts. As in other Confucian cultures, teachers are highly respected, and their authority and knowledge are never to be questioned. Combined with the emphasis on rote memorisation, this creates an environment in which analytical and creative thinking do not flourish. Additionally, this system has a negative impact on the development of verbal aptitudes.

The focus on applying learned concepts is clearly revealed in the strength in science and maths of Asian students. The recent Third International Maths and Science Study[7] showed that students of Singapore, South Korea, Japan and Hong Kong took the top four places in maths. Singapore, Japan and South Korea were among the top four places in science as well. *The Economist* points out that, while maths and science scores are far superior among Asian nations, efforts are being made to improve the analytical ability of Asian students and balance their ability in synthetic thinking. Singapore is currently spending $1 billion over the next 5 years to promote innovative thinking and problem-solving in schools.[8]

We may theorise that the writing systems of the Chinese, Japanese and Korean languages, which use Chinese pictographs, favour the development of an *associative* means of remembering images. We associate pictures (or characters) with words and their actual objects. Thus memory is orientated towards remembering the image as a whole. Western languages, being phonetic, favour development of a *dissociative* means of remembering by dissociating words into the basic units of syllables and letters. Thus memory is orientated towards remembering the components that form the complete image. This is significant in that writing systems may influence the visual orientation and capabilities of members of a culture.

Communication styles

Communication styles are distinctly culture bound. They are influenced by a culture's low context or high context orientation (specific versus diffuse culture in Trompenaars' terminology). A low context culture relies for its communicative power on specificity, an 'I mean what I say' mentality. A high context culture relies for its communicative power on mutually understood implicit meanings and context. To communicate in a high context style, both parties must share the same cultural meanings in order to understand the implicit meanings.

A high context culture requires a language that conveys implicit messages. In spoken Japanese, for example, 'The manner of speaking perceptibly shifts in register between more than twenty subtly different forms according to the age, sex, and social position of the conversation partner, as well as the relative positions of the speakers in the social hierarchy.'[9] A language of this type requires a high context orientation so that speakers have the opportunity first to form a relationship and get to know one another well in order to communicate clearly. Thus the time allotted to 'small talk' and relationship-forging prior to doing business is absolutely necessary.

The difference in high/low context communication styles also affects an individual's ability to comprehend implicit symbolism. Many observers comment on the highly abstract style of Japanese advertising. What may seem 'strange' or 'incomprehensible' to Western eyes and ears, however, may be an example of high context communication. Just as Japanese individuals communicate with one another in an indirect and unexplicit fashion, advertisers communicate with consumers in an abstract style. Those missing the same cultural background, particularly those from low context cultures, may lack the ability to interpret the implicit messages.

Whether a culture is high context or low context will also affect the emphasis put, according to cultural norms, on talking, listening and silence. In a low context culture, since the focus is on being explicit, the emphasis is put on talking. The feeling is that two people must communicate through words. Silence is experienced negatively and is considered to be a sign of a breakdown in communication. In a high context culture, words are not the only means of communication. Talking is only one component out of many, including gestures, body language, context, eye positioning (for example, cast down), tone of voice and even silence. In Japanese culture, silence is considered part of communication; messages are implicit and are interpreted through context. Words are, in fact, the least trusted component of communication in Japan. The extensive use of ritual expression and the necessity of portraying a *tatemae* appropriate to the situation means that words do not necessarily communicate *honne*, or true feeling. Context and mutual understanding are far more powerful tools of communication.

Perceptions

Each day our senses are bombarded with stimuli in the form of sights, smells, sounds, tastes and so on. Perception is the process by which external stimuli are selected, organised and interpreted. Meaning is assigned to the stimulus according to the individual's beliefs and feelings, and then the stimulus is interpreted. Since an individual's beliefs and feelings are extremely culture dependent, the interpretation of stimuli such as signs, names and symbols varies greatly across cultures. There are cultural differences in the ability to perceive certain stimuli as well as in the feelings and images they evoke. Different cultures do not necessarily build equivalent symbolic associations for the same stimuli.

Aesthetic sensibility and symbolic associations

A general concern for aesthetics, that is, for an attractive look, touch, feel and attention to detail, is common throughout Asian cultures. Although there is significant variation in aesthetic style across Asian countries, the three principles present in varying degrees that guide Asian aesthetic sensibility are: (1) complexity and decoration, (2) harmony, and (3) naturalism.

Chinese, Thais, Malays and Indonesians value complexity and decoration. The display of multiple forms, shapes and colours is found to be highly pleasing. Harmony, the second principle, is regarded as one of the highest goals of aesthetic expression. The third principle, naturalism, can be found in the many images of mountains, rivers, gardens, trees and other natural objects portrayed in Asian art and also in the advertising and packaging of consumer goods. Japanese people, in particular, are fond of miniaturised nature such as exists in Japanese gardens, where moss can represent oceans and stones signify mountains.

The aesthetic sensibility of the Japanese reflects the strong desire for group conformity, in that autonomous aesthetic expression is generally discouraged. Instead, it is believed that artistic creation should be attuned to the surrounding environment and especially to social occasions.[10] Ostentatious, conspicuous creativity is therefore disdained as being in bad taste, while simplicity, modesty and refinement are esteemed as true signs of aesthetic sophistication. In a culture in which social behaviour is characterised by acute attention to proper form, this aesthetic sensibility takes on heightened importance and extends to the most mundane aspects of life. For example, Japanese mothers go to enormous lengths reading special cookbooks and spending hours in preparing creative and aesthetically appealing *bento* ('lunchboxes') for their children to take to school.

Symbolic associations exist in all cultures for colours, shapes, animals, numbers and so on. The symbolic attributes of colours in Asia are quite different from those in the West. Red means happiness and good luck, and is therefore the most appealing. Blue carries rather sinister associations. Yellow is considered pleasant and signifies authority, while white is linked with death. While Americans associate green with freshness and good health, in Japan green is considered an appropriate colour for high-tech products. Across Asia, purple is associated with luxury and expense, while it is associated with cheapness in the USA. Even smells can carry different symbolic associations. In the Philippines, lemon scent connotes sickness, whereas it connotes freshness in the USA. Numbers also carry different meanings; the number 4 connotes death in Japan and China, and the number 7 is considered unlucky in Singapore. The symbolic associations surrounding lucky and unlucky numbers is revealed in the fact that the Mandarin Hotel in Hong Kong has no thirteenth floor, as 13 is an unlucky number in the West. In contrast in Macau, which is more Chinese in its symbolic associations, the Mandarin Oriental Hotel has a thirteenth floor but neither a fourth nor a fourteenth floor. The value of the lucky number 8 clearly documents itself in Hong Kong, where number plates for cars are auctioned off at extremely high prices.

The entrenchment of symbolic associations is not specific to Asia. It may, however, have a deeper meaning than in the West because of the widespread belief in the supernatural found in many Asian cultures, including an orientation towards an external locus of control and a belief in fate and *karma* (as discussed above).

The Shinto religion in Japan, for example, with its many rituals and practices related to nature and spirits, encourages faith in the supernatural. In earlier ages, fortune-telling and divination played a major part in Japanese life, and oracles were often consulted before the undertaking of a new project. Today, horoscopes, almanacs and palm-reading remain popular, and fortune-telling, in particular, has seen a surge in popularity over the past few years, largely among women. Such beliefs reflect light-hearted speculation over what the future might hold rather than a belief in the overriding power of fate. However, the importance that Japanese place on such things as blood types and the animal year during which they were born as factors determining personality is distinctive. For example, women born during the year of the horse are considered profoundly unlucky and, even today, may discover that finding a potential spouse presents an extra challenge. The Chinese are also strong believers in the associations implicit with animal years.

In China, luck is a pervasive value and certain colours as well as certain characters of the Chinese language are considered distinctly more lucky than others. Many companies, when choosing a brand name, will consult a fortune-teller to determine the 'fate' of a name. *Feng shui* ('wind and water') refers to the ancient art of geomancy and is widely used in China, Hong Kong, Singapore, Vietnam and Japan. Geomancy is defined as divination by means of lines, figures or dots on the earth or on paper, or by particles of earth cast on the ground. *Feng shui* reflects the belief that man's destiny can be enhanced through correct alignment of the earth's invisible energy with human energy. Such alignment of one's living and working conditions will contribute to good health, which will in turn lead to success and prosperity. Companies will arrange their furniture, decide where to install windows and decide which way the building should face according to *feng shui*. They may believe that customers will have more confidence in their products if they have the foresight to adhere to the principles of *feng shui*. For example, both the Bank of China in Hong Kong and the Hyatt Hotel in Singapore have gone to great expense to make necessary changes to their construction in order to correct their previously bad *feng shui*. The Meridian Hotel in Singapore effectively had to eliminate its pedestrian entrance in order to conform to the principles of *feng shui*.

Product names

Asian firms spend extraordinary amounts of time and resources on selecting product names. In the West, research on ideal names has shown that an effective brand name should be short, distinctive, memorable and indicative of the product's functions. In Asia, while these qualities are also important, additional considerations complicate naming decisions. For example, the strong belief in luck and fate prevalent among Asian cultures makes the brand-naming decision crucial. In China, the characters used to write the name and whether or not the name is a 'lucky name' were identified as significant predictors of brand attitude.[11] In Hong Kong, the phonetic name of Philip Morris cigarettes was changed from three syllables (*mo-li-see*) to four syllables (*mor-ha-li-see*). This change transformed the interpretative value of the product from one literally associated with no luck to one in which a mere touch conferred luck upon the user.[12] The importance of the 'fate' of a name leads many firms to consult fortune-tellers as part of the naming process.

Although many Western firms might consider such practices irrational, the example of Coca-Cola's success demonstrates the importance of a careful selection of a name. The drink's Chinese name resembles the English pronunciation in both Mandarin (*ke-kou-ke-le*) and in Cantonese (*ho-hau-ho-lohk*) and means 'tasty and happy', a meaning consistent with the worldwide positioning of the brand.[13] Revlon's name in Chinese offers another example of a fortuitous translation. Its name is linked to a famous poem describing the love between a Tang Dynasty king and one of the four most beautiful women in Chinese history. Revlon is translated as '*lu-hua-nong*', the last three characters in the second sentence of the poem, which mean 'the fragrance of flowers that are covered with morning dew'[14] – certainly an evocative image for a cosmetics manufacturer.

The ideographic nature of many Asian writing systems is an additional consideration in the creation of corporate and brand names as well as in the marketing communications used to promote the company and its products. Whereas advertisers in the West use jingles to improve the memorability of a corporation or a brand, Asian consumers have a more lasting impression of a unique or distinct style of writing of the corporate and brand names as well as the product benefits.

The type of writing system used in naming a company or a product also communicates a certain cultural meaning. In modern Japanese, for example, four writing systems are used: Chinese character-based ideographic *kanji*, two phonetic systems called *hiragana* and *katakana*, and Roman letters called *romaji*. Brand names that use *kanji*, the oldest writing system, are perceived as 'traditional'. Thus *kanji* may be appropriately used as a brand name for Chinese tea but not for a diet soft drink. *Katakana*, the most 'modern' language system, is usually used for foreign products and products associated with foreign lifestyles, so is the most appropriate for Western or technology products.[15] *Hiragana* has a somewhat feminine image and is frequently used for beauty products, hair salons and kimono shops.[16]

In some cases, it may be beneficial to maintain the Western name and spelling of a firm. This approach seems to work best for companies or brand names that are short and catchy, such as 3M, IBM, AT&T and M&M. In such cases, the name becomes a visual symbol or logo and is remembered by its graphic qualities rather than as a linguistic unit.

Country of origin

Depending on the country the product is from, the country the product is selling in and the product category, a product's country of origin can be an advantage or a hindrance. Product categories become associated with certain countries, for example French perfume, German machine tools, Scottish salmon and American jeans. Consumers also use the country-of-origin concept on a symbolic level as an associative link. For example, Japanese consumers have been shown to associate countries with the following stereotypes: Germany and France with a long history and tradition, Switzerland and Australia with a rich nature, California and Brazil with plentiful agricultural products, the USA and Germany with advanced industrial technology, and France with a sense of design and up-market products.[17] The country-of-origin cue is just one evaluative criterion, but it is especially pronounced when little is known about the product category.

Consumers in industrialised countries such as Japan tend to rate their own products and those of other advanced countries highly. In many developing countries and also in Asia, imported products tend to be more appreciated, especially when they come from industrialised countries.[18] Thus having the right national origin/product category associative link may be particularly valuable in countries with developing economies. In China, for example, a clear distinction is made between imported products, those produced locally by a foreign-affiliated firm and those made by local manufacturers for a number of product categories. In Vietnam and Indonesia, for example, a clear distinction is made between cigarettes produced locally and those officially imported or smuggled in – even for the same brand. A Marlboro made outside the country will demand a premium price over the locally produced brand. Thus multinationals may find it in their best interest not to manufacture locally. However, the governments of developing economies may demand that investment be made in the country and that manufacturing facilities be established. Thus many multinational corporations, pressured by governments, set up small manufacturing plants in such markets for no other purpose than to legitimise the existence of their brands in the market. At the same time, they tolerate the further inflow of their own brands from across the border.

The value of country-of-origin perceptions varies across national cultures, although many similarities do exist. An awareness of such perceptions can serve as an advantage. The Japanese cosmetics giant Shiseido, aware of the symbolic value of the 'made in France' label, strategically chose to manufacture and market its perfumes *L'eau d'Issey* and *Le Mâle* as being made in France. It does not even mention its own name on the packaging. In Japan, Coca-Cola tried to market its canned Chinese tea under the brand name *Simba* written in Roman characters. When the product failed, they decided to emphasise its Chineseness and renamed it *Sa Ryu Sai Sai*, written in Chinese characters. The change had an extremely positive impact on sales.[19]

Brand names, especially Japanese, European or American ones, are important to consumers because they function as an implicit guarantee of status and high quality. When little is known about the brand or product category, the country of origin is often used as a proxy for quality. A Hong Kong Chinese entrepreneur exploited this phenomenon by calling his garment company 'Giordano', benefiting from the image of Italian fashion without having any connection with the country. A poll of consumer attitudes on the Chinese mainland revealed that six out of the top ten foreign brands identified were Japanese.[20] Although Chinese brands are still favoured in rural China, Asian brands (excluding Japanese brands) are gaining credibility overseas only gradually. Japanese consumers in particular are often wary of Asian brand names. Thus the Tokyo signboard of the Korean company BIF reads 'Italian design furniture' and gives no clue to its actual origin. 'An Asian brand name is an outright impediment', says Hong Kong jewellery designer Kai-Yin Lo. Lo sells her jewellery through Mitsukoshi department stores in Tokyo under the brand name 'Lumia', although 'by Kai-Yin Lo' is written in smaller type. Thus, in the short term, having a Western brand may serve as an advantage in many Asian countries depending on the product category and the perceptions of the country of origin.

Company image

In the West, while great attention is paid to enhancing brand image, far less attention is typically paid to company image. In Asia, the way in which the company is perceived is supremely important since a positive image serves as a means of assuring consumers of the quality of the company's full line of goods and services. Particularly in collectivist cultures, where informal channels of communication such as word of mouth are much more influential than mass marketing, projecting a positive company image is important.

Consequently, most television commercials by major consumer goods manufacturers end with a shot of the company logo. Japanese advertisements often highlight the company *more* than the product. In a well-known commercial for Yamaha pianos, a stern teacher drills his pupil in how to pronounce 'Yamaha'. The brand name is the only word in the script, except for the teacher's final '*hai*' of approval as the pupil says it correctly.[21] Mitsubishi's three-diamond logo is regularly seen on prime-time television without a link to any concrete product.

The attributes that Asians consider important in evaluating a company reflect Asian values. For example, communication of tradition and long-term commitment serves to enhance image. In more traditional business sectors in Asia, there are many manufacturers or service providers with names such as 'Company No 1' or 'The First Seafood Restaurant'. The preference for such names is related to the hierarchical nature of Asian societies. 'No 1' or 'First' serve to communicate either the status of the longest established and thus most trusted company in the sector, or alternatively the status of the market leader. A recent Standard Chartered Bank advertisement assures potential customers that 'The financing of international trade has been a core business of Standard Chartered Bank for over 140 years... Standard Chartered Bank has a long-established reputation as a leader in financing international trade.' Similarly, a Sanwa advertisement states: 'Our commitment to Asia... has a long history.'[22]

In its annual nomination of Asia's company of the year, the magazine *Asian Business* uses the following criteria to evaluate companies operating in the region: the quality of management; the quality of products and services; the contribution to the economy; the size and type of charitable donations and the establishment of educational foundations; a concern shown for the environment; the image projected of being an honest, ethical and considerate employer; and the potential for growth.[23] The heavy emphasis placed on social and communal activities and responsibilities reflects the collectivist orientation of Asian cultures.

The confidence that the consumer places on brands has its foundation in the importance of corporate identity. Japanese consumers have traditionally limited their choice set to large, well-known companies. Consumers have believed that they could avoid risk by buying from such companies and that brands from these companies differed little in terms of benefits. Buying a new brand from an unknown company might result in dissatisfaction and (Japanese culture being high on Hofstede's uncertainty avoidance dimension) should therefore be avoided. Thus consumers had no need to search outside the existing choice set unless they were totally dissatisfied with its existing members. In such an environment, the positive perception of the corporation may give a particular brand an edge in the marketplace.

Changes are occurring in Japan, however, as the risk-averse traditional Japanese consumer has become far more willing to search outside his traditional choice set for brands providing a superior price/quality proposition. This creates a market far easier to enter for newcomers, both foreign and domestic. The new, less culturally bound consumer is more global in his consumption techniques.[24] Although some observers might consider these changes as merely a reaction to the recent recession in Japan, many assert that the change is a permanent one reflecting the increasing awareness among Japanese consumers of international products and their decreasing willingness to pay higher prices in order to protect Japan's market.

An example of how to cope with the changes in both the market environment and in Asian consumer behaviour is represented by the case of Cartier Japan.[25] At the beginning of the 1990s, the company faced a very different Japanese market for its luxury goods. Japan's economic 'bubble' had burst, taking with it much of the prestige associated with being able to brag about the ridiculous price paid for a luxury item. Although Japanese consumers had always been rather price conscious in personal-use purchases, they were now being forced towards practicality even for status items. Value for money was the new name of the game. Many luxury brands that had proliferated during the bubble years disappeared, and those which remained could no longer rely on the traditional strategy of *'Le produit se vend.'* In other words, the product could no longer be assumed to sell itself. Luxury goods companies were faced with the dilemma of how to maintain the exclusivity and prestige of their brands while also responding to such changes in economics and consumer sentiment.

Although Cartier had been introduced to Japan in the early 1970s, a wholly owned subsidiary was not established in Japan until 1989 and a flagship boutique on the exclusive Namiki-dori in Tokyo opened. The Cartier brand name in Japan was synonymous with high-quality leather goods, but the company wanted to improve awareness of Cartier's jewellery and wristwatch products to ensure its exclusive cachet while maintaining sales in the face of a national recession. For three years, Cartier advertising featured only these products and was restricted to quality magazines targeting the high-end consumer attracted to French luxury products. Additionally, Cartier Japan increased the selectivity of its distribution outlets for its jewellery and watches. Cartier jewellery and timepieces would now be sold in boutiques and mini-boutiques in only the leading department stores of each city.

For Cartier, the most perplexing problem was pricing. Between 1989 and 1991, Cartier Japan had increased its prices each year in order to maintain the traditional differential between prices in Japan and those overseas.

Japanese consumers, however, were increasingly well travelled and well shopped, and were aware that the prices that they paid were the highest in the world. The renewed appreciation of the yen against the dollar, beginning in 1990, provoked a dampening of demand for foreign luxury goods among Japanese consumers. In March 1992, a run of decreasing aggregate sales began for Japanese department stores, which would last for the next 45 months.

In response, Cartier took action that would go against accepted consumer behaviour wisdom, change the pricing structure for the entire market and establish the company as the market leader in Japan. On 15 May 1993, a full-page advertisement placed in all the leading daily newspapers announced that Cartier would cut its prices of jewellery and timepieces in Japan to bring them into alignment with world levels. The advertisement explained that this new pricing policy was to demonstrate Cartier's sense of good citizenship in Japan, in view of the strength of the yen. Using such a justification was extremely shrewd as it improved Cartier's image as a company of high social responsibility. Other luxury goods companies appeared to be pillaging the Japanese people in comparison. Competitors soon followed suit and cut prices as well. Cartier has remained the clear market leader with exceptionally strong growth in sales despite lower prices over the years since these events. It also has secured for itself an unquestionable image as a top brand from a trustworthy company.

Attitudes

Individuals form and hold on to lasting evaluations, or attitudes, regarding every aspect of life. An understanding of Asian attitudes to various issues related to consumer behaviour allows a better positioning of products and understanding of consumer motivations, and more effective marketing communication. In this section, we will discuss some of the many important differences between attitudes in Asian and Western cultures as well as across Asian cultures.

Brand loyalty

In collectivist-orientated cultures, product and brand preferences are more likely to express attitudes arising from social norms than from internal drives or motives. Thus product or brand preferences represent expressions of what is considered socially acceptable rather than individual preferences.

This is good news for the marketer, since publicly held views are far easier to monitor than privately held views.

Chinese cultural characteristics lead to a consumer with whom it takes far longer to establish brand loyalty than it does with a Western consumer. Once such a loyalty is formed, however, it tends to be lasting. The loyalty is not individually established but is a reflection of conformity with group norms. Extremely sensitive to social risk, the Chinese consumer will not deviate in his purchases from the brand or product recommended by his reference group. Thus, once a product is established as the normative standard of the group, loyalty is extremely strong. An individual will be unlikely to deviate from the group standard, particularly for social-use products; indeed, one survey revealed that brand loyalty for famous XO (extra old) cognac brands such as Camus, Hotard and Hennessey stands above 80 per cent.[26] Thus the product life-cycle for non-durable items can be considerably longer than in the West.

The relatively weak attachment to objects that is characteristic of the Chinese works counter to brand loyalty. The strong emotional ties which a Western consumer feels towards a product that might make him feel younger, reminds him of his happy childhood or makes him feel powerful, for example, do not really exist for the Chinese consumer. Instead, pragmatism makes the price–quality relationship the chief concern in purchasing private-use items. Chinese like branded products because of the stronger assurance of good quality, but the emotional links are far weaker in comparison with those of Western consumers.

In traditional Chinese society, new things were often regarded with scepticism and accepted only after long resistance. A number of observers have noted the inhibitions of the Chinese when presented with new situations for which they have no prescribed mode of action or solution. For the Chinese, creativity raises the spectre of *luan*, or chaos; hence creativity is generally not encouraged.[27] However, the current torrent of new products compared with prior decades may be changing traditional consumption habits, at least for consumer durables. One survey revealed that 95 per cent of Chinese respondents felt that they had 'too much choice' in their lives and felt encumbered by too many options. This sudden flood of new brands into China has impeded the creation of brand loyalties. Chinese are particularly enamoured with technology and, in the case of consumer durables, will switch brands to the most recent offering in the belief that the latest model provides the newest technology. One four-city survey reported that 74 per cent of those surveyed 'like to learn more about new products and brands', while 71 per cent 'like to try the latest things to keep up'.[28] Thus there is a dilemma: in a country where brands are highly regarded and serve as reassurance of quality to a risk-averse consumer, launching a product early can provide valuable brand awareness. However, since 'new' connotes latest technology to the Chinese consumer, it is necessary for existing brands constantly to reinvigorate themselves and retain an image of embodying the latest technology.

The curiosity Chinese currently exhibit about brands leads to a high level of variety-seeking brand-switching. If a product fails to deliver on important product attributes, however, the pragmatism of the Chinese and their relative lack of emotional ties with specific products or brands allows them to try without hesitation another brand, provided that such a move does not conflict with group norms.

As described in the section on company image, above, traditional Japanese consumers have tended to be *company* loyal but not necessarily *brand* loyal. Believing that they could not go wrong if their consumption choices stayed within the traditional choice set of brands of big, well-known companies, they did not actively seek out or try new brands. This type of consumer is still prevalent in Japan, particularly among older Japanese. However, the emerging openness of many Japanese consumers is quite significant and is changing traditional, conformist-seeking consumption patterns. The new Japanese consumer emerged as a result of changing lifestyles and the recession that hit Japan when the 'bubble' burst in the early 1990s. This consumer is highly aware of the price–value relationship and is no longer willing to pay higher prices for domestic products for the sake of national welfare. This consumer is focused on individualistic satisfaction and is willing to search for value.

As a result, discount retail stores are growing dramatically, are taking business away from department stores and are increasingly providing private-label goods such as cola and film.[29] When Kou's, Tokyo's first warehouse-style discount wholesaler, recently opened, it became one of the world's busiest stores almost overnight. The size of three football fields, the store offers items in bulk, does not wrap goods and has only 18 full-time employees for the entire store.[30] Direct mail sales from overseas are also rising in Japan because the stigma against foreign products is waning as Japanese become more global in their consumption habits and enjoy buying goods for far less than their domestic price.[31] Loyalty continues to exist, but it is increasingly focused on specific *brands* rather than on the *company*. Such changes in consumer behaviour are forcing even the best established players to change their approach; Hitachi, the appliance-maker, noting the trend towards more practical, casual and affordable items, recently launched a basic product to sell at 20–30 per cent less than traditional Hitachi products.[32]

Status-seeking consumption in Japan is not following the same trend. As younger Japanese move towards greater individuality, change has been accompanied by the belief that an individual's personal identity can be expressed through his other consumption choices. The emotional connection with certain high-status brands becomes particularly intense when the brand is linked strongly to self-identity. Thus brand loyalty in the case of status-seeking consumption is very high but is established in line with the normative standards set by the reference group or the aspirational reference group.

Risk aversion and diffusion of innovation

Most Asian cultures rate strongly on Hofstede's uncertainty avoidance dimension, resulting in consumer behaviour exhibiting high brand-name consciousness, brand loyalty, a greater insistence on quality, the active use of reference groups and opinion leaders, group shopping and a slower acceptance of new products. In this section, we will discuss the types of risk-aversion characteristic of Asian consumers and their subsequent effect on the rate of diffusion of innovation.

Social risk

All consumers are concerned to a greater or a lesser extent, depending on individual circumstances, with monetary, functional, physical, psychological and social risks. However, Asians as a whole tend to be more sensitive to social risks than are Western consumers. This sensitivity (as well as economic constraints that increase monetary and functional risk) leads consumers to a greater hesitancy in trying new products and thus to a different rate of diffusion of innovation from that in the Western context. Additionally, in the Asian context, brand loyalty may sometimes be more due to 'inertia'[33] than to 'brand loyalty' as defined in a Western context, in which a conscious decision to continue buying the same brand is involved. Brand loyalty arises chiefly from the psychological comfort provided by avoiding social risk through sticking to the brand chosen by reference group norms.

The Asian sense of status propriety may also play a part in fostering risk-averse behaviour towards new products. In a recent five-city survey in China, about 54 per cent of those surveyed said that they would hesitate to try a fancy new product ahead of their boss. One Hong Kong market researcher comments, 'There is a high desire to try new things, but a very keen sense of social position and not screwing up the system.'[34] In much of Southeast Asia, a mid-level manager might prefer to smoke the Marlboro brand but feel that he must smoke the domestic brand his boss uses when in the presence of his superior.

The focus on quality and brand-name consciousness that most Asian consumers exhibit is partly a reflection of risk aversion as a recognised brand name serves as a proxy for quality. This suggests that non-branded or generic products, particularly those intended for social-use consumption, meet with a less than favourable response. In social-use situations, the quality of a product demonstrates not only the level of living standard, but also the sensibility and taste of the persons who buy or own the product.[35] Levy points out, however, that without adequate information, consumers do not appreciate the value and promise of a quality brand. According to Gallup, only 30 per cent of Chinese consumers nationwide purchase leading brands of consumer durables. Urban residents are somewhat more favourably disposed towards branded goods, with 41 per cent purchasing leading brands.[36]

Monetary and functional risk

In Western cultures, risk aversion is most likely to be orientated towards monetary or functional risk, depending on the product type, cost, complexity and so on. Such risk aversion in a Western context would typically lead to extended problem-solving. The consumer collects as much information as possible, from both internal and external sources, evaluates each product alternative carefully, considers the attributes of each brand and finally selects the brand to purchase based on this evaluation. This process is abbreviated or extended depending on the importance of the decision. The important point, however, is that while risk aversion leads to active involvement of the Western consumer in the search process, it leads to more passive, conformist behaviour in the Asian consumer. Among Chinese consumers, for example, if the risk is perceived to be too high, it may prevent problem recognition entirely instead of triggering a search.

Rate of diffusion of innovation

Such risk aversion leads to a distinctly different rate of diffusion of innovation among Asian consumers compared with Western consumers. In traditional diffusion theory, consumers are categorised in relation to other consumers in terms of when they adopt a new product. The five adopter categories frequently cited are: innovators, early adopters, early majority, late majority and laggards. In a Western context, these categories are generally depicted as a normal distribution curve with innovators, early adopters and laggards accounting for 2.5 per cent, 13.5 per cent and 16 per cent, respectively (Figure 3.1). The early and late majorities each account for 34 per cent of the total population ultimately adopting a product.

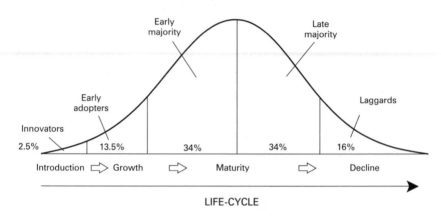

Figure 3.1   Diffusion of innovation[37]

Very few Asian consumers are prepared to take the social risk of being innovators and trying a new product first. The discomfort of being left behind, however, induces them to follow suit if they think that others have tried it. Trials by early buyers thus soften the perceived risk for followers, who are then inclined to 'pile in' in their haste to buy. This suggests that the percentage of both innovators and laggards – which form the two tails of the distribution curve – is much lower among Asian consumers, resulting in a steeper distribution curve. Additionally, the curve will no longer be symmetrical; the left tail of the curve will be longer, reflecting the hesitancy to try the new product, whereas the right tail of the curve drops off sharply as consumers are ready to switch brand once the normative standards of their reference group change (Figure 3.2). No published data exist so far to prove the validity of a shorter and biased diffusion curve. Product life-cycles in Japan, for consumer durables in particular, do, however, lend support to a different penetration pattern of innovative products into consumer markets.

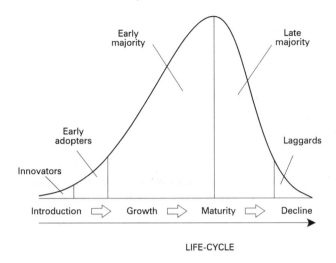

Figure 3.2   Diffusion of innovation in an Asian context

Diffusion of innovation in the Asian context reflects the fact that referral is a highly powerful way of expanding product trial by the first wave of consumers.[38] Thus the most effective way of reducing risk and winning acceptance for an innovation lies in accessing the Asian consumer's referral network and utilising positive word of mouth.[39] Once a brand has gained acceptance among early adopters, the rate of diffusion will proceed rapidly in societies with homogenous cultural and socio-economic backgrounds (Japan, South Korea and Taiwan). Product life-cycles will tend to be shorter. In more heterogeneous societies, such as those of Malaysia and Singapore, the transfer of ideas takes longer and diffusion of innovation proceeds at a slower and more even pace.

Firms marketing to Asian consumers face the difficulty of stimulating trials of their products and identifying innovators and early adopters. Researchers have found that, not surprisingly, the consumers in China most willing to try new products are among the young, the educated and the affluent. Entrepreneurs and workers in the private sector are more likely to experiment with products than are government employees. Residents of Shanghai and the prosperous coastal, southern provinces such as Guangdong and Fujian tend to be more receptive to trying new products than those in Beijing and the industrialised northern provinces. Variations also exist between product categories; trials are higher in more familiar product categories such as beer and alcohol than among relatively unfamiliar product categories such as cosmetics and two-in-one shampoos.[40]

Being an innovator also reflects an *active*, or 'doing', orientation, which is more characteristic of Western than Asian cultures. The Buddhist cultures of Asia are strongly orientated towards a 'being' orientation, which does not engender behaviour such as actively seeking out new products for trial. Only once a product has been established as the normative standard of an individual's reference group would he or she be inclined to follow suit. If social risk is involved, conformity is the result of normative social influence, in which individuals conform to meet the expectations of the group. If the risk involved is monetary or functional, for example, conformity is the result of informational social influence in which the group's behaviour is taken as evidence of reality. Several types of risk may exist simultaneously, creating an overlap of social influences.

The marketer should try to use to his advantage social interdependence and reliance on informal channels of communication. A popular and effective way of generating positive word of mouth is to conduct consumer promotions at retailer venues. Sampling encourages trial and builds consumer knowledge about particular brands. It is, therefore, a widely used method, particularly for food and beverages. Tang and Maxwell House, for example, entered the Chinese market with samples complementing their usual advertising media.[41] Premiums are the second most popular type of promotion. The extreme price sensitivity of Chinese consumers, for example, when purchasing items for themselves, makes them more responsive than Westerners to discount price offers and 'good deals'.[42] The aim of 'delayed benefit' promotions, in which consumers must make several purchases to be eligible for special offers, is aimed at encouraging repeat purchases.

Attracting the attention of potential customers, educating them and encouraging brand loyalty are key objectives in a market where consumers are not affluent enough to experiment with brands. In China, Johnson & Johnson backed a prime-time television baby-care series in which a young couple puzzled over the care of their newborn infant. Each vignette ended with a Johnson & Johnson baby-care expert who provided the necessary advice.[43] Singer Sewing Machines has introduced its products to the Chinese consumer by opening a showroom in Shanghai where it offers sewing classes to Chinese women. Leading cosmetics manufacturers have cosmetic counters in department stores where they teach women how to wear make-up, and distribute samples of skincare products.

Häagen-Dazs is aware of the importance of attracting opinion leaders and generating positive word of mouth among Asian consumers. The

Häagen-Dazs strategy in each Asian country is to establish one flagship location to get its luxury image rolling. In Tokyo, the flagship location is on the expensive and fashionable Omotesando Dori. In Shanghai, the beachhead is on Nanjing Road, an up-market shopping area. The image is then supported by hardwood furniture, gourmet coffee, and waiters in tuxedo-like outfits. The strategy has paid off richly: in 1995, 40 per cent of the company's sales were in Asia, where Häagen-Dazs had 50,000 retail outlets carrying its products and 150 of its own stores.[44]

Network marketing is another effective means of taking advantage of the tight social structure of Asian cultures. Risk aversion can be overcome through the development of personal, on-going relationships with product representatives, education through demonstrations, samples and trials. Since many women are full-time housewives as long as their children are of school age, home-use products are particularly suited to network marketing. In Japan, a variety of cultural organisations from college clubs to tea ceremony schools provide ready-made distribution frameworks.[45] Home shopping parties make use of informational social influence, arising from the expertise of the sales representative, and normative social influence, since a woman's buying behaviour is being observed by her peers. Risk aversion is further overcome as the bandwagon effect begins to take place and de-individuation, in which individual identities are submerged within the group, occurs. Solomon claims that a psychological 'risky shift' occurs in which group members are more willing to consider risky alternatives after group discussion than if the individual had made a decision alone without any group discussion.[46] Amway, Tupperware, Avon and Mary Kay have had considerable success in Japan by utilising network marketing. Mary Kay's use of network marketing in mainland China has been so successful that, within six months of beginning operations in Shanghai in 1996, the company was selling more cosmetics than all the department stores in town.[47]

Thus, although a high level of risk aversion among Asian consumers poses a challenge, innovative ways can be found to overcome risk aversion, stimulate interest and trial, and eventually establish brand loyalty.

Concern for safety/hygiene

Perhaps a trait more representative of Japan than of the rest of Asia is a virtual obsession with cleanliness. Proper appearance and form are an integral part of the Japanese culture and are often manifested in a high degree of fastidiousness. The emphasis on cleanliness can be observed through everyday details such as the individual wrapping of food items, handtowels being provided at restaurants, the wearing of face masks in public when sick, special toilet slippers and so on. To some extent, such customs were developed to maintain public health under crowded conditions. In the present environment, however, the tendency seems to have developed to such an extreme that it has prompted national discussion about a virtual cleanliness 'syndrome'.

Although we might imagine that extreme behaviour is limited to a few individuals, there appears to be a market for products appealing to the super-fastidious: germ-free writing instruments; sanitary coatings on telephones, faxes and dishwashers; an automated bank teller that irons and sanitises the bills it dispenses; and washing machines with a separate section for socks and other 'contaminated' items of laundry.[48] An increasing fear of bad breath and concern for oral hygiene has driven the sales of mouthwash and liquid toothpaste from an estimated $19.3 million in 1991 to nearly $114 million in 1995.[49] A recent, highly successful innovation is the Travel Washlet, a portable, battery-run bidet about the size of a small cordless telephone.

This trend, which can be traced to the ritualistic perfectionism and precision of the purification rites of Shinto worship, sheds light on the Japanese attitude towards nature. Japanese prefer nature that has been tamed by human hands. Many housewives state a preference for organic vegetables but do not buy misshapen cucumbers or slightly blemished fruit, and discard vegetables showing the slightest signs of insects. Peaches are always sold individually packed in styrofoam padding. Cheaper, slightly less perfect peaches are simply not available in the Japanese market. Perfection is the norm. When Japanese refer to a love of 'nature', it is the nature of spotlessly kept parks and ornamental gardens. In many ways, Japanese are rather pro-urban. People are more likely to retire to the city than to the countryside.[50]

Related to the emphasis on cleanliness and perfection is the demand for freshness. Much of Japanese cooking involves raw or slightly cooked ingredients in which the emphasis is on freshness. Sushi relies for its appeal on the freshness of the fish. Japanese find *ikitsukuri sashimi* the best since it is the freshest – the fish is sliced up while still living, and served immediately while still wriggling. Asahi has overtaken Kirin as the number one beer in Japan partly through effectively emphasising the freshness of its beer. Asahi's 1,600 'market ladies' regularly visit retailers and check production dates. Any beer older than three months is taken back. Asahi's general manager of marketing says, 'You've got to treat beer like a vegetable.'[51]

Similarly, there is a great concern about safety in Japan. In a country relatively devoid of violent crime, the Japanese abundantly use the words *abunai* ('dangerous') and *kiotsukette* ('be careful') in daily conversation. These extreme concerns for cleanliness, freshness, perfection and safety create marketing opportunities that may not exist in other cultures. The marketer who can appeal to and exploit such concerns may find success with the Japanese consumer.

Attitude towards authority

The rigidity of social hierarchy common among most Asian cultures creates a different attitude towards authority from that found in the West. Asian religions, educational systems and societal norms all favour an acceptance of one's position in life, respect for those positioned above oneself and a sense of status propriety, all of which are deemed essential for the maintenance of social harmony. High power distance implies high tolerance for a discrepancy in power between individuals. Power is centralised at the top, and individuals have a clear understanding of their place in society.

Confucius' five cardinal relations provide the basis for the Chinese respect for hierarchy. The Chinese are orientated towards finding their place in this hierarchy and working within its dictates. The alternative to hierarchy is chaos and anarchy, the combination of which is worse than harsh authority. Deference to authority is perceived as upright, prudent and to the benefit of the society rather than cowardly, unprincipled or weak, as it may be perceived through Western eyes.

Most Western educational systems attempt to engender in students a certain ability to analyse situations and question accepted beliefs. Posing questions to the teacher and defending one's viewpoint, even if it is opposed to the teacher's, is considered perfectly acceptable. In Asia, however, such behaviour would be perceived as extreme and would not be tolerated. The education system's focus on the rote memorisation of knowledge does not encourage questioning. A teacher is there to transfer knowledge to students, not to be challenged. Bond asserts that Chinese students will feel that they are not learning if they are asked to express their opinions or to solve a problem by themselves. Chinese-style respect for superiors entails silence and the reproduction of what the teacher regards as important.[52]

The difference between Japan and the USA in the conception of democracy illuminates the Japanese attitude towards authority. Whereas Americans believe it a fundamental part of democracy to question their leaders, the Japanese are apt to assume that those in power are in full command. Although the wave of scandals that has swept across Japan in recent years has somewhat changed such complacency and increased opposition to and criticism of the dominating LDP party (which has held the leadership in Japan for almost the entire post-war period), the average Japanese remains largely unpolitical and tends to rely on government mandate.

Status and seniority are also an integral part of life in Thailand, with many levels in the hierarchy. The traditional *wai* gesture with the hands is not just a greeting without words. Instead, it is an action of respect and is the most significant of the many social actions that reinforce Thai social structure. Its basic rule is simple and clear: in any social encounter, the inferior person takes on a physically inferior position and the superior assumes a posture of physical superiority.

The heightened respect for authority in Asian cultures has profound marketing implications. In the case of motivation, since problem recognition and motive activation are largely externally stimulated through the opinions and actions of others, advertising that utilises opinion leaders to recommend products and services will be persuasive. Consequently, it is important to identify the persons or institutions that influence consumption habits in a particular society. As in the West, television personalities, movie stars, sports stars and so on serve as opinion leaders in the Asian context. In China, Jianlibao, a Chinese sports drink company, used China's famous medal-winning badminton players to promote its product.[53] However, Asian opinion leaders will also be found more often than in the West among older people, political leaders and authority figures. It should be noted, nevertheless, that informal channels of communication remain the most influential, and opinion leaders come from within an individual's reference group. One market researcher in China commented that, as Chinese become increasingly sceptical in their evaluation of advertising, their lack of confidence creates an even stronger need to rely on the validation of product choices from informal sources, such as family and friends.[54]

This respect for authority also makes the role of the salesperson crucial. As are all human relationships, the salesperson–customer relationship is considered important. Particularly because shopping is seen as a social outing for the traditional Chinese consumer, a warm, lasting relationship with store personnel enhances the experience. Once trust is established with customers, the salesperson can be much more influential in motivating purchases than can in-store promotional techniques such as point-of-purchase displays.[55] The Asian customer typically likes to deal with a salesperson he can trust, thus diminishing the risk associated with the purchase. The tendency towards dependency and *amaeru* leads the Japanese individual to feel a sense of relief if he can rely on the care of the knowledgeable salesperson familiar with his likes and dislikes.

Attitude towards products

Consumers form an attitude towards the advertising of a product as well as towards the act of buying the product. They also form an attitude towards the actual product itself. Together, such attitudes lead the individual to form an intention to either purchase the product or not purchase the product. Many other uncontrollable factors may come into play to prevent the individual from fulfilling his intentions. However, this behavioural intention is one of the best predictors of actual behaviour. Much of consumer behaviour theory is devoted to developing proper tools of measurement for behavioural intentions. In this section, we will discuss whether such tools, the majority of which were constructed and tested in the West, apply equally in an Asian cultural context.

The functions of attitudes

An attitude 'is a lasting, general evaluation of people, objects, or issues'.[56] An individual's attitude towards an object or idea will lead him to certain evaluations, emotional feelings and behaviour. Understanding consumers' attitudes is important in designing the advertising message. Since attitudes are enduring, an effective advertising message will generally adhere to existing attitudes in the specific cultural context.

People can form attitudes toward objects for very different reasons according to the purpose the object serves for the individual: (1) utilitarian function, (2) value-expressive function, (3) ego-defensive function, or (4) knowledge function (Table 3.1). Applying these concepts to products, the utilitarian function refers to whether a product provides pleasure or pain. If you like ice cream, despite its high calorie content, you can somehow persuade yourself to concentrate on the fact that it is a source of calcium and thus still form a positive attitude towards it. The value-expressive function refers to a consumer's view of a product as a means of expressing his core values or self-perception. If a certain product seems counter to his self-concept, he might form a negative attitude towards it. For example, if an individual has a negative perception of tattoos and sees an advertisement of a model with a tattoo, the individual may form a negative perception of the brand being advertised. The ego-defensive function forms certain attitudes in order to protect the individual from external threats to internal feelings. Should a product seem to offer a solution to an insecurity, for example, it would serve an ego-defensive function. Advertisements that portray how a product can save an individual from embarrassment, such as deodorant commercials, appeal to the ego-defensive function. Finally, the knowledge function is in action when a product seems to provide order, structure or meaning in a seemingly disordered situation. For example, when a product seems to offer information about possible solutions to a poorly understood problem, it serves a knowledge function.[57] Complex product categories such as technology products provide an opportunity for the marketer to appeal to the knowledge function.

Table 3.1 Functions of attitudes

Function of Attitude	Utilitarian	Value-expressive	Ego-defensive	Knowledge
Refers to	Pleasure or pain provided by attitude object	Central concept or values expressed by attitude object	Protection provided from external threats or internal feelings provided by attitude object	Clarity needed in an ambiguous situation provided by attitude object
Product example	Ice cream	Mercedes-Benz cars in Singapore	Frozen vegetables in Japan	Johnson & Johnson baby-care products in China
	⇓	⇓	⇓	⇓
	Positive attitude formed due to pleasure provided	Positive attitude formed due to expression of one's success and status	Negative attitude formed due to threat to house-wife's conception of herself as a capable home-maker	Positive attitude formed due to helpful baby-care advice provided in advertisements
Advertising focus	Communicate straight-forward product benefits	Communicate image of lifestyle associations of the product	Communicate avoidance of negative consequences or feelings through product's benefits	Communicate clear information about product category and product's attributes

Understanding what functions a product serves for a consumer provides insights into consumer behaviour and permits the effective positioning of the product. Marketing communications and packaging can be designed to reflect the benefits related to the function. In the case of the Asian consumer, all four functions may be present as they are for the Western consumer. However, there may be significant differences between which products serve which function and why. For example, frozen vegetables may be regarded positively by the Western housewife because of their convenience of use. However, in Japan, where the housewife may feel that serving frozen vegetables rather than fresh betrays a lazy and uncaring attitude towards her family, this product may serve a negative ego-defensive function. Additionally, there may be differences between Western and Asian societies in the frequency of occurrence of such functions. For example, high conspicuous consumption among wealthier Asian consumers reflects a high rate of value-expressive function of products.

The ABC model of attitudes and hierarchy of effects

An attitude can be broken down to its three components: (1) affect, (2) behaviour, and (3) cognition (Figure 3.3).[58] In the context of consumer behaviour, *affect* refers to a person's feelings about a product, which do not always have a basis in objective fact. *Behaviour* refers to his intention to do something about the product, that is, to approach it, reject it, buy it and so on; it is not yet actual behaviour. *Cognition* refers to his knowledge about and belief in the product and is thus the perceptual component of attitude. Together, these three components make up what is referred to as the ABC model of attitudes.

Figure 3.3   The ABC model of attitudes

All three components are involved in forming an attitude towards a consumer product. However, the relative importance of each component will depend on the consumer's level of involvement in the purchase decision. Thus there are different hierarchies of effects that describe the sequence of components that appear in forming an attitude. Three such hierarchies are summarised below:[59]

High-involvement hierarchy

Cognition ⇨ Affect ⇨ Behaviour ⇨ ATTITUDE

The high-involvement hierarchy characterises purchase decisions in which cognitive information-processing is involved. The consumer forms beliefs (cognition) about a product from sources such as friends and advertising. The consumer then evaluates the relevant information to form a feeling (affect) about the product and, based on this feeling, forms an intention (behaviour) to purchase or not purchase the product. This hierarchy reflects an independence of thinking and emotion on the part of the consumer that may be less common among Asian consumers than among Western consumers.

Low-involvement hierarchy

Cognition ⇨ Behaviour ⇨ Affect ⇨ ATTITUDE

The low-involvement hierarchy characterises low-involvement purchase decisions in which an attitude towards the product is formed through behavioural learning processes. In other words, the consumer does not have strong beliefs about the product or brand but instead forms a behavioural intention to purchase or not purchase based on limited information. Only after having experienced the product does the consumer form feelings towards it. This hierarchy can be found equally among Asian and Western consumers. However, because of the fact that some products are low involvement for Westerners but not for Asians, and vice versa, this hierarchy may be present cross-culturally in different product categories.

Experiential hierarchy

Affect ⇨ Behaviour ⇨ Cognition ⇨ ATTITUDE

The experiential hierarchy characterises purchase decisions that are highly influenced by external stimuli and reflect the consumer's overall evaluation of the product. The consumer first has a feeling towards the product that arises from stimuli such as advertising, the brand name and the opinions of others. Based upon this feeling, the consumer forms an intention to purchase or not purchase. Only after having experienced the product will the consumer form a personal belief towards it. This hierarchy can be seen in the conspicuous consumption of Asian consumers. Products which communicate status are valued for their expressive ability, and attitudes towards such products will be formed based less on the individual's personal beliefs but strongly on the overall image of the product communicated by brand and the opinions of important referent others.

Notes

1. Usunier, J. (1996) *Marketing Across Cultures*, Hertfordshire: Prentice-Hall, p. 116.
2. Usunier, J. (1996) *Marketing Across Cultures*, Hertfordshire: Prentice-Hall, p. 86.
3. Sakaiya, T. (1993) *What is Japan?*, Tokyo: Kodansha, p. 118.
4. Bond, M.H. (1991) *Beyond the Chinese Face*, Oxford: Oxford University Press, pp. 20–32.
5. Hofstede, G. (1991) *Cultures and Organizations*, London: McGraw-Hill, pp. 159–74.
6. Hofstede, G. (1991) *Cultures and Organizations*, London: McGraw-Hill, p. 171.
7. 'Who's top?', *Economist*, 29 March 1997: 21–5.
8. 'Billion dollar ideas', *Asiaweek*, 10 January 1997: 41.
9. Usunier, J. (1996) *Marketing Across Cultures*, Hertfordshire: Prentice-Hall, pp. 371–3.
10. Lebra, T.S. (1976) *Japanese Patterns of Behavior*, Honolulu: University of Hawaii Press, p. 19.
11. Schmitt, B.H. and Pan, Y. (1994) 'Managing corporate and brand identities in the Asia-Pacific region', *California Management Review*, 36(4): 32–48.
12. Mcdonald, G.M. and Roberts, C.J. (1990) 'The brand-naming enigma in the Asia-Pacific context,' *European Journal of Marketing*, 24(8): 6–19.
13. Schmitt, B.H. and Pan, Y. (1994) 'Managing corporate and brand identities in the Asia-Pacific region', *California Management Review*, 36(4): 32–48.
14. Yan, R. (1994) 'To reach China consumers, adapt to *guo qing*', *Harvard Business Review*, 72(5): 66–74.
15. Sherry, J.F. and Camargo, E.G. (1987) 'May your life be marvellous: English language labelling and the semiotics of Japanese promotion', *Journal of Consumer Research*, 14(2): 174–88.
16. 'Interbrand – it's all in the name', *Focus Japan*, May 1994: 7.
17. Nishina, S. (1990) 'Japanese consumers: introducing foreign products/brands into the Japanese market', *Journal of Advertising Research*, 30(2): 35–45.

18. Johansson, J.K. (1989) 'Determinants and effects of the use of "made in" labels', *International Marketing Review* (UK), **6**(1): 47–58.
19. 'Interbrand – it's all in the name', *Focus Japan,* May 1994: 7.
20. 'China's known brands are most often Japanese', *New York Times,* 16 February 1995: 6.
21. 'The hard sell', *Far Eastern Economic Review,* 24 November 1994: 101.
22. Seen in *Far Eastern Economic Review,* 1 December 1994: 38.
23. Schmitt, B.H. and Pan, Y. (1994) 'Managing corporate and brand identities in the Asia-Pacific region', *California Management Review,* **36**(4): 32–48.
24. Hotaka, K. (1997) 'The two consumers: what's happening to Japanese marketing in the 90s?', *Journal of Japanese Trade and Industry,* **16**(1): 12–17.
25. Schütte, H. and Probert, J. (1996) 'Cartier Japan', Fontainebleau: INSEAD-EAC. The complete text of the case study can be found in Chapter 9.
26. *Far Eastern Economic Review* (1990) Asian affluents, Hong Kong: *The Far Eastern Economic Review,* p. 82.
27. Bond, M.H. (1991) *Beyond the Chinese Face*, Oxford: Oxford University Press, p. 43.
28. Levy, G.R. (1996) *Consumer Marketing in China: Chasing Billions, Catching Millions*, Hong Kong: Economist Intelligence Unit, p. 47.
29. 'Japanese shopper power', *Asian Wall Street Journal*, 10 August 1994: 6.
30. 'The price is right in Japan', *Financial Times*, 4 February 1997: 1.
31. Brown, D.L. (1996) 'The changing Japanese consumer: new attitudes, purchasing habits on quality, value, and imports', *East Asian Executive Reports,* **18**(5): 8–16.
32. Brown, D.L. (1996) 'The changing Japanese consumer: new attitudes, purchasing habits on quality, value, and imports', *East Asian Executive Reports,* **18**(5): 8–16.
33. Solomon, M.R. (1996) *Consumer Behavior*, Englewood Cliffs, NJ: Prentice-Hall, p. 290.
34. 'Market shifts, study finds', *Asian Wall Street Journal*, 27 April 1995: 1.
35. Huang, J. and Jaw, Y.L. (1991) 'Consumer marketing in Taiwan: changing environment and implication', *Singapore Marketing Review,* **5**: 53–63.
36. Levy, G.R. (1996) *Consumer Marketing in China: Chasing Billions, Catching Millions*, Hong Kong: Economist Intelligence Unit, pp. 48–9.
37. Rogers, E.M. (1962) *Diffusion of Innovations*, New York: Free Press, p. 162. Cited in Kotler, P., Ang S.H., Leong, S.M. and Tan, C.T. (1996) *Marketing Management: An Asian Perspective*, Singapore: Prentice-Hall, p. 416.
38. Yan, R (1994) 'To reach China consumers, adapt to *guo qing*', *Harvard Business Review*, **72**(5): 66–74.
39. Yang, C.F., Ho, S.C. and Yau, O.H.M. (1989) 'A conception of Chinese consumer behavior', in Yang, C.F., Ho, S.C. and Yau, O.H.M. (eds) *Hong Kong Marketing Management: A Case Analysis Approach*, Hong Kong: Commercial Press, pp. 317–42.
40. Yang, C.F., Ho, S.C. and Yau, O.H.M. (1989) 'A conception of Chinese consumer behavior', in Yang, C.F., Ho, S.C. and Yau, O.H.M. (eds) *Hong*

Kong Marketing Management: A Case Analysis Approach, Hong Kong: Commercial Press, pp. 317–42.

41. Tan, C.H. (1991) 'Marketing in China: special emphasis on advertising', *Singapore Marketing Review,* **5**: 64–74.
42. Kindel, T.I. (1983) 'A partial theory of Chinese consumer behavior: marketing strategy implications', *Hong Kong Journal of Business Management,* 1: 105.
43. Baiyi, X. (1992) 'Reaching the Chinese consumer', *China Business Review,* **19**(6): 41.
44. 'More than a scoop,' *Business Asia,* 23 September 1996: 12.
45. 'They've got their feet in the door', *Business Week,* 31 May 1993: 20.
46. Solomon, M.R. (1996) *Consumer Behavior,* Englewood Cliffs, NJ: Prentice-Hall, pp. 351–2.
47. 'Window shopping in Shanghai', *Economist,* 25 January 1997: 71.
48. 'To buy an antiseptic pen in Japan, launder the money', *International Herald Tribune,* 28 July 1995: 10.
49. 'In a cold sweat', *Asiaweek,* 24 January 1997: 36.
50. Sakaiya, T. (1993) *What is Japan?,* Tokyo: Kodansha, p. 17.
51. 'High and dry: Asahi's deft moves win over Japan's beer drinkers', *Far Eastern Economic Review,* 3 October 1996: 98–9.
52. Bond, M.H. (1991) *Beyond the Chinese Face,* Oxford: Oxford University Press, pp. 20–32.
53. Schütte, H. and Ching, P. (1996) 'Consumer behaviour in China – an exploratory study', Working Paper No. 38, Fontainebleau: INSEAD-EAC.
54. Forestier, K. (1994) 'Researchers pick the consumer mind', *China Business Review,* 4 August: 3.
55. Kindel, T.I. (1983) 'A partial theory of Chinese consumer behavior: marketing strategy implications', *Hong Kong Journal of Business Management,* 1: 108.
56. Baron, R.A. and Byrne, D. (1987) *Social Psychology: Understanding Human Interaction,* 5th edn, Boston: Allyn & Bacon. Cited in Solomon, M.R. (1996) *Consumer Behavior,* Englewood Cliffs, NJ: Prentice-Hall, p. 157.
57. Katz, D. (1960) 'The functional approach to the study of attitudes', *Public Opinion Quarterly,* **24**: 163–204. Cited in Solomon, M.R. (1996) *Consumer Behavior,* Englewood Cliffs, NJ: Prentice-Hall.
58. Solomon, M.R. (1996) *Consumer Behavior,* Englewood Cliffs, NJ: Prentice-Hall, pp. 160–2.
59. Adapted from Solomon, M.R. (1996) *Consumer Behavior,* Englewood Cliffs, NJ: Prentice-Hall, pp. 160–2.

4 Driving Forces in Asian Consumer Behaviour

While culture helps us to understand a society's consumer behaviour, the reverse is true as well: observation of a society's consumption behaviour illuminates aspects of culture. Consumption choices can reflect how an individual perceives himself, his gender and his role as part of a larger whole or as an isolated individual. Culture and consumer behaviour are therefore intimately and inextricably linked. As it is necessary to understand one in order to understand the other, we began with a discussion of the distinctive features of Asian culture compared with cultures of the West. We will now tie these observations to an explanation of current consumer behaviour among Asian cultures and provide an analysis of corresponding marketing implications.

Motivation and needs

In order to understand consumer behaviour, we must understand the motivating forces driving consumption decisions. In other words, we need to know *what* needs consumers are seeking to meet and *why* they choose to meet them in the way they do. In this section, we will investigate these issues in the Asian context and reveal whether these needs, motivations and means of fulfilment differ from those of Western consumers.

Maslow's hierarchy of needs

The psychologist Abraham Maslow proposed a means of understanding motivation through his five-tiered 'hierarchy of needs'. Each level of the hierarchy specifies a certain type of need.[1] The existence of an unfulfilled need creates tension within the individual, which motivates the individual to fulfil that need in order to reduce the tension and return to a balanced state of homeostasis. This hierarchy, although originally proposed as a means of understanding personal growth and the attainment of 'peak experiences', serves as a universal approach to motivation, appropriate also for explaining the needs and motivations of consumers.[2]

Maslow's theory of motivation proposes five levels of prepotent human need: physiological, safety, belonging, prestige and self-actualisation (Figure 4.1). These five basic levels of human need rank in order of importance from lower-level, biogenic needs to higher-level, psychogenic needs. The individual's lower-level needs must be satisfied before higher-level needs can emerge. The lowest-level need that an individual experiences as yet unsatisfied serves to motivate the individual's behaviour. Once satisfaction of that need is achieved, a new and higher need emerges that the individual is motivated to fulfil. Upon satisfaction of that need, a still higher need will emerge, again motivating the consumer to fulfil it.

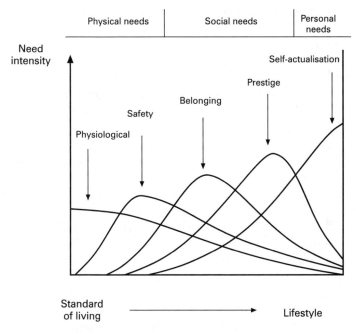

Figure 4.1   Maslow's hierarchy of needs

The theory assumes some overlap between each level as no need is ever completely satisfied. While all the needs below those which remain unsatisfied continuously motivate behaviour to some extent, it is the lowest level of unsatisfied need that serves as the dominating motivating force of an individual's behaviour. Thus the theory asserts that dissatisfaction is a stronger motivation than satisfaction.[3]

While Maslow's theory is agreed to be broadly applicable across many social disciplines, his needs hierarchy seems particularly suited to Western culture, specifically American culture. Maslow himself dismissed the question of cross-cultural transposability. He writes, 'It is a common experience of anthropologists that people, even in different societies, are much more alike than we would think from our first contact with them, and that as we know them better we seem to find more and more of this commonness. We then recognise the most startling differences to be superficial rather than basic...'.[4] In light of the fact that Maslow himself conceded that he did not know what self-actualisation would mean to the Chinese,[5] one may wonder how or whether his theory can actually apply to Asians. Kindel asserts that Maslow's needs hierarchy 'is inappropriate for Chinese particularly at its stages of self-esteem and self-actualisation'.[6]

Such criticism is not to say that Maslow's hierarchy is completely inapplicable. It is useful in outlining human needs and in raising our awareness that consumers may have different need priorities at different times. However, applied cross-culturally, it may require adaptation according to the cultural context in order appropriately to describe how a consumer moves up his own personal ladder of needs.[7]

In the case of the Asian consumer, not only are modifications to Maslow's ranking of needs required, but also the definition of and even existence of such needs must be questioned. As Asians, like everyone else, must be fed and then protected in order to survive, changes are not required as far as physical needs are concerned. However, it is debatable whether self-actualisation as a personally directed need actually exists for the Asian consumer. Instead, it may be a socially directed need reflecting the desire to enhance an individual's image and position through contributions to society. Among the collectivist cultures of Asia, the idea that personal needs are the highest level of need would be neither readily accepted nor regarded positively by others. Indeed, the emphasis on achieving independence, autonomy and freedom characteristic of the individualistic value system of Western cultures is visibly absent from Asian cultures. In the Asian context, socially directed needs are considered those of the highest level.

Rather than redefining Maslow's self-actualisation need as a socially directed self-fulfilment need, we hypothesise that personal needs in Asia tend to be subordinated to social needs. As a consequence, the highest level of satisfaction is not derived from the actions directed at the self but from the reactions of others to the individual. Therefore, a more accurate hierarchy of needs in the Asian context is one which eliminates the personally directed self-actualisation need and instead emphasises the intricacies and importance of social needs. What Maslow has identified as the social needs of belonging and prestige can in fact be broken down into three levels: (1) affiliation, (2) admiration, and (3) status (Figure 4.2).

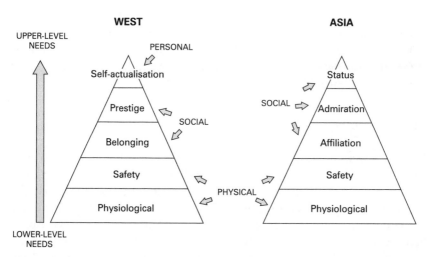

Figure 4.2   Maslow's hierarchy of needs and the Asian equivalent

Affiliation is the acceptance of an individual as a member of a group. In the family, this acceptance is automatic, but in most other groups certain qualifications must be met in order to gain membership. In terms of consumer behaviour, the affiliation need will encourage conformity with group norms. Once affiliation has been attained, the individual will desire the admiration of those in his group. This is a higher level need and requires effort, as *admiration* must typically be earned through acts that demand the respect of others. Once the individual feels sufficiently admired within his group, he will desire the *status* that comes from the esteem of society at large. Fulfilment of this level of need requires the regard of outsiders, whereas fulfilment of the admiration need is on a more intimate level. This status level of needs most closely resembles Maslow's prestige need and manifests itself in highly visible conspicuous consumption.

One example is the new company recruit. His first need is affiliation within the group. This will be achieved by conforming to corporate culture norms such as seriousness and working long hours, dressing appropriately in a suit and tie, and expressing interests similar to those of others in the group. Once affiliation is achieved, he will be motivated by his unfulfilled need for admiration from the others in his group. He will seek to fulfil this need for admiration in ways that depend on the norms of the group. If volunteering for extra projects results in admiration, then he will do so. If being an expert golfer garners admiration, he will work on perfecting his golf game. Once the admiration need is fulfilled, he will desire status. He may strive to attain that new car or expensive watch, or drink only the best cognac. The objects or activities that connote status are extremely culture dependent. This hierarchy of needs is, however, fairly representative throughout Asia.

Trio of needs

Maslow's work is complemented by a number of other attempts to classify human needs and their impact on behaviour. The marketer's understanding of such needs allows him to position his product such that consumers respond accordingly. One theory groups together three human needs with the most significant ramifications for consumer behaviour as a 'trio of needs': the needs for power, affiliation and achievement (Figure 4.3).[8] These needs can be related to Maslow's needs hierarchy and go even further in delineating the contrasts between Western and Asian consumers in terms of the nature and importance of each need and the type of consumer behaviour each need inspires. We find that, while these needs can often be personally directed in the case of the Westerner, among Asians these needs are far more often socially directed.

Power

The need for power refers to an individual's need for control. This control can be directed towards the individual's environment as well as towards other persons or objects. When an individual feels that controlling other people or things increases his status in the eyes of others, this need for power is socially directed and is related to Maslow's prestige need. When an individual experiences increased self-esteem as a result of such control, this need for power is personally directed and is related to the individual's need for self-actualisation.

In our Asian hierarchy of needs, the need for power would relate to the status need when the individual feels that greater power brings with it

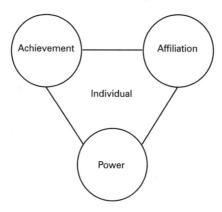

Figure 4.3   Trio of needs

greater esteem from others. The collectivist Asian consumer, however, is typically more satisfied to remain a part of the group rather than to control it, and the personally directed motivation the Western consumer experiences is therefore relatively absent in the Asian context. Since Asian and Western consumers share similar safety needs, the form of power need that relates to the desire for control of one's environment for safety reasons is consistent among Asian and Western consumers.

Affiliation

The need for affiliation is very similar to Maslow's social need and therefore ranks as extremely important in motivating consumer behaviour among individuals with a high dependence on the acceptance and approval of others. As our modified Asian hierarchy of needs in Figure 4.4 reveals, the affiliation need is of particular importance in collectivistic cultures and may therefore be a greater motivator than in the Western context. People with high affiliation needs often select goods that they feel are in accordance with group norms and will thus meet with the approval of their group. In the Western context, this need is relevant to products and services that are consumed in groups and alleviate feelings of loneliness, such as team sports, coffee bars and shopping malls.

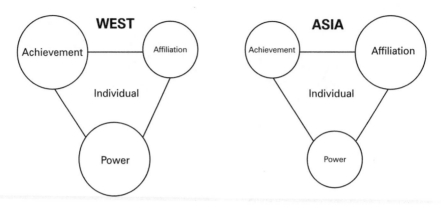

Figure 4.4   Modified trio of needs

Achievement

In the Western context, the achievement need is related to both the socially directed prestige need and the personally directed self-actualisation need. People with a need for achievement tend to be more self-confident, enjoy taking calculated risks, actively research their environments and are very interested in feedback.[9] Products and services that signify success are particularly appealing as they provide feedback about the realisation of their goals. In the Western context, products associated with the need for achievement include cigarettes, candy, alcohol, ice cream and cookies because they serve as rewards for achievement.[10] For the Asian consumer, achievement is a primary means of satisfying the social need for admiration from the peer group as well as status from society at large. The self-satisfaction that achievement brings to the Asian consumer is derived not from providing a means of setting oneself apart from or above the group, but from the social rewards in terms of status and acceptance that it brings. In other words, achievement in the Asian context is very much a socially directed need in contrast to the personally directed self-actualisation needs of Western consumers.

Figure 4.4 illustrates the different weighting of needs between Western and Asian consumers. For the Western consumer, the individualistic needs of achievement and power are more prevalent and motivating than is the need for affiliation. In the collectivist Asian cultural context, social needs (affiliation/admiration/status) are far more motivating than the need for individualised self-fulfilment in the form of achievement and power. The needs for power and achievement are most motivating to the Asian consumer when they are socially directed, thus being subsumed by the affiliation need.

Hence, for the Asian consumer, it is the 'social self' that motivates. The 'private self' is sublimated to concern over the effects of one's actions and behaviour on others. It is therefore more important to monitor the motivations of the social self than the private self. Motivational research techniques designed to uncover hidden motives may provide interesting detail, but the outward, social self is the active participant in consumption choices. Since this social self is far easier for the marketer to measure and respond to than the private self, it may be relatively easy to predict responses of Asian consumers to product-offering and promotional activities.

The cultural meaning of consumer goods

Consumer goods represent more than their simple utilitarian and commercial value. Consumer goods have the additional attribute of carrying and communicating cultural meaning.[11] McCracken illustrates the impact of culture upon consumption choices by emphasising the fact that consumer goods are imbued with cultural meaning from the 'culturally constituted world' through instruments such as advertising and fashion. Thus to our model of product we must add an extra dimension: the meaning imparted from the culturally constituted world. All aspects of the product are then transferred to the individual through consumption rituals.

McCracken holds that culture determines both the way in which individuals view the world and the way in which they interact together. The beliefs and assumptions of an individual's culture create his own 'culturally constituted world'. The individual organises what he observes in the world according to categories in order to derive meaning from those observations. The categories he deems essential in organising the world are determined by culture and may include gender, age, class, status and so on. Each culture thus establishes its own vision of the world with its own unique set of appropriate norms of beliefs and behaviour. From this 'culturally constituted world', meaning is transferred and attached to consumer goods through such mechanisms as fashion and advertising.

In other words, culture contributes to how an individual views the world. In turn, how an individual views the world determines how he interprets the messages that fashion and advertising attach to consumer goods. By purchasing the good, the consumer seeks to transfer that meaning to himself or the recipient of the gift. Consumption is a form of meaning transfer. Understanding this meaning is essential to understanding consumer motivation and behaviour.

Once purchased, the consumer seeks to transfer the meaning of the good through consumption rituals. McCracken has identified four consumption rituals: (1) exchange ritual, (2) possession ritual, (3) grooming ritual, and (4) divestment ritual. Each consumption ritual involves a process by which meaning is transferred from the consumer good to the life of the consumer. Exchange rituals, for example, are those in which the giver seeks to transfer to the receiver certain symbolic properties. This is often the type of exchange ritual occurring in gifts of perfume or jewellery; the attempt is to add elegance and luxury to the life of the recipient. An item purchased from an expensive department store will transfer to the recipient the properties of status and class essential in Asian gift-giving. Exchange rituals are very significant in Asia since gifts communicate meaning in terms of status for both the giver and the receiver, and communicate the importance of the relationship between the giver and the receiver.

In the case of possession rituals, individuals use display and discussion of their consumer good in order to claim possession of it. In doing so, they seek to draw from the good the qualities it has been given by marketing forces, such as sophistication, prestige and elegance. In this way, goods are given the ability to draw distinctions between such cultural categories as class and status. In the case of conspicuous consumption, possession rituals are especially prevalent.

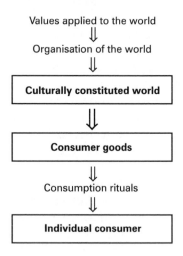

Figure 4.5   The movement of meaning[12]

Figure 4.5 illustrates how consumption patterns are a means of transferring meaning from consumer good to individual. The meaning of the good has been imparted from the culture and is then transferred to the individual through consumption rituals.

Private-use consumption versus public-use consumption

The behaviour of consumers from individualistic cultures is primarily motivated by internally focused, personal needs such as self-fulfilment or enrichment. The consumer will focus on the *private meanings* that the item holds for him personally. What other people think is of lesser concern. This consumer's self-concept is orientated towards an *independent* self.

The behaviour of consumers in collectivist cultures will tend to be motivated by externally focused, social needs such as affiliation, admiration and status. It is the *public meanings* (that is, those meanings attributed to the product which the individual believes are held by others) that motivate purchase decisions for this consumer whose self-concept is orientated towards an *interdependent* self. This consumer's identity lies in familial and social relationships.

This orientation towards the interdependent self motivates the Asian consumer in both public-use purchases and private-use purchases, but in different ways (Figure 4.6). Whereas the interdependent self pushes the Asian consumer towards low-involvement, conformist consumption in the case of private-use purchases, it leads the consumer towards high-involvement, status-seeking consumption in the case of public-use purchases. When a product is used to reflect social status, to maintain and advance social relationships or to seek social approval, social risk is high and involvement must therefore be correspondingly high. It is this difference that illuminates the distinction between private-use and public-use consumption.

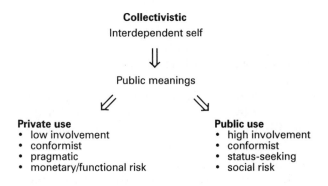

Figure 4.6   Private-use versus public-use consumption in Asia

Private-use consumption

Asian consumers are characterised by a pragmatic approach when it comes to private-use purchases. The purchase decision is typically based on utilitarian features of the product such as physical characteristics and price-to-quality ratio. Even among the Japanese, who take great pains not to appear publicly overconcerned with pecuniary issues, the housewife carefully purchases daily, private-use items with a great attention to price. After all, it is this Japanese housewife who creates for Japan its high household savings rate. The Chinese are similarly very price conscious when purchasing items for personal use and take great pride in being smart in money matters. When purchasing items destined for public use, however, the Asian consumer in general is far less concerned with price and practicality.

Some scholars have theorised that the individualistic orientation of Western cultures leads to a greater personal attachment to 'things' such as automobiles, pets and clothes, whereas the high level of interdependence of Chinese individuals corresponds with a lesser personal attachment to material objects and a greater attachment to human beings. Thus, for private-use purchases, Chinese base their evaluation of goods more on product features and utilitarian features than on emotional appeal. Therefore, private-use purchases are low-involvement items when compared with high-involvement social-use purchases, which must reflect the complex Chinese conception of human relations.[13]

The interdependent self influences private-use purchase decisions by encouraging conformist consumption. As the Asian consumer regards his own identity in the context of society, he does not want to stray far from socially acceptable norms, even in private. Thus, even among his consumption of items for private use, he will choose the same products and brands chosen by other members of his group. An example of this strong group-orientated conformist consumption pattern can be seen from the fact that Korean people living in the same area, such as an apartment building, tend to use the same brand of detergent. The Japanese, when choosing between brands they have never tried, will also typically choose the one that they have seen used by others. This is not an exclusively Asian feature. Westerners, too, will choose the brand that is familiar. What is different, however, is the Asian motivation: to maintain homogeneity among the group and to feel within the safety of societal norms. In other words, it is the conformist orientation that motivates Asian consumers in their low-involvement, private-use purchase decisions.

Public-use consumption

The Asian orientation towards the interdependent self is also revealed in the case of public-use consumption. The distinctly status-seeking consumption patterns among Asian consumers in public-use purchases reflect the inherent social risk and lead to high-involvement purchase decisions. The purchase decision criterion for products for social use is the capacity of the product to convey the right meanings according to accepted norms and standards. Such meanings are transmitted through signals such as price, brand name and packaging rather than inherent product qualities. In a situation in which a product is purchased as a gift for a person who is socially significant to the giver, the choice of product is often based less on its intrinsic quality or the probability of it being liked by the recipient, and more on a precise calculation of what kind and level of relationship needs to be demonstrated in the particular social context.

The high level of development of conspicuous consumption in Asia reflects the importance attached to and resources devoted to public-use consumption. For luxury goods companies, Asia is regarded as the area of greatest importance. Louis Vuitton–Moët Hennessey, for example, sells over half of its production to Asians, as do many other cognac and luxury goods companies. While conspicuous consumption may seem to clash with such traditional characteristics of Asian cultures as pragmatism, collectivism and modesty in self-presentation, the explanation lies in the meaning that luxury products convey and the importance in Asian culture of status and face-giving. The symbolic meaning associated with ownership and gift-giving forms the foundation of conspicuous consumption in Asia. Conspicuous consumption is a means of securing the social recognition and adhering to the norms of reciprocity and gift-giving so important in collectivist cultures. While the desire to assert the independent self can serve as the stimulus for conspicuous consumption in a Western context, in an Asian context interdependence can similarly serve as the stimulus: one buys products that fit with a socially desirable image of a public self.[14]

Conspicuous consumption in action

The importance of gaining social recognition in a collectivist society turns Asians into probably the most image-conscious consumers in the world. In one Hong Kong survey, 70 per cent of respondents indicated that earning a great deal of money and acquiring luxury goods (particularly expensive cars) were among the most important goals in life.[15] The importance of status and face-saving makes it imperative to project the 'right' image, which usually means classy, up-market and prestigious. The social acceptability of conspicuous consumption in Asia corresponds with the high ranking of most Asian cultures on the power distance dimension. In high power distance societies, differences in power are expected to translate into visible differences in status.[16] Conspicuous consumption corresponds directly with status propriety.

Status-conscious Asians will not hesitate to spend freely for premium brands such as BMW, Mercedes-Benz and the best Scotch whisky and French cognac. Mercedes-Benz's highest market share worldwide is in Asian markets. Johnnie Walker's recent line extension, Honour, has been developed specifically for the East Asian markets. Using the British spelling, a proprietary bottle shape and distinctive box design with a seal and satin lining, great efforts were made to position the brand at the premium level.[17] According to Joseph Kanoui, chairman of the Vendôme Luxury Group, 'The ultimate need is for recognition. Whether you have good taste or not, at least you are shrewd enough to understand that [buying luxury goods] is a way to show you have good taste.'[18]

Throughout Asia, advertising reflects the distinctly status-seeking nature of conspicuous consumption. A Singapore Airlines advertisement, for example, assures customers that 'Your status as a valued passenger is your passport to our Priority Passenger Service... the mere mention of your name assures you of a world of privileged treatments.' An advertisement for Patek Philippe watches targets those who desire subtle distinction: 'The day that you take delivery of your Patek Philippe, you will have acquired the best. Your watch will be a masterpiece, quietly reflecting your own values.'[19] These advertisers clearly communicate the meanings that status-conscious consumers seek for themselves.

Japan

Of all the countries in Asia, Japan is the most seasoned in consumerism. It has therefore lived through different phases of consumption patterns. The Japanese are particularly sensitive to maintaining status propriety. Therefore, consumption has traditionally been motivated by the need for belongingness through conformity. A person buys those objects which allow him to fit into his group. In a climate of sustained economic growth and prosperity, status elevation becomes a more important motive, and individuals seek to buy something that will set them apart somehow – something a bit more up-market, different or rare. This is where a sort of competitive consumption that becomes increasingly conspicuous begins to develop. The 1980s in Japan witnessed the beginning of such status-seeking consumption on a mass level.

Many Western consumer goods manufacturers, noting the obsession with branded everything in Japan, have developed goods specific to the Japanese market. Dunhill, for example, does not sell handkerchiefs or socks anywhere in the world but Japan. 'People take off their shoes a lot in this country. They like a designer label on their socks', explains a Dunhill manager. Burberry's makes umbrellas with its distinctive plaid only for the Japanese market. Japan is also the only country in the world where you can buy a Pierre Cardin toilet seat cover.[20]

Although most Japanese claim to be 'middle class' and the traditional moral code discouraged ostentatious displays of wealth, the desire for social status has motivated the modern phenomenon of competition to possess, display or consume whatever is the most modern or most famous item of its type, whether it be the latest-model commodity or the newest words. During the 1980s, as the Japanese took the leap towards conspicuous consumption, the items chosen to communicate status were typically Western brands.

The 'awakening of individuality' in Japan produced by contact with the West in the early 20th century has been proposed as an explanation for the choice of Western brands as the means of conveying status in modern Japan.[21] Western culture and material objects came to represent to the Japanese those qualities of the West which most contrast with Japanese culture: individualism, freedom of expression, modernity and so on. As consumption became more conspicuous in the late 1980s, it moved away from conformist-orientated consumption and became more orientated towards status-seeking consumption. The Japanese use Western brands to express the meanings of individuality, worldliness and status. Language is also used to convey cultural meanings; today, expressions of individualism tend to be couched in Western terms. For example, Japanese use the English pronoun 'my' (*mai*) for Japanese expressions such as 'my home' (*mai homu*), 'my car' (*mai kaa*) and 'my privacy' (*mai puraibashii*), which indicate a new social order emphasising the priority of one's family and one's private realm. Japanese singers express individualised feelings such as love and sexual desire by using English words.[22] Finally, the new, smaller households formed since 1985 are termed *nyufamiri* ('new family'), representing a turn away from the traditional family structure to the Western nuclear structure.[23]

In the wake of the speculative bubble and the conspicuous consumption of the late 1980s, there appears to be a shift in Japanese values in the 1990s. According to consumer goods manufacturers, Japanese consumers now want simpler, more functional products, with the emphasis on utility rather than design. They are learning how much they have been paying for such things as convenience and presentation, how much they have been paying for substance, and how much for frills – for image, prestige and excessive redundancy. Japanese consumers in the 1980s were reluctant to complain about inflated prices because it was not culturally acceptable, but today's generation of consumers are more worldly, sophisticated, knowledgeable and pragmatic about goods and have an acute sense of the price/value equation.[24]

Japanese are increasingly willing to buy less expensive products without famous brand names as long as they can be assured of reasonable quality. The success of retailers such as Toys-R-Us, Gap and Daiei reflects the growing popularity of discount stores and non-brand products. Even traditional department stores are making changes accordingly. Isetan department stores, for example, which formerly operated a sales strategy based heavily on the promotion of big name brands, have had notable success selling a wide variety of competitively priced quality goods, regardless of brand name.[25] As one observer notes, 'You learn there's more to life than a Burberry coat.'[26]

It should not be assumed, however, that brands have lost their lustre for the Japanese consumer. In fact, today's Japanese market is one in which the youth market is inspiring what has been termed Japan's third 'brand-name boom'. However, the consumption of brands is now far more selective. No longer will just any new Western brand sell. Particularly in the categories of handbags, shoes and other accessories, consumers choose only the top brands – Chanel, Hermes, Louis Vuitton, Prada, Gucci and Ferragamo.[27] Young consumers have the means to buy such products but only selectively.

It has been argued that the Japanese, particularly the younger generation, have interpreted individualism as representing a sort of hyper-materialistic self-centredness. The songs, novels and media geared towards Japanese youth serve to reinforce this image. *Nantonaku Kurisutaru* (Somehow, Crystal), a novel that uses footnotes to identify and thus advertise the boutiques and clubs that the protagonists frequent, became a bestseller of the 1980s. Tobin remarks that the central notion of this sort of conspicuous consumption is 'to create an identity of one's own through enlightened consumption'. Expressing a sense of personal identity through one's consumption habits is fundamentally different from Western-style individualism based on personal autonomy and responsibility. As Tobin notes, however, 'One purchases not things in themselves but a life-style defined by things. The new ideal is the man or woman who is not self-made but self-consumed.'[28] One example of the obsessive power of brands is the recent 'Chaneler' boom in Japan.[29] Wealthy Japanese women and even schoolgirls are infatuated with Chanel and have decided that Coco Chanel's 'CC' logo is an essential for which they will happily pay.

ASEANIEs[30]

The economic growth experienced in recent years in the ASEANIEs has allowed enormous growth in status-seeking conspicuous consumption throughout the region. Bright new shopping centres sporting expensive boutiques such as Versace, Hugo Boss and Valentino can be found in places such as Seoul's downtown area and Bangkok's Gaysorn Plaza. Among consumers with the financial means, conspicuous consumption is the rule rather than the exception and is distinctly motivated by the pursuit of status. As economic growth progresses, families feel compelled to display their increasing wealth and status. Lavish spending on the children of the family is common. For example, teenagers in Thailand make up 80–90 per cent of the spending in major categories ranging from motor bikes to brand-name clothes.[31]

The pursuit of status is the leading determinant of such consumer behaviour, and it is Western brands that connote status. Thai consumers, for example, are eager to be modern and so adopt Western consumption habits, buying French perfumes, German appliances, American cigarettes and Swiss watches. In Malaysia, the hunger for imported sports cars and perfumes has contributed to the swollen current account deficit. Products intended for display are regarded as an important vehicle for self-enhancement.[32] Even Korean consumers, who were traditionally encouraged to 'Buy Korean', began enthusiastically buying Western products. Reflecting this new attitude, pent-up demand and a growing desire to try new things, personal consumption in Korea began to increase at a rapid pace. In particular, imports of apparel, cosmetics, automobiles and cigarettes have seen enormous increases over the past few years.[33]

Although such spending may seem incongruous against the still relatively low incomes in many ASEANIE countries, the pursuit of status is so important that some of these consumers have shown themselves willing to go into debt to buy products. For example, it is not just the small number of Malaysian millionaires who partake in conspicuous consumption, but also middle-level managers on shopping sprees with their year-end bonuses. Even teenagers sport expensive running shoes. From an economic standpoint, the governments of many ASEANIE countries have grown increasingly concerned about the foreign shopping sprees of their nationals and their consequent 'shopping deficits'.[34] From a cultural standpoint, they are concerned about the strong growth in consumerism and its apparent opposition to many of the values, attitudes and behaviours associated with their traditional cultures.

Vietnam

Even in Vietnam, which only instituted *doi moi*, the policy enabling a partial return to a market economy, as recently as 1986, there has been a rapid movement towards consumerism in urban centres such as Hanoi and Ho Chi Minh City. Obviously, with an average annual per capita income of US$250, most Vietnamese consumers restrict their purchases of branded products with status appeal to low-value items such as cigarettes and beverages. However, it is impressive how quickly consumerism has caught on in Vietnam's urban centres.[35]

China

In China, the relatively low income level precludes all but a small minority of *nouveaux riches* from being able to afford the luxury of status-seeking consumption through top luxury brands. Some studies estimate that only around 120 million Chinese have a high enough income to afford even modest branded items such as detergent or packaged food.[36] For most Chinese, a desire to conform is the more probable motivation of purchase decisions. Whether buying household products, luxury items or clothes, for example, Chinese tend to choose the 'middle-of-the-road' style or brand rather than one that would make them stand out.

Part of the reason for the more conformist-orientated consumption patterns in China lies in the fact that consumerism is still rather new to China. In the 1970s, Chinese were acquiring bicycles, watches and sewing machines; in the mid-1980s, they were acquiring refrigerators, television sets and washing machines. The Chinese consumer of today is buying air-conditioners, telephones, video cameras and modern toilets. If the economic growth of China continues at the same pace that it has in recent years, the next purchase could be personal cars.[37] People aspire to Western brands because they have an image of higher quality compared with national brands. Part of the attraction, however, does lie in status-seeking, as can be seen by the tendency to leave tags on sunglasses and labels on the sleeves of suits. As for the Japanese, Western products also carry the connotation of a 'new, international lifestyle' for most Chinese.[38]

Faddism

Instilled from childhood, reinforced by the educational system and solidified by peer pressure, the desire to conform is the engine behind the faddism to which the Japanese are particularly prone. The rapid speed of cultural diffusion in Japan is an outcome of this particular motivational factor, but it is facilitated by a homogenous population and an efficient, widespread and centralised mass media. Faddism covers not only the rapid diffusion of material culture or gadgetry, but also the modes of behaviour that come into vogue, including vocabulary and hobbies.[39] New words, typically a mix of Japanese and English, seem to be born overnight and spoken by everyone the next day.

From an outside perspective, some trends are absolutely perplexing. One example is the craze in early 1997 for the Tamagotchi, a video game the size and shape of an egg that functions as a pet chick. The owner feeds it, plays with it and cleans up after it with the click of a button. Should the owner not care for it adequately, it will grow sickly and mean-looking. This is not just a child's amusement; middle-aged business people play with them on the subway. The craze for Tamagotchi has grown so fierce that news of a new delivery at a toy store in Tokyo has led to pandemonium and a line of overnight campers sleeping on the sidewalk waiting for the store to open.[40] Japan Airlines has even provided its passengers with Tamagotchi on certain flights.

Although such fads may seems rather innocuous, there may be a dangerous and disturbing side to such pack consumerism. One example is the recent spate of schoolgirl prostitution. High-school girls and even junior high girls have realised that an easy means of financing their taste for expensive brands such as Chanel, Fendi and Prada is to sell sex. In 1995, Japanese police picked up 5,481 schoolgirls under the age of 18 for prostitution and related activities. Says one 16 year-old girl, 'If I want to buy Prada and Vuitton bags that cost $600 to $700, I have to have this kind of job. Everybody wears them. I feel like a more valuable person if I have them.'[41]

One excellent example of the systematic creation of a fad in the entertainment industry is the 'J.League', Japan's first attempt to professionalise soccer and make Japanese soccer teams world class.[42] Baseball had long been the most popular – and the only professional – sport in Japan. In contrast, soccer was a minority sport in Japan throughout the 1970s and 1980s. Soccer matches attracted only a few thousand spectators from the companies whose teams were playing. There was no nationwide support for individual teams, and there were no players who attained international fame.

The launch of the 'J.League' entailed (1) finding corporate sponsors to lend their names to league championships in return for financial support, (2) creating home town spirit by linking individual teams to certain cities, (3) bringing in famous foreign soccer players to raise the standard of play to international levels and create 'stars' for fans to cheer for, and (4) using a centrally organised marketing machine to promote soccer on a national basis. Marketing included the co-operation of Sony CP to design, manufacture, distribute and license products sporting team mascots and logos or the J.League logo, ranging from mascot puppets, hats, scarves, flags, towels, suitcases and sweaters to bicycles, batteries, underwear, curry, candy, drinks, beer and even bank passbooks. Mizuno manufactured the team uniforms in jazzy team colours such as bright orange, lime green and yellow, and pink and pale blue, and also sold 'replica kits' of shirts, shorts, socks and so on to fans who wanted to wear the team uniform during the games.

In 1993, Japan's first professional soccer matches kicked off amid tremendous fanfare. The launch of the J.League turned professional soccer into an overnight success and a hugely fashionable spectator sport. J. League tickets became like gold dust.

Although the J.League initially targeted its appeal to soccer fans who had once played soccer in school and to children (whose parents would indulge them by going to matches and buying the corresponding souvenirs) who would become fans, perhaps the most fanatical support initially came from Japan's notorious OLs. Dressing in brightly coloured team uniforms and screaming for the cute players chasing the ball around was right up their alley. Fashion magazines provided tips on how to cheer 'correctly'. Soccer also became a family affair and offered a new leisure amusement in a country where there were not many possibilities for family recreation.

In July 1996, the whole of Japan went crazy over the victory of the national team over Brazil in the opening round of the 1996 Olympic Games in Atlanta, its first appearance at the Games in nearly 30 years. However, as could be expected of consumers bent on faddism, the glamour of soccer soon began to fade for the fickle OLs. In 1996, the average crowd per match dropped by 21 per cent. The J.League then turned to attracting more loyal fans among young boys and men in order to protect the political and commercial investments of the previous 4 years and to continue working towards co-hosting the 2002 World Cup along with South Korea.

The story of how the J.League gained overnight national awareness and enthusiasm for a sport that had long been a sleeper is a tale of skilful and inventive marketing combined with a society with a tendency towards pack consumerism. The homogeneity of the Japanese, their desire not be left behind by the crowd and a powerful, centralised media allowed professional soccer to become a nearly instant national craze that filled stadiums with 60,000 screaming fans, their faces painted in team colours, decked out in team uniforms and chanting and dancing to the team songs. Professional soccer in Japan today serves as a prime example of conformist consumption. It also illustrates how the Japanese can take a Western concept or tradition and interpret it in a distinctly Japanese fashion.

Purchase intention and process

One might assume that an individual's attitude towards a product would serve as a sufficient predictor of his behavioural intention to purchase or not purchase. However, it has been found that attitude towards product alone is insufficient in explaining purchase intentions. In this section, we shall look at how other factors come into play in determining purchase intentions.

Behavioural intention model

Fishbein's behavioural intention model[43] was designed to account for the various factors influencing behavioural intention. In the context of consumer behaviour, the decision to purchase or not purchase a product is influenced greatly by the individual's intention to purchase the product or not. The Fishbein model explains how this intention is formed. It proposes that behavioural intention is influenced by two factors: (1) the individual's attitude towards the act of purchasing the product and his belief about the consequences of this act, which represents the personal component, and (2) a subjective norm characterising what the individual perceives to be the attitude of important others towards the act of purchasing the product, and the motivation of the individual to comply with that attitude, that is, the social component of the intention (Figure 4.7). In other words, a person forms intentions to behave or not behave in a certain way, and these intentions are based on the person's attitude toward the behaviour as well as his perception of the opinions of significant others.

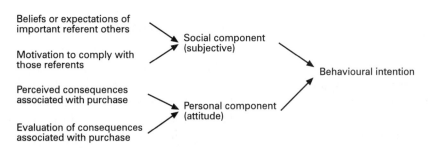

Figure 4.7   Fishbein's behavioural intention model

This model is the most widely known consumer behaviour model and has been found to be highly effective in predicting the behaviour of American consumers across a wide range of products and choice situations. It is rather obvious that both the social component and the personal component may be greatly influenced by cultural context. Thus, it is necessary to question the validity of the model when applied to Asian consumers.

It has been argued that, in the Asian context, the Fishbein model falls short because the social component simply assesses the subjective perceptions of others' opinions rather than the social pressure of those opinions. As we have already seen, in Asian culture and specifically in those cultures influenced by Confucianism, a person's behavioural intentions are greatly influenced by the social influences of group conformity and face-saving pressures. Thus the social component of Fishbein's model appears to require modification when applied to Confucian consumers. Additionally, the Fishbein model does not take into the account the fact that, in the case of Asian consumers, social influences (that is, subjective norms) will affect personal attitudes (in other words, attitudes towards the purchase).

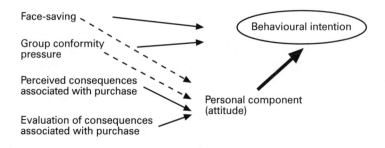

Figure 4.8   Modified Fishbein model

In a study conducted in 1990,[44] Chol Lee proposed a modified Fishbein behavioural intention model to account for the most significant social influence factors in Confucian culture: group conformity pressure and the concept of face. Lee's premise is that incorporating these constructs could improve the predictive ability of the model in explaining consumer behaviour in Confucian-based cultures. In Lee's modified Fishbein model, the social component and the factors contributing to it are replaced with the face-saving and group conformity pressures put upon consumers (Figure 4.8). Face-saving pressure is more than thinking about and complying with others, since it is a reflection of one's own role in comparison with others. Face-saving is especially important when purchasing a socially visible product such as a watch and is determined by the status of the person. Group conformity, on the other hand, depends on the person's group orientation and his perception of the importance of group norms. Group conformity pressure is prelevant when purchasing less socially visible products such as toothpaste.

Recognising the pervasive influence of social factors on personal attitude, a causal link between these two social components and the formation of personal attitude (attitude towards purchase) is also established. This applies, according to Lee, particularly to face-saving pressures because of the link between the concept of face and the personal sense of shame. If a person does not satisfy the expectations of the group concerned, the moral integrity of his character is in doubt.

While Lee found that his modified model produced superior results in predicting Korean consumers' behavioural intention formation, a study he conducted in 1991 revealed that the unmodified Fishbein model does predict behavioural intention even in the context of Confucian culture, although not as accurately as for American consumers. Importantly, however, the way in which the model works is different because of the greater weight of the social component relative to the personal component in determining the behavioural intentions of Korean consumers. This difference is due to the strong social pressure put on them in a collectivist culture.[45]

As a conclusion of their work, Lee and Green remind marketers to take into account face-saving pressure and/or group conformity pressure when developing a marketing mix programme targeted at Confucian consumers such as those in Korea. According to them, 'group acceptance of a product will often be an essential forerunner of acceptance in the market place'.[46]

Decision-making

Throughout previous chapters, we have touched upon the various factors influencing decision-making, such as perceptions, attitudes, motivation and needs. Additionally, we have discussed the impact of culture on thought processes and problem-solving. We will now integrate these concepts to look specifically at the impact of culture on decision-making in the Asian context.

The child-rearing practices and socialisation processes in China and Japan orientate individuals towards a particularist, or pragmatic, way of viewing situations, which is reflected in the different conception these consumers hold of consumer products. Consumer products are viewed as a means to a specific end and are not endowed with emotional connections. Additionally, the collectivist orientation of most Asian cultures leads to a greater value being placed upon human connections, in the form of group belonging, relative to material objects. Thus the emotional connections that Western consumers are likely to form with products are distinctly absent among most Asian consumers. For example, Gallup reports reveal that 88 per cent of Chinese consumers surveyed claim that they rely on facts rather than feelings when making purchasing decisions.[47] Additionally, purchases by Asian consumers are less motivated by emotions because of the necessity of adhering to the norms of status propriety.

Such pragmatic attitudes towards consumer goods leads to a far lesser frequency of impulse-buying in the Asian context. Gallup reports that, nationwide, only 8 per cent of Chinese consumers ever buy on impulse, compared with 80 per cent of purchases that are planned.[48] While Westerners tend to be alone when making impulse purchases and tend to be more influenced by personal factors such as prior mood states, for example depression or boredom, shopping is more of a group activity in Asia. This more collectivist orientation of Asian consumers means that purchasing is less an expression of personal preference and more determined by input from various sources such as family, friends and peers. Ultimate satisfaction with a product not only may derive from the individual's own expectations of the product, but is also determined largely by the reactions of group members.

The impulse-buying characteristic of Western consumers is very much an individualistic experience. One study on impulse-buying among American consumers described the impulse-buying urges of American consumers as 'relatively extraordinary and exciting', 'more emotional than rational' and 'intensely preoccupying'. In certain instances, consumers perceived the objects of their desire to be 'empowered with motility and a will. The impulse object demands attention, directs the consumer's activity, and ultimately determines the outcome.'[49] Such endowment of nearly human attributes to consumer goods is difficult to imagine among pragmatic Asian consumers.

When making different types of decision, different approaches may be appropriate. Traditionally, consumers were regarded as *rational* decision-makers who went through the following steps:

Problem recognition ⇨ Information search
⇨ Evaluation of alternatives ⇨ Product choice
⇨ Outcomes

It is unrealistic, however, to think that a person can go through all of these steps for every purchase. Consumers may use a variety of other decision-making frameworks, such as a *behavioural influence* framework, in which the consumer's decision is a learned response to environmental cues such as product packaging, placement and so on. A high-involvement decision may be approached more holistically than rationally, as outlined in the *experiential* framework.

In the context of the Asian consumer, although all three approaches are used in decision-making, the frequency with which each is used and the way in which they function may differ from the Western consumer context. For example, problem recognition for the Asian consumer is less frequently internally generated. It is the social self who guides the process of problem recognition. The collectivist orientation of most Asian cultures means that the processes of problem recognition and motive activation tend to arise from environmental stimuli. In other words, an individual tends not to identify a need and a corresponding want through internal generation such as drive or self-reflection. Instead, problem recognition most often occurs through external inducement provided by reference groups or opinion leaders. Additionally, Asians tend to employ a less linear and analytical approach in their decision-making and instead take into account all the different factors important in the purchase decision beyond merely product attributes, such as opinion of others and status propriety. Such a disposition leads to a greater frequency of behavioural intention and experiential approaches to decision-making.

Post-purchase behaviour

Consumers form an attitude towards a product prior to purchase that evolves further once the product has been purchased and consumed. If the product is consistent with the consumer's prior expectations, the consumer will experience satisfaction. If the product fails to live up to the consumer's prior expectations, dissatisfaction will result. Many of the causes of satisfaction and dissatisfaction (for example, breakage or poor quality) with products are universal, but variation does exist according to cultural context. Additionally, the rate of dissatisfaction expression and the way in which it is communicated are affected by culture. In the Asian context, properly measuring and responding to consumer dissatisfaction is extremely important because of the significance of word-of-mouth communication.

Expressing dissatisfaction

In most Asian cultures, the value placed upon maintaining smooth and harmonious interpersonal relationships and protecting the face of others discourages the expression of negative emotions such as dissatisfaction. To complain or return or exchange products would be regarded as extreme or aggressive behaviour with the potential to cause embarrassment or loss of face towards the salesperson. In Thailand, an act of direct criticism is regarded at best as a sign of bad manners, and at worst as a deliberate attempt to offend. Additionally, the orientation towards an external locus of control allows customers to attribute the failure of products to external forces such as fate or lack of *yuarn* with the product, rather than holding the manufacturer or store responsible.

Western consumers, with an internal locus of control and a correspondingly higher view of personal potency, feel a greater sense of personal failure should their choice of consumer good lead to dissatisfaction. Such a consumer would feel a need to express his dissatisfaction to the store or the manufacturer and seek redressment. The Asian consumer, typically of a lower potency viewpoint, would not take the failure of a consumer good to provide satisfaction nearly as personally and may not regard expressing his dissatisfaction to the store or manufacturer as important or necessary. This consumer will simply 'vote with his feet' and not purchase the same product again.

The fact that Asian consumers tend to express dissatisfaction with products less frequently than Western consumers means that Western methods of measuring dissatisfaction are not adequate in the Asian context. The marketer must take a more active and initiative role rather than waiting for consumer feedback. Nissan provides an example of a proactive approach in the way in which it calls Nissan owners after car servicing to monitor customer satisfaction with their service.[50] As Asian economies grow and Asian consumers gain more experience with consumer products, become more aware of their rights as consumers and develop a sophisticated view of the price–value relationship, we may see an increasing rate of consumer feedback.[51] However, until that time, a low level of expression of consumer dissatisfaction should not be considered to be the equivalent of a high rate of consumer satisfaction.

Importance of after-sales service

In many ways, Asia is fundamentally a service culture. The ritual surrounding host–guest relationships, gift-giving, packaging and the serving of tea and food illustrates the institutionalisation of the service concept in Asia. For the Japanese, service is related to the concept of *giri*, reflecting the sense of obligation that the seller has to the buyer. The Asian sense of continuous time means that the obligation to the buyer does not end with the actual transaction but continues for the life of the product. Thus after-sales service is not considered an 'extra' but is every bit as much a product attribute as quality or price.

In Japan, it is not uncommon for a customer to have a lifelong relationship with his car dealer. The purchase of the car is just the beginning. The car dealer will call every few months or so to see how the car is running and to make sure that the customer is experiencing nothing but satisfaction. When the time comes for a tune-up, the car dealer will bring a replacement car to the customer's home for use while the car is in the workshop, and will later bring the customer's car back. A personal relationship develops through such personal attention which is very difficult to break. In this case, after-sales service can create customers for life.

Notes

1. Maslow, A.H. (1970) *Motivation and Personality,* 3rd edn, New York: Harper & Row, pp. 15–61.
2. Solomon, M.R. (1996) *Consumer Behavior,* Englewood Cliffs, NJ: Prentice-Hall, pp. 126–33.
3. Schiffman, L.G. and Kanuk, L.L. (1994) *Consumer Behavior,* 5th edn, Englewood Cliffs, NJ: Prentice-Hall, pp. 109–16.
4. Maslow, A.H. (1970) *Motivation and Personality,* 3rd edn, New York: Harper & Row, p. 28.
5. Redding, S.G. (1982) 'Cultural effects on the marketing process in Southeast Asia', *Journal of Market Research Society,* **24**(2): 98–114.
6. Kindel, T.I. (1983) 'A partial theory of Chinese consumer behavior: marketing strategy implications', *Hong Kong Journal of Business Management,* **1**: 101.
7. Solomon, M.R. (1996) *Consumer Behavior,* Englewood Cliffs, NJ: Prentice-Hall, p. 133.
8. Schiffman, L.G. and Kanuk, L.L. (1994) *Consumer Behavior,* 5th edn, Englewood Cliffs, NJ: Prentice-Hall, pp. 116–18.
9. Schiffman, L.G. and Kanuk, L.L. (1994) *Consumer Behavior,* 5th edn, Englewood Cliffs, NJ: Prentice-Hall, pp. 116–17.
10. Solomon, M.R. (1996) *Consumer Behavior,* Englewood Cliffs, NJ: Prentice-Hall, pp. 131–7.
11. McCracken, G. (1986) 'Culture and consumption: a theoretical account of the structure and movement of the cultural meaning of consumer goods', *Journal of Consumer Research,* **13**(1): 71–84.
12. Adapted from McCracken, G. (1986) 'Culture and consumption: a theoretical account of the structure and movement of the cultural meaning of consumer goods', *Journal of Consumer Research,* **13**(1): 71–84.

13. Yang, C.F., Ho, S.C. and Yau, H.M. (1989) 'A conception of Chinese consumer behavior'. In *Hong Kong Marketing Management at the Crossroads: A Case Analysis Approach,* Hong Kong, Commercial Press, pp. 317–42.

14. Yang, C.F., Ho, S.C. and Yau, H.M. (1989) 'A conception of Chinese consumer behavior'. In *Hong Kong Marketing Management at the Crossroads: A Case Analysis Approach,* Hong Kong, Commercial Press, pp. 317–42.

15. Tai, S.H.C. and Tam, J.L.M. (1996) 'A comparative study of Chinese consumers in Asian markets – a lifestyle analysis', *Journal of International Consumer Marketing,* 9(1): 25–42.

16. Hofstede, G. (1984) 'Cultural dimensions in management and planning', *Asia Pacific Journal of Management,* 1(2): 81–99.

17. Schmitt, B.H. and Pan, Y. (1994) 'Managing corporate and brand identities in the Asia-Pacific region', *California Management Review,* 36(4): 32–48.

18. 'Snobs like us', *Far Eastern Economic Review,* 27 October 1994: 80.

19. Seen in *Far Eastern Economic Review,* 1 December 1994: 2.

20. 'Crazy for European luxury', *International Management,* December 1987: 24–8.

21. Tobin, J.J. (1992) *Re-made in Japan,* New Haven, CT: Yale University Press, pp. 22–9.

22. Passin, H. (1977) *Japanese and the Japanese,* Tokyo: Kinsheido. Cited in Tobin, J.J. (1992) *Re-Made in Japan,* New Haven, CT: Yale University Press, p. 23.

23. 'Japanese shopper power', *Asian Wall Street Journal,* 10 August 1994: 6.

24. 'Japan's consumers want a new deal', *Wall Street Journal,* 28 March 1995, Japan advertising supplement.

25. 'Tricks of the Japan trade', *Asian Business,* February 1992: 20.

26. 'Teens may be linked by malls, TV, and Nike, but they're far apart on hopes and values', *Asian Wall Street Journal,* June 24 1996: 21.

27. 'Third brandname boom coming?'(1997) *Tradescope,* 17(3): 12–13.

28. 'Teens may be linked by malls, TV, and Nike, but they're far apart on hopes and values', *Asian Wall Street Journal,* 24 June 1996: 21.

29. 'Chanel surfing in Tokyo', *Far Eastern Economic Review,* 11 January 1996: 80.

30. Here are grouped together the middle-sized developing and industrialising countries of ASEAN (Thailand, Indonesia, Malaysia and the Philippines) and the four NIEs (Hong Kong, Taiwan, Singapore and South Korea).

31. 'Children of plenty', *Far Eastern Economic Review,* 5 December 1996: 54–5.

32. Onkvisit, J.S. and Shaw, J. (1985) 'A view of marketing and advertising practices in Asia and its meaning for marketing managers', *Journal of Consumer Marketing,* 2(2): 5–17.

33. 'Cracking the market: Korean consumers snap up previously shunned imports', *Asian Wall Street Journal,* 12 September 1996: 1.

34. 'Shopping till they drop' (1996) *Asian Business,* 32(5):14.

35. Shultz, C.J., Pecotich, A. and Le, K. (1994) 'Changes in marketing activity and consumption in the Socialist Republic of Vietnam', *Research in Consumer Behavior: Consumption in Marketizing Economies,* Vol. 7, Greenwich, CT: JAI Press: 235–57.

36. 'Window shopping in Shanghai', *Economist,* 25 January 1997: 71.
37. Hong, J. (1994) 'The resurrection of advertising in China', *Asian Survey* 34(4): 326–42.
38. 'Local versus foreign food', *Beijing Review,* March 1993: 15–21. Quoted in Hong, J. (1994) 'The resurrection of advertising in China', *Asian Survey,* **34**(4): 326–42.
39. Lebra, T.S. (1976) *Japanese Patterns of Behavior,* Honolulu: University of Hawaii Press, p. 29.
40. 'A demanding toy chicken takes over Japan', *International Herald Tribune,* 25–26 January 1997: 13.
41. 'For the price of a designer bag, Japanese schoolgirls offer sex', *Asian Wall Street Journal,* 2 October 1996: 1.
42. Schütte, H. and Probert, J. (1997) 'Goal! Japan Scores in Soccer', Fontainebleau: INSEAD-EAC. The complete text of the case study can be found in Chapter 9.
43. Fishbein, M. (1967) 'Attitudes and the prediction of behaviour'. In Fishbein, M. (ed.) *Readings in Attitude Theory and Measurement,* New York: John Wiley, pp. 477–92; Ajzen, I. and Fishbein, M. (1980) *Understanding Attitude and Predicting Social Behavior,* Englewood Cliffs, NJ: Prentice-Hall.
44. Lee, C. (1990) 'Modifying an American consumer behaviour model for consumers in Confucian culture: the case of Fishbein behavioral intention model', *Journal of International Consumer Marketing,* 3(1): 27–50.
45. Lee, C. and Green, R.T. (1991) 'Cross-cultural examination of the Fishbein behavioural intentions model', *Journal of International Business Studies,* **22**(2): 289–305.
46. Lee, C. and Green, R.T. (1991) 'Cross-cultural examination of the Fishbein behavioural intentions model', *Journal of International Business Studies,* **22**(2): 302.
47. Levy, G.R. (1996) *Consumer Marketing in China: Chasing Billions, Catching Millions,* Hong Kong: Economist Intelligence Unit, p. 48.
48. Levy, G.R. (1996) *Consumer Marketing in China: Chasing Billions, Catching Millions,* Hong Kong: Economist Intelligence Unit, p. 48.
49. Rook, D.W. (1987) 'The buying impulse,' *Journal of Consumer Research,* **14**(2): 189–99.
50. Kotler, P., Ang, S.H., Leong, S.M. and Tan, C.T. (1996) *Marketing Management: An Asian Perspective,* Singapore: Prentice-Hall, p. 348.
51. 'All of a sudden the customer is king in South Korea', *Asia Times,* 19 September 1996: 1–2.

5 An Example of Asian Consumer Behaviour: The Leisure Industry

Countries in Asia have been concentrating their energies on economic development and modernisation, and leisure has been relatively low on the list of priorities. As economic development progresses and the personal wealth of the average Asian continues to improve, attention will turn increasingly towards leisure activity. We can expect that in 10 or 20 years, by which time Asians will make up two-thirds of the world's population, the leisure industry in Asia will have developed enormously. In this section, we will look at the leisure industry as an example of Asian consumer behaviour to illustrate the concepts discussed in earlier chapters.

Concepts of leisure

The Western concept

As discussed at the beginning of Chapter 4, Maslow's hierarchy of needs proposes that, as the standard of living increases, people progress from satisfying their basic physical needs such as those for food, sleep, shelter and protection to satisfying the social needs of belonging and prestige. Once those needs have been met, they engage in satisfying the higher personal needs of self-actualisation, such as self-fulfilment.

Using Maslow's model, it is clear that leisure in the Western cultural context is largely a means of achieving the personal needs of self-actualisation and fulfilment.[1] Work, for its part, is primarily the means of attaining leisure. Westerners perceive a progressive linear relationship between work, leisure and fulfilment in life. Westerners have a positive overall attitude towards leisure. It is something they consider rightfully earned by working. They believe they deserve leisure time and have no qualms about using it in any way they see fit. They see little need to consult with others on how to spend their leisure time and do not feel guilty about using it purely for their own benefit.

Furthermore, Westerners, particularly Europeans,[2] see a relatively clear boundary between work and leisure. This distinction is possible largely because, at work, Westerners primarily exchange such 'universalistic' resources as money, information and products. These exchanges have a beginning and an end, which allows the exchangers to place a finite beginning and end to their work life.[3,4,5]

Club Mediterranée,[6] the French package tour organiser and the world's largest operator of holiday resorts, offers the prototype of a Western leisure concept. What makes Club Med's holiday experience unique is the emphasis on freeing its guests from the pressures and hassles of modern life and allowing them an escape back into nature. Prices are all inclusive; there is no need to carry money and, until recently, rooms were not equipped with locks, telephones or televisions. Enthusiastic young GOs (*'gentils organisateurs'*) are available to cater to guests' requests, provide sports instruction, look after children and so on. The emphasis is on relaxation and 'letting your hair down' in an environment that is very different from that at work.

In 1979, Club Mediterranée KK (Japan) was established to market Club Med's products in Japan, and in December 1987 Club Med opened its first in-country facility at the ski resort of Sahoro, 140 km east of Sapporo, as a 'showroom' village. The resort was a success and contributed to the increase in the number of Japanese frequenting holiday resorts in Asia and other parts of the world that were mainly located on beaches.

The easy-going, hedonistic, 'sun, sex, sea' concept for which Club Med has traditionally been known stood in stark contrast to the traditional Japanese leisure behaviour described below. Despite extensive promotional efforts, the percentage of Japanese opting for a Club Med experience remained low. This was surprising as, in many ways, the Club Med concept should be well suited to the Japanese customer. The concept of membership in the Club Med network, as well as the emphasis on social activity within the resorts, meets the social needs of belongingness and prestige that are strong among Japanese. The European image of Club Med enhances the prestige value further. Additionally, the strength of the brand name and the all-inclusive concept removes much of the risk associated with vacationing. Finally, the Japanese expectation of a high level of service is largely satisfied by the GOs who are available to cater to guests' every need. All of this was, however, not enough to overcome the fundamental differences in the perception of the role of leisure between the West and Asia.

The Asian concept

As previously described, Maslow's hierarchy of needs is limited in its ability to explain Asian needs and motivation because of the overarching precedence of social needs and the limited level of personal needs among individuals in Asian cultures. Thus, in the Asian context, leisure may serve to fulfil socially orientated needs such as group belonging or prestige rather than personal needs such as self-fulfilment.

Asians do not recognise the West's linear, progressive relationship between work, leisure and fulfilment in life. To Asians, the relationship between work and fulfilment in life is more direct; life fulfilment is achieved directly through hard work.[7] Furthermore, the nature of work in Asia blurs the boundary between work and leisure. Compared with work in the West, which requires the exchange of universalistic resources, work in Asia often requires the exchange of 'particularistic' resources of service, status, trust and human interconnection. These resources have no clear-cut beginning, and the exchangers cannot therefore place finite boundaries on their work life.[8,9,10]

Similar particularistic resources are also required for duties prescribed by Asian culture towards other entities such as family, clan, community and even ancestors, none of which is exclusive, and all of which must be fulfilled concurrently.[11] Given this heavy burden of duties, one may even be tempted to go a step further and argue that, in Asians' minds, life is divided between work and 'other responsibilities' as opposed to work and 'leisure'.

It is not surprising, then, that Asians have a generally negative attitude towards leisure. They are uncomfortable with the perception that it is something to which they are entitled, no matter how hard they have worked, and appear to harbour an underlying sense of guilt in using leisure time to satisfy only their personal needs. As a consequence, it seems that any leisure pursuit requires justification.

Asian motivations for leisure

There are many underlying motivations for leisure activities, such as relaxation, escapism, fun and pleasure, that are common to all human beings. However, given the fundamental differences in the concepts of culture and leisure identified in the previous sections, it is hardly surprising that, in Asia, certain specific motivations for leisure activities are stronger than in the West. It is not that such motivations do not exist among Westerners, but simply that in Western societies they are less pronounced determinants of leisure activity.

Family/group engagement

Reflecting the collectivist orientation of most Asian cultures, leisure in Asia is distinctly group orientated. One of the most important purposes of an individual's leisure hours is to spend time with his family and/or the group to which he belongs. Leisure time spent fortifying bonds of group belongingness appears to generate the least need for justification or rationalisation. As the time spent away from the home in work-related activities grows, especially for Asia's urban middle-class families, leisure time spent with the family will continue to grow in importance.[12] Illustrative of the growing emphasis on family-orientated leisure activity is the fact that the fastest growing segment at Club Med's Asian villages is families with small children, which today already account for approximately 30 per cent of their Japanese clientele. This represents a sharp increase from a mere trickle a decade ago.

The orientation towards group-related leisure activity can be witnessed across Asia. *Karaoke* is a form of entertainment in which small groups sing at home, in bars, in specially designed soundproof boxes at cafés and even on tour buses. *Karaoke* originated in Japan, where it now claims 60 million enthusiasts and is sung about 16.5 million times daily.[13] Countless more millions including the Chinese sing *karaoke* across Asia. Today, if an Asian song is to be a hit, it must be easy to sing along with.[14] Although *karaoke* is sometimes sung alone, such solo singing is typically a preparation for group outings. Another example of Asian group-orientated leisure is the recent bicycling boom in Indonesia, which is centred around group cycling and membership of bicycling clubs. Some clubs have as many as 8,000 members of all ages.[15]

Learning

The Confucian emphasis on learning and continuous self-improvement can be seen in the appeal of certain leisure activities to Asians. Learning is perhaps the most viable justification for Asians who spend leisure time on their own. For example, Asians widely regard travel as an opportunity for learning and personal enrichment. In a recent survey, two-thirds of South Koreans and Taiwanese named culture and sightseeing – basically learning experiences – as their preferred activity while vacationing abroad.[16] Japanese men often head for Australia and Southeast Asia to learn to play golf, scuba dive or learn other sports that are less accessible at home,[17] while the OLs of Japan throng European museums to learn about European art.

Realising that many Japanese need a means of legitimising their vacation time, Club Med Japan began offering courses in English, French, computers and cooking, for example. The brochures stressed the opportunities for learning tennis, wind surfing or diving, as well as for sightseeing. This certainly appealed to the Japanese, although the expectations of the guests became difficult to fulfil because of the limited length of their holidays and their preference for taking 3–4 day holidays in each season rather than the 15 days common in France. The value perception of men and women can, however, differ considerably, even if they belong to the same age group or have a similar educational background. While OLs were attracted to Club Med's offer of learning and experiencing a new 'international' world of leisure, the 'office boys', young men in their twenties, stayed away as they had to concentrate on their career. This led to imbalances in the mix of guests in the resorts.

Learning and education are central themes in daily leisure activities not only in Japan, but also throughout Asia, particularly for children. Their extracurricular lessons may cover a dizzying array of activities, including singing, violin, piano, art, dance, swimming, martial arts and Chinese calligraphy. Many of these 'leisure' lessons are strongly encouraged by parents. Recently, some parents have also begun to send their children to religious camps during school breaks to learn about Buddhism and Islam.[18,19]

Asian adults also take lessons in a wide variety of activities as a form of daily leisure. One of the most popular leisure pursuits across Asia is to take English lessons at a foreign language school. While many undoubtedly take these lessons because they need to learn the language, many others engage in them, especially the conversation-orientated ones taught by native speakers, as an entertaining and easily justifiable form of leisure.

Status propriety/elevation

As discussed in Chapter 2, maintaining proper status is an important prerequisite for joining or staying in Asian peer circles and other groups. As the Asian middle class rounds out its possession of modern consumer goods, there are signs that leisure behaviour is becoming an important means for someone to elevate his status to join a group, or simply to stay in a group whose status is in transition.

In Japan, golf is nearly mandatory for conducting business. While corporate mid-level managers are members of golf driving range clubs, their superiors may join exclusive golf course clubs whose annual memberships can cost up to $1 million. Status is an integral part of playing golf in Japan and increasingly throughout many parts of Asia. An executive of Dentsu, Japan's largest advertising agency remarked, 'One condition for becoming the president of Dentsu is a hole in one.'[20] Senior members of the Vietnamese government have also taken to the golf courses since their country became part of ASEAN.

No-one can fail to notice the desire of Asian tourists to be photographed in front of famous monuments, landmarks and works of art. This tendency is related to status-seeking. A photograph of a retired Korean farmer in front of the *Mona Lisa* at the Louvre in Paris, for example, does wonders to elevate his status among friends back home. The adult children of these friends soon hear about the trip and feel the need to send their parents on *hyodo,* or filial piety, tours to level the socialising field for both their parents and themselves.

Culture-driven constraints

While cultural values in Asia may serve to motivate certain leisure activities, they may limit others. Thus culture serves as both a motivating and a constraining factor influencing aspects of consumer behaviour that involve leisure activities.

Family/group responsibilities

The cultural value of responsibility towards their group leads Asian employees to take far less time off from work than their Western counterparts. The exchange of particularistic resources in professional life requires far more energy and time than the exchange of universalistic resources in the West.[21] This difference in professional life, combined with the sheer number and variety of duties and responsibilities prescribed by Asian culture, all of which must be fulfilled simultaneously, means that Asians have even less leisure time available than Westerners.

The most significant reason behind the Japanese worker's reluctance to take all of his holiday entitlement is his desire to avoid consigning more work to colleagues remaining in the office. In contrast, during public holidays when everyone has time off, workers will happily take the vacation. The time is usually spent, however, fulfilling family obligations such as visiting and paying respect to ageing parents, relatives and even superiors at work.

The role that family obligations and filial piety play in most Asian cultures is illustrated by the fact that the first big wave of overseas tourists from Korea in the 1980s consisted largely of two segments: honeymooners and older retirees being sent by sons and daughters on the aforementioned *hyodo* tours. It was widely accepted that grown children should first fulfil their filial duties before indulging themselves in such high-profile leisure excursions as overseas tourism.[22]

Religion

Another powerful culture-driven constraint is religion. Religious constraints to leisure are most visible in the mixed-culture countries of Singapore, Indonesia and Malaysia. Islam, for example, is stringently opposed to the consumption of alcohol. In Indonesia, 90 per cent of whose population is Muslim, there has been little increase in alcohol sales and consumption despite heavy marketing and the wide availability of liquor.[23] Muslim groups in Indonesia are pressuring the government to abolish the 'Philanthropic Donations with Prizes', or national lottery, whose name symbolises the government's attempt and failure to appease religious pressures.[24] In 1990, the predominantly Malay state of Kelantan in Malaysia voted into office an Islamic administration bent on making the state more Islamic. As a result, currently banned activities include carnival rides, most public performances that include singing and dancing, and other leisure activities where there is contact between the sexes.[25] In order to serve non-Moslems and tourists, however, privately owned lotteries, horse racing, sweepstakes, digit-betting and a casino were left intact.[26] In 1997, Moslem females were arrested in another state of Malaysia for parading in bathing costumes during a beauty contest.[27] Questions soon surfaced concerning whether Malaysian swimmers of Moslem belief could continue to participate in national or international swimming competitions.

State/government

In some Asian countries, the most powerful constraint to leisure activity is state or government regulation. For example, not only does the Singaporean government outlaw the ownership of satellite dishes, but the Singapore Broadcast Authority (SBA) also has authority over the many Singapore-based international broadcasters, who must abide by its editorial guide-lines.[28] Malaysia bans certain MTV programmes and local music bands sporting improper attire or having inappropriate musical content,[29] while pressure from the Chinese government influenced Star TV to drop the BBC and tailor its programmes to be acceptable to the Chinese leadership.[30]

Government constraints to leisure do not always appear in such obvious forms. The Asian group orientation applies to the state as well, and individuals are expected to subjugate their needs, including leisure needs, to those of the state, even if they are not officially told to do so. In 1987, the Japanese Ministry of Transport announced a programme to double the number of its citizens travelling overseas within the following 10 years. This announcement was numerically of little importance because the doubling was expected to occur easily within that time frame. The announcement was important, however, for it represented an official endorsement of overseas travel by the state to its subjects and suddenly turned foreign travel into a patriotic pastime.[31]

Implications for future leisure behaviour of Asians

At least until the current generation of teenagers, who have experienced the benefits of fast and continuous economic growth, become parents themselves, the importance of Asian cultural values such as family/group orientation, learning and status propriety/elevation will continue to influence and permeate leisure behaviour in Asia. This will be apparent both in terms of the conceptualisation of leisure and in the motivation and constraints surrounding certain leisure activities. Also at play will be the myriad forces originating from the various national, regional and religious traditions that make up Asia, as well as other physical factors such as space and geography.

Western influences will undoubtedly continue to play a significant role in developing and providing activities for leisure in Asia. However, it would be a mistake to interpret the warm reception of new Western leisure concepts as an indication that Asian leisure behaviour will become fundamentally Westernised in the immediate future. Although Asians are experimenting with Western concepts in what they sing, listen to, watch on television and at cinemas, eat at restaurants and play at casinos, they eventually adapt such concepts to their own tastes and preferences. Tokyo Disneyland, for example, is not successful because the Japanese continue to be fascinated by the same American culture. Instead, the $100 million the park spends annually to adapt continuously to Japanese tastes allows it to maintain its appeal.

This is not to say that unaltered Western leisure concepts have no future in Asia. Curiosity will encourage Asians entering the middle class to experiment with Western culture and leisure activities. Western leisure providers looking towards Asia face a choice that includes: (1) keeping their original concept whole and appealing to a Western-orientated niche market, and (2) adapting their concept partially to the local cultural context and appealing to a larger market. If the latter choice is made, it seems advisable to consider the following adaptations while strategically planning for the Asian market:

- Tailor the facilities and services to maximise group/family activities.
- Promote learning experiences that can be used to justify fun and pleasure.
- Present visible signs of achievement (such as certificates) that contribute to the recipient's status.
- Provide souvenirs and memorabilia that can be shared with those back home.
- Make the facilities easily accessible in terms of the constraints on space, time, transportation and religious and government constraints.

In 1981, 2 years after the opening of its Sahoro resort, Club Med membership reached 6,706 and then grew to 49,300 in 1989. However, this membership still represented only 0.04 per cent of the Japanese population, whereas 0.66 per cent of the French population were Club Med members. Certainly there was potential for growth. With the European market already at maturity, the American market nearing maturity and the Asian leisure market just beginning to take off, growth in Asia was an integral part of Club Med's long-term strategy.

It was at this point that the company faced the decision of whether or not to change its leisure format fundamentally in order to suit the traditional Japanese leisure concept more closely. Should it consider its 'escape from civilisation' vacation concept as its core competence and maintain it unadulterated even for Japanese consumers unused to this type of vacation? Or, if Club Med wanted significant growth, would major changes such as stressing learning be needed in order to appeal to the mainstream Japanese consumer? Would such changes constitute cultural sensitivity or simply a strategy of differentiation? Additionally, with the understanding that the idea of 'untamed' nature was less appealing to most Japanese, should Club Med villages for Japanese guests offer telephones and air-conditioning in rooms with a more hotel-like, sterile quality compared with the thatched roof bungalows common in Club Med's Mediterranean villages?

After a long internal debate and extensive market research, Club Med decided to stick to its traditional formula and adjust its offering only marginally. The strong corporate culture of Club Med, best described as a company of fun-seeking beachboys, did not lend itself to a major change towards a more serious, learning-orientated and tightly structured holiday provider. The decision to stick to its free-spirited French image meant accepting the role of niche player in Japan in the short term. This strategy, however, also prevented other Asian leisure companies from competing directly with Club Med. In targeting younger, more modern Japanese, Club Med was able in the 1990s to attract an increasing number of loyal customers, successfully extending its marketing activities to most of the other Asian countries in the meantime.

Notes

1. Unger, L. and Kernan, J. (1983) 'On the meaning of leisure: an investigation of some determinants of the subjective experience', *Journal of Consumer Research,* **9**(4): 381–91.
2. Kaufman, C. and Lane, P. (1992) 'Crisscrossing the cultural time gap', *Cultural Dimensions of International Marketing,* 1: 30–49.
3. Foa, V. and Foa, E. (1974) *Societal Structures of the Mind,* Springfield, IL: Charles C. Thomas.
4. Hall, E. (1976) *The Hidden Dimension,* New York: Anchor Press-Doubleday.
5. 'How cultures collide', *Psychology Today,* July 1976: 66–74.
6. Schütte, H. and Ishida, E. (1990) 'Club Med Japan', Fontainebleau: INSEAD-EAC. The complete text of the case study can be found in Chapter 9.
7. Manrai, L. and Manrai, A. (1995) 'Effects of cultural context, gender, and acculturation on perception of work versus social/leisure time usage', *Journal of Business Research,* **32**(2): 115–28.
8. Foa, V. and Foa, E. (1974) *Societal Structures of the Mind,* Springfield, IL: Charles C. Thomas.
9. Hall, E. (1976) *The Hidden Dimension,* New York: Anchor Press-Doubleday.
10. 'How cultures collide', *Psychology Today,* July 1976: 66–74.
11. Manrai, L. and Manrai, A. (1995) 'Effects of cultural context, gender, and acculturation on perception of work versus social/leisure time usage', *Journal of Business Research,* **32**(2): 115–28.
12. 'Coping with kids', *Asiaweek,* 8 September 1993: 36–9.
13. 'Karaoke goes higher tech', *International Herald Tribune,* 13 March 1996: 2.
14. 'Sweet Chinese sirens', *Forbes,* 20 December 1993: 78–9.
15. 'The rich way to pedal', *Asiaweek,* 30 June 1994: 33.

16. 'Asia lifestyles', *Far Eastern Economic Review,* 11 August 1994: 35–47.
17. 'Tee masters', *Far Eastern Economic Review*, 29 December 1994: 80–2.
18. 'Little emperors', *Asiaweek,* 1 December 1995: 44–50.
19. 'Camping with a difference', *Asiaweek,* 15 September 1995: 42.
20. 'Tee masters', *Far Eastern Economic Review*, 29 December 1994: 80–2.
21. Foa, V. and Foa, E. (1974) *Societal Structures of the Mind,* Springfield, IL: Charles C. Thomas.
22. 'Here come the Koreans', *Asia Travel Trade,* July/August 1989: 38–9.
23. 'To drink or not to drink', *Asiaweek,* 20 October 1993: 30.
24. 'A losing gamble', *Far Eastern Economic Review,* 2 December 1993: 28.
25. 'Getting serious about fun', *Asiaweek,* 10 November 1995: 37.
26. 'A controversial gamble', *Asiaweek,* 10 February 1993: 25.
27. 'Hot-seat experience', *Far Eastern Economic Review,* 31 July 1997: 17–20.
28. 'A TV extravaganza', *Asiaweek,* 20 October 1995: 32.
29. 'It's only rock 'n' roll', *Asiaweek,* 28 April 1993: 34–8.
30. 'TV is exploding all over Asia', *Fortune,* 10 January 1994: 24–8.
31. 'The impending tourist tide', *Asian Business,* February 1990: 56–8.

6 Marketing Implications

Market segmentation is the process of dividing a market into distinct groups of consumers with different characteristics, needs and behaviours. Among the various segments identified, the marketer selects one or more of the most attractive or suitable target groups, to which he will tailor appropriate activities within the marketing mix. The marketing mix activities in turn create a certain positioning of the product or service that is appealing to the targeted segment.

In this chapter, we will first propose some specific ways to define market segments in Asia. We will then discuss some generic positioning options for the region. Finally, we will look at a number of aspects of the marketing mix that are specific to Asia.

Segmentation

Geographic segmentation

Segmentation cuts across markets in various ways using geographical, demographic and psychographic dimensions. The geographical dimension can be applied across several countries or within the borders of a given country (Figure 6.1).

Segmentation across Asia

There are at least two segments in Asia in which the target groups in the various countries across the region show a great deal of similarity with each other but at the same time differ considerably from other segments in their respective countries. The first of these two segments comprises the rich, well-educated, well-travelled élite. They may meet in international meetings or on well-known golf courses within or outside Asia, and frequent the same five-star hotels around the world. Members of the group with 'old money' have certain Asia-specific characteristics, such as a strong attachment to family traditions. Alternatively, those who belong to groups that have more recently acquired wealth feel less dependent on the value system at home that helped them to succeed. This élite segment is basically the Asian segment of a global group of cosmopolitan consumers with very similar preferences and attitudes across the globe. Consequently, they can be reached through international media such as *Time, Newsweek,* the *Far Eastern Economic Review* or Cable Network News (CNN).

The second segment cutting across the region includes young, trendy, superficially Westernised people who are well educated, often travel abroad and spend considerable time searching for new ideas and values. The open-mindedness of these individuals from any country in Asia unites them across borders with the other members of their segment, but this unity is more imaginary than real. Despite listening to similar Asian pop stars and wearing the same designer jeans, they remain firmly rooted in their own national environment. Star TV from Hong Kong reaches most of them, providing them with different language channels while following the same programme, often consisting of music shows and other forms of entertainment.

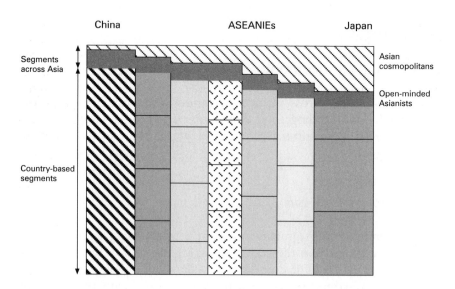

Figure 6.1   Concept of geographical segmentation

Country-based segmentation

Geographical segmentation also reveals substantial differences in consumer behaviour within countries, particularly in large countries. Differences exist between geographically separated parts of the country that are either, as in China, very far apart or separated by water, as is the case for the islands of Indonesia or the Philippines. On the other hand, different segments can also be found between urban and rural areas that may geographically not be very distant from each other but which often represent different worlds as far as consumer behaviour is concerned.

China's best known and most prosperous regions, such as the Yangtse Delta around Shanghai, the Beijing–Tianjin corridor, or Southern China centred around Guangdong Province, display consumption patterns very different from each other, let alone compared with provinces in the hinterland. People from Shanghai tend to be more fashion conscious, while those from Beijing are considered more serious and sober. This puts them in stark contrast with consumers in the south, who are more lively and materialistic. Different mentalities, different dialects spoken and different foods eaten can also be found in Indonesia, where consumer behaviour in Java is not the same as in the so-called Outer Islands of Sumatra, Sulawesi and Kalimantan.

In most of Asia, however, the differences in consumer behaviour between the regions within individual countries are smaller than the differences between the urban and rural segments and subsegments. Urban populations tend to be more exposed to advertising, are attracted by higher-quality products and are more brand conscious. This is, of course, largely a result of the higher income levels generally found in the urban centres. The phenomenon is clearly visible in the ASEANIEs and China, although much less so in Japan. The gap between the urban and rural segments serves as a stark reminder that, as far as consumer behaviour is concerned, Shanghai is not representative of China nor Jakarta of Indonesia, just as New York is not representative of the USA.[1] A growing suburban population represents a segment somewhere in between the often backward countryside and the glittering cities of Asia. However, even in the rural agglomerations, leading households develop consumption patterns not dissimilar to those of the middle segments in urban areas. They thus become interesting targets for consumer goods, although they are much more difficult to reach than consumers in urban or suburban areas.

Demographic segmentation

Demographic segmentation can take into account a number of criteria such as age, gender, household size, race, income, expenditure and saving rates, education, occupation and so on. Some segments are more important in certain countries than in others, and different products and services will also require specific criteria in segmenting the market. A number of criteria are correlated, such as age and income, or income and education. These relationships, however, work less well in China, where income has in the past been used as an equaliser rather than a factor differentiating younger and older, or unskilled and highly trained workers.

Dramatic demographic changes can be expected to occur in Asia over the next few decades. They will have a decisive impact on future market opportunities. The most important demographic change is the general decline in population growth. However, this does not mean that the size of Asia's populations is stabilising. As Table 6.1 below shows, Indonesia's population is expected to increase from 201 million in 1995 to 283 million over the next 30 years.

Table 6.1   Actual and projected population size in millions

Country	1990	1995	2025
Indonesia	184	201	283
Philippines	62	69	105
Thailand	55	58	72
South Korea	43	45	50
Malaysia	18	20	31
Hong Kong	6	6	7
Singapore	3	3	3
China	1153	1238	1540

Source: World Resources 1994–95, World Resources Institute, Oxford University Press, 1994.

Declining population growth is primarily a result of reduced child-bearing. However, this phenomenon is partly compensated for by reduced infant mortality and longer life expectancy. As a consequence, the structure of the population is changing and the percentage of young people is shrinking. While Japan has by far the oldest population in Asia, the newly industrialised economies (NIEs) follow, with the ASEAN countries representing the youngest populations.

As a result of these shifts, three major changes now taking place will have a direct impact on consumption patterns. First, because of the increasing number of young adults with disposable income, the number of households will rise sharply. These nest-building households will be considerably smaller and will need to be accommodated and equipped. Demand for housing and consumer durables will therefore remain strong for the foreseeable future. Second, relative spending power is slowly shifting from the younger to the more mature households who have completed their family. Among these households, demand will shift from daily necessities to transportation, better housing, entertainment and education. Third, as women are freed of their maternal responsibilities, they will increasingly join the workforce. This will in turn create a higher demand for labour-saving goods and restaurant services.

Table 6.2   Percentage of population 25 years and older

Country	1995	2020
Hong Kong	67	76
Japan	69	75
Singapore	62	69
Taiwan	58	69
South Korea	58	69
China	56	66
Thailand	50	61
Indonesia	46	59
Malaysia	44	59
Philippines	42	53

Source: Calculated from World Population Projections: Estimates and Projections with Related Demographic Statistics 1994–95, World Bank, John Hopkins University Press, 1994.

In addition, the trend towards urbanisation can be expected to continue. The presence of consumers within easier reach, in terms of both logistics and communication, will lighten the task of marketing products and services. Urban dwellers, although on average much better off financially than their rural counterparts, will nevertheless pay much higher prices for housing, which will leave them with a smaller disposable income than their total income would indicate. Traffic congestion in the main cities will worsen, and the existing infrastructure will be put under extreme stress. Governments will be forced to spend heavily just to keep up with the demand for utilities and public services. Smaller families with fewer children will allow households to save more for their retirement – a system already obligatory in Singapore – and will also force parents to rely less on their children as a source of security in their old age. However, as an increasing percentage of the adult population reaches retirement age, adults will begin to draw on their savings rather than accumulating more wealth. This could have the effect of reducing the net savings rate, as is already apparent in Japan.

Segmentation in the ASEANIEs

As the income level in the ASEANIEs is still low compared with that in Japan, Western Europe and the USA, income and expenditure criteria play an overwhelming role in developing segments typical for these countries. Each segment has to be defined differently for each of the ASEANIEs and for each product category.

Market research firms generally divide the consumer population into segments A, B, C, D and E, using relative income levels as the main criteria for differentiation.[2] It is obvious that, in developing countries with a low average income, the top segments are very small, while the overwhelming majority of people still live in relatively poor circumstances and have only very limited purchasing power. The simplified segmentation for a less developed country (LDC), shown in Figure 6.2, may be typical of Indonesia. It looks quite different from a typical segmentation in an NIE such as Singapore, where a large group of relatively affluent spenders has emerged even though the majority of the population still has limited purchasing power. It must be noted here that segments always relate to each other within one given country: a member of the E segment in Singapore is probably better off than the C or even B consumer in Indonesia.

It is only when a country has reached the status of a developed country (DC), such as the USA or Germany, that the segmentation takes the shape of a diamond, the majority of consumers belonging to the middle class and a similar percentage of the population lying either above or below that level. The Scandinavian countries represent the extremes of middle-class countries because of high taxes on the rich and welfare payments to the poor. Almost everyone lives on a similar net income. It is interesting to note that the development of a capitalist society from the status of an LDC to a NIE, and later to a DC, occurs not through a rapid growth of the D segment but instead through the growth of B and C consumers (on account of the D segment), while the fate of the E segment remains unchanged in relative terms for quite some time.

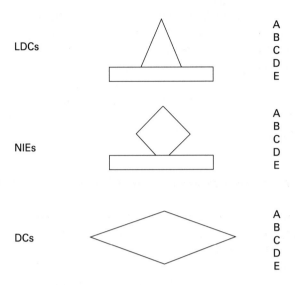

Figure 6.2   Class structures in development stages

Adding psychographic and behavioural characteristics to income criteria, we propose a segmentation into three types of consumer for the
markets of the ASEANIEs, which can serve as the next step towards
targeting specific consumers in a given product market (Table 6.3).

Table 6.3   Consumer segments in the ASEANIEs

The élite segment	
	(...where money does not matter)
The transition segment	
	(...where things are changing)
The traditional segment	
	(...where one gets through the day)

The élite segment consists of a tiny minority of business, government
and military leaders who, by any Western standard, are rich. They live in
the capital but frequently travel abroad. Their consumer behaviour and
tastes do not differ significantly across borders and are on the whole similar
to those of the rich in the West and Japan. Although their total number is
small, their frequent public appearances and their role as trendsetters in
these societies make this élite group important in marketing terms.

Those who have benefited from the economic growth of recent years represent the transition segment. The members of this segment have above-average incomes and live mainly in urban areas. They are open-minded, active, consumption orientated and modern without necessarily being Westernised. They live in a world that is entirely different from the one their parents knew 20 or 30 years ago. They have neither inherited nor accumulated substantial wealth but possess managerial and technical skills that their parents may not have had. For this reason, this segment is not yet called middle class – a term that implies a certain degree of stability over generations.

Members of the transition segment are well educated, often thanks to sacrifices their parents made, and belong to the sector of the workforce that is currently most in demand in the ASEANIEs. The majority of Singaporeans belong to this segment (Singapore being, in fact, a country in transition) and perhaps 10 per cent of all Indonesians. The percentages for the other ASEANIEs lie between these extremes.

Demand from the transition segment creates the most dynamic markets in the region for products ranging from up-market clothing to motorbikes and cars, and services such as insurance and travel. Non-essential product markets like these, which aim to improve the quality of life, benefit more than others from the growth in income of the transition segment. This purchasing pattern confirms the economic law stating that as income increases, the percentage spent on food will decrease, the percentage spent on housing and household operations will stay roughly constant and other purchases will increase. The number of people belonging to the transition segment is also increasing as a higher percentage of the population becomes better educated, moves into urban areas or is absorbed into the modern workforce.

In the traditional segment, income is limited to the purchase of daily necessities and the occasional acquisition of cheap consumer durables. Most of the people in the countryside belong to this segment, but so too do the poor masses living in urban areas. Modernisation and industrialisation of the country have hardly affected such people. The members of this segment are very price conscious and are laggards in the adoption of new products.

For foreign firms who aim exclusively at the small, élite segment, it is not essential to make a major marketing effort in each country. The high prestige value of the brands themselves creates the necessary pull. Regional promotional activities, combined with a controlled distribution of products in Singapore and Hong Kong, may suffice, as brands with a strong appeal will find their way into the other countries through indigenous channels, thereby avoiding high tariff barriers.

A greater marketing effort will be required over time to cater to the transition segment. The sales response function in Figure 6.3 shows the shape of the classical S-shaped curve. Adaptation of the marketing mix to the characteristics of the respective markets is usually necessary, and positive results can only be achieved over time. Those who have started to cultivate the market at an early stage will have a considerable head start over latecomers. Western firms have most firmly established themselves in the fields of food, cosmetics and pharmaceuticals. In consumer durables, product offerings are almost exclusively Japanese, with competition emerging from Korean and Taiwanese producers.

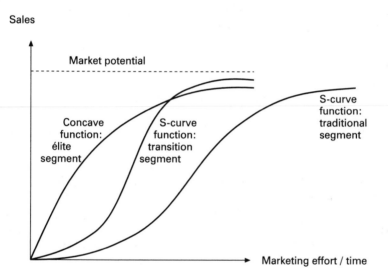

Figure 6.3   Sales response function

For the traditional segment, the sales response function again follows an S-shaped curve, but it is flatter and more stretched. In this segment, consumers are reluctant to switch to new products because their limited purchasing power makes them extremely averse to taking risks. They are also more loyal to traditional products, preferring tea to soft drinks for example. Foreign firms need to keep their costs well under control to penetrate this segment. They also have to build up elaborate distribution systems to reach the consumers in the countryside, a major effort that will only show results over a considerable length of time.

Segmentation in China

Until recently, communist ideology had ensured that income differentials in China remained small. For this reason, the segmentation used to describe the ASEANIEs is inappropriate, at least during the current phase in China's history. To cite one example, China's most highly qualified specialists still earn roughly the same wages as its unskilled workers and have a similar standard of living. However, the inflow of foreign investment and the Chinese success in export markets have resulted in very high income growth rates in the Special Economic Zones, in Guangdong province and in the urban areas of the coastal belt. In these regions, a group of 60–100 million people has emerged who are estimated to earn about three times the income of the average Chinese. These relatively affluent consumers have reaped the lion's share of the benefits of the country's rural and urban reforms, and now constitute a group almost comparable to the transition segment we identified in the ASEANIEs.

There is also a small group of people in China who have made enough money as entrepreneurs or speculators to afford to buy a car or expensive electronic gadgets. Estimates of their number range from a few hundred thousand to 5 million, although it is impossible to verify these figures given that conspicuous wealth still carries the residual risk of persecution should the political winds change. At the other end of the spectrum is a group of people living in poverty, either unemployed or living in isolated rural areas (Figure 6.4).

Unemployment has grave consequences for the individual in China's urban areas, where the state and the communist party still use a comprehensive social welfare system to control freedom of movement and residence to a degree unimaginable in the West. Estimates of the unemployed therefore range from 50–150 million people, but again official data are not available since the government maintains the claim that it provides the population with an 'iron rice bowl', or basic food and shelter.

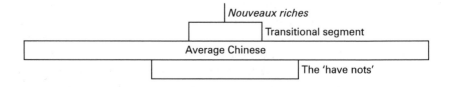

Figure 6.4   Income segmentation in China

This still leaves the marketing man with about one billion Chinese of average income, who have over the past few years shown a surprisingly strong appetite for soft drinks, more up-market food products, cosmetics, toys and ready-to-wear apparel, all of which are frequently sold at relatively high prices. The demand for consumer durables such as bicycles, watches, television sets and cameras has also grown exponentially, although today's consumers are moving up the income ladder and are acquiring video recorders, air-conditioners and motorcycles.

Chinese consumers have shown a willingness to accept higher prices in exchange for better product presentation and quality. This is surprising considering that the World Bank calculates an average Chinese income of only US $750 per annum (World Bank estimate for 1996). Various studies have tried to come to grips with this phenomenon.[3] They conclude that, in quantitative terms, the low income figures grossly underestimate the purchasing power and the standard of living in China for a number of reasons, including the soft exchange rate of the renminbi and the fact that housing, health, education and transportation are still either entirely financed or heavily subsidised by the state. In terms of quality of life, greater consumer choice and improved distribution have increased consumer satisfaction. However, diminishing economic security, increasing environmental degradation and unequal access to education and medical care have negatively influenced the welfare of many people since the beginning of the reforms.

As income differentials grow in China, income criteria will become more important in future for segmentations based on demographics. Today, however, age has almost as great an impact on consumer behaviour as income. The turbulence of the country's recent history has created very distinct generational groups of people with very similar experiences, which in turn have a strong influence on their attitudes.[4] These experiences, such as the strong indoctrination with communist ideology in the 1950s, the suffering from hunger during the period of the Great Leap Forward, the suspension of education during the Cultural Revolution and the experience of consumer choice after the opening of China in the 1980s, have left very clear marks on the mind-set of different generations of Chinese and on their consumer behaviour.

Consequently, we propose a segmentation of the market into: (1) the 'Socialist' generation, which was born before 1945, (2) the 'lost' generation, which was born between 1945 and 1960 and had great difficulty in obtaining any education, and (3) the 'lifestyle' generation, born after 1960.

It is this last generation that is spearheading the move from traditionalism and egalitarianism towards differentiation and modernism (Figure

6.5). It is most visible in Guangdong province, where the largely urban consumers are strongly influenced by Hong Kong's consumption patterns via exposure to Hong Kong television and radio stations and constant contact with Hong Kong Chinese.

The Hong Kong-isation of Guangdong represents an extreme caricature of Chinese consumerism. For the moment, it must be considered an exception for it is not at all representative of the overall state of the Chinese consumer market. While younger consumers may be very open-minded and keen to opt for new, modern and foreign brands, the vast majority of the population still show more conservative consumer behaviour by sticking to proven and traditional Chinese products.

While an increasing number of consumers want to flaunt their wealth and differentiate themselves from their neighbours and colleagues, others still adhere to egalitarian principles and refrain from conspicuous luxury consumption.

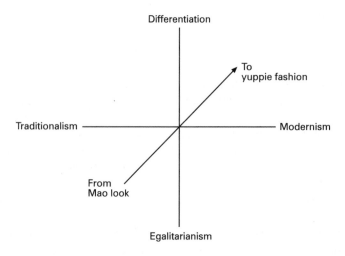

Figure 6.5   Change in consumer behaviour in China

Psychographic segmentation

Segmentation based on income differentials combined with other criteria works sufficiently well for most consumer markets in the ASEANIEs and even China, yet it provides little help in the case of Japan. Here, other criteria determine consumer behaviour. First, the historical separateness of Japan from the rest of the world and the strong Japanese belief in the uniqueness of their culture and society mean that Japanese consumer behaviour differs greatly from that found in other world markets. One striking example of this difference is the longstanding Japanese emphasis on service rather than price. Second, within the Japanese market, differences in behaviour are more subtle. The overwhelming majority of the Japanese still consider themselves members of the middle class, if not the middle of the middle class. Small wage disparities, similar living conditions in largely urban areas, a lack of minorities and subcultures, a generally high degree of education and the rapid spread of new trends by the omnipresent media throughout Japan created a society whose members enjoyed a uniquely homogenous standard of living and tended to act in conformity with the group.

Today, however, the growing integration of Japan into the world economy, the presence of foreign products and services, and the exposure of Japanese consumers to foreign cultures and values through the media or foreign travel have blurred the previously clear demarcation between what was 'Japanese' and what was 'foreign'. Western firms now offer typical Japanese goods with Japanese specifications and Japanese names, while Japanese firms sell foreign novelties under foreign names. The confusion of product origin, brand images and perceptions has created, at least superficially, a sense of internationalisation in both the Japanese marketplace and the mind of the Japanese consumer.

Not all Japanese consumers, however, are open to these new influences. Not surprisingly, the younger generation has eagerly followed new trends and has tried to distinguish itself from the older generation by a different type of consumer behaviour. Traditional Japanese values are increasingly questioned by this group, and have been replaced with more modern values that have many similarities with Western values but are nevertheless not exactly the same. Table 6.4 below sets out some shifts in values and behaviour.

In Japanese terms, the *shinjinrui* ('rebellious youth') exhibit a very untraditional type of consumer behaviour. They represent the first generation of Japanese who have lived neither in a wartime society nor in a postwar reconstruction society, with their emphasis on frugality and sacrifice to future generations. The *shinjinrui* came of age in a relatively affluent society, in which the ownership of consumer durables was already widespread and the future appeared financially secure. Consequently, and in marked contrast to their parents and elders, this younger generation has been much less hesitant to purchase on credit and easily spends money on fads and fashions, entertainment and leisure. Conditioned by this new type of consumer, Japanese markets have become more fickle, and product life-cycles have become extremely short.

Table 6.4   Values in Japan

Traditional	Modern
Work	Leisure
Diligence	Quality of life
Thrift	Conspicuous consumption
Deferred gratification	Instant gratification
Non-material	Material
Conformity	Differentiation
Collectivism	Individualism
Loyalty	Independence
Security	Risk-taking
Age	Youth
Position	Performance
Dedication	Detachment
Japaneseness	Eclectic/imitative

Consumption for this particular consumer group is in general very lifestyle orientated and strongly influenced by the specialised media. In this context, consumption has become more conspicuous, more expressive of individuality and more concerned with impressing the consumer's immediate peer group. From the marketing perspective, two separate and clearly defined target groups stand out: young men prior to the acceptance of their first career ladder job, and young women – OLs – prior to marriage and/or child-bearing. Within these groups, consumption patterns again exhibit a high degree of conformity.

The new trend towards consumption and even superficial individuality does not necessarily herald the dawning of a new era in Japan. Much depends on whether the new generation will turn back to traditional Japanese values once they become *shakaijin*, that is, full members of society with responsibilities towards their families or firms. There are indications that this may well be the case.

Positioning

Adjustment and appropriateness

Positioning is the process through which an image of a product or service is established, maintained or changed in the perception of the targeted consumer. The marketer will always stress meaningful differences to distinguish his own product's offer from that of his competitors. Positioning, therefore, is always relative to others. It is also geared towards an ideal offering in the mind of the consumer and is thus relative to the ideal brand.

Positioning is influenced by all marketing mix instruments and is always the result of perceptions rather than objective performance tests or results of technical measurements. Changes in product, in price or distribution, in advertising or service can all have an impact on the positioning of an offer. Positioning is therefore dependent on the actions a company takes. It is, however, also dependent on the actions of its competitors with regard to its own positioning and the perception by the target group of an ideal brand. Across countries, the same targeted segment of consumers may have different perceptions about the brand in question relative to others, as well as about the ideal brand.

As a consequence, even with the use of the same or similar marketing mix instruments, the positioning of a brand can differ considerably across countries. An extreme example is Mercedes-Benz, whose whole product range is firmly perceived in Asia as luxury cars, yet in Germany some of the models are considered to be workhorses, ideally suited to serve as taxis and as a long-serving means of transportation for people living in the countryside. IKEA's furniture in Europe stands for value-for-money and in the USA for low quality. The company has, however, established itself with an above-average image in Singapore.[5] Conversely, some internationally known brands of beer, when introduced into China, were seen as premium brands by its producers. The Chinese consumers, however, not affected by international advertising campaigns did not rate these brands as highly as the leading domestic products firmly established in the market for many years. Positioning and repositioning therefore have to begin with a good knowledge of consumer needs, attitudes and perceptions. Solid market research serves as the basis for any positioning activities.

The need for adjustment to a different marketing environment is universal, although each case may require a different solution. There are, however, a number of specific issues related to positioning in Asia that apply to almost all products and services.

First, markets, with the exception of Japan, are relatively immature and in consequence are still very volatile. Not only new brands, but also the introduction of new product categories can dramatically reshape the positioning of established products. By the end of the 1980s, Foremost Thailand had established itself as the producer of premium ice cream – until the launch of Wall's ice cream by Lever Brothers. The appearance in the market of imported, highly priced Häagen-Dazs ice creams again changed the positioning of the various brands. Wall's product range is now perceived as suitable for the middle-class consumer rather than being a premium brand. Similarly, long-established and leading products with broad distribution through tens of thousands of neighbourhood stalls may be vulnerable to newcomers gaining access to new and modern distribution channels. Suddenly, the established product looks old fashioned. The need continuously to watch your product's positioning versus your competitors', constantly to check the perception of ideal brands, and frequently to adjust to changing situations seems to be greater in the rapidly evolving markets of developing Asia than in the mature markets of Japan, the USA and Europe.

Following our argument that consumer behaviour in Asia is directed more towards social than individual needs, the second issue concerns the appropriateness of an ego-centred positioning in the Asian context. Such positioning would stress the benefits for the individual rather than the group, would focus on indulgence rather than sacrifice, on disrespect rather than harmony. While a more Western type of positioning, with the consequent image campaigns, may be acceptable for some niche products, larger market segments will be difficult to penetrate without appropriate changes. Nutritional supplements, marketed in the West as energy-providers appealing to free spending, athletically inclined yuppies, would therefore have to be positioned as beneficial to children's health. Television sets would not only provide entertainment, but also bring the family together in their free time. Educational values are always considered to be important investments, especially as far as the next generation is concerned.[6] The sort of positioning adjustment needed obviously depends on the individual case.

Club Med was confronted with the question of appropriateness when it introduced its French, or Western, type of holiday-making to Asians. The easy-going, freewheeling style of mixing with other guests from other parts of the world in a restricted, although well-equipped, camp seemed almost frightening. Not many Asians found the opportunity to let their hair down in front of others rather than save face particularly appealing. The individualistic, sometimes hedonistic or narcissistic, attitudes of other guests who just wanted to have fun and did not want to take anything seriously did not help to convince more than a handful of potential Asian customers to become members. Adjusting Club Med's positioning to the Asian market would have meant – at least in the perception of the Asian customers – making holidays more structured and disciplined, shifting the emphasis to organised fun rather than improvisation and converting the Club into training camps for new sports rather than hangouts for relaxation.

Repositioning towards a more serious holiday destination was an option for Club Med, as shown on the simplified perceptual map in Figure 6.6.

However, the company did not want to isolate Asians from non-Asians, and its corporate culture was simply not geared towards a structured, serious approach. As discussed in Chapter 5, Club Med therefore decided against a change in positioning and as a consequence settled for a niche market in Asia, a strategy very much in line with its worldwide attempts to move up-market towards more select target groups.

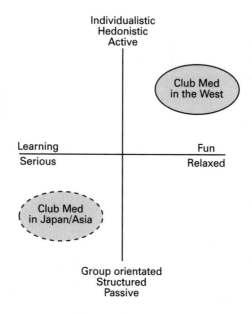

Figure 6.6   Perceptional map of Club Med's positioning options

Branding

If a product is clearly positioned in the eyes of the consumer as an offer distinctively different from others, a brand has been created. Brands are intangible, yet they are often the most valuable asset a company can have. The value of a brand arises from the positive perceptions and associations held by individuals and consists not only of ideas about functional products or services, but also of feelings and associations.[7] The goodwill generated by a successful brand often results in a high degree of brand loyalty. This 'brand equity' gives powerful branded products an edge over average brands or unbranded products and is the result of long-term heavy financial investment in building a brand image. Branding is therefore of prime importance to the marketer and represents more than simply giving a product a name. It is a complex task as it consists of an image-building process that involves the brand name and eventually the company name, the country of origin and the country of production.

Western companies in Asia have been immensely successful in building and exploiting brands. This is particularly true of European companies in lifestyle-related product categories. Some, like Louis Vuitton–Moët Hennessy, Cartier or Chanel, sell more than 50 per cent of their output to Asian consumers, either directly in the region or indirectly when these consumers are travelling in the rest of the world. A number of these Western firms have concentrated on the top segments of the market and have simply transferred their image-building techniques to Asia.

They have benefited from the desire of Asian consumers for prestige products (see Chapter 3). Their main long-term problems stem on the one hand from the danger of faddism, which makes demand fickle and therefore unpredictable. On the other hand, their continuing drive for expansion carries the risk of losing or diluting their exclusivity, the prominent feature of their positioning. In Japan, for example, many luxury brands achieved a higher market penetration in the middle of the 1990s by gaining acceptance among a clientele in their twenties, formerly considered too young an age group. Equally, further geographical expansion into countries such as China or Vietnam may negatively influence the image of brands perceived as being available only to the very rich.

In many cases, companies with luxury brands have benefited from the image of their country of origin, which is in turn shaped by the success of their brands. A French perfume therefore has a better chance than fragrances from Denmark, Italian top couture is easier to position than German fashions, and European luxury cars automatically enjoy a better reputation than those from the USA. As production is limited, governments in Asia rarely force these companies to manufacture locally. If they do, very low local content requirements are imposed, although import duties are high. In such a case, the positioning of a top luggage brand, for example, remains untainted by the image of a country in which local production is mandatory but where the reputation for quality work is questionable. A negative country-of-production effect like this will make it almost impossible for domestically produced Volkswagens or Audis in China to establish for themselves brand images that can compare with those of Mercedes, BMW or even Toyota.

Japanese brands have been as successful in Asia as Western luxury goods companies, although their success lies primarily in technical areas. Having entered the Asian markets at the low end, offering value for money rather than prestige, they subsequently consistently upgraded their image. Today, Sony stands out as a first-class producer of consumer electronics, which can demand a higher price for standardised products than its competitors, almost without reference to the country of production.

Local companies in the ASEANIEs and China find it much more difficult to build their own brands. Acer and Pro-Kennex from Taiwan, Samsung and Daewoo from Korea, and a few others have gained name recognition, but as leading companies rather than leading brands. They carry little brand equity in comparison with products from Japan, Europe or North America.

Asian companies have also discovered the fragility of their brands when attacked by world-class marketing firms introducing international brands and expertise. Certain well-known Chinese names almost collapsed when foreigners challenged them in their own territory. Over time, however, companies such as television manufacturer Sichuan Chonghong or the pharmaceutical firm Taita have learnt to invest systematically in their brands, sometimes with the support of foreign experts or foreign-affiliated advertising agencies. The result is a much more level playing field and the emergence of the first properly positioned Chinese brands.

Southeast Asian packaged goods markets often are dominated by a single brand with a high market share. Deeply entrenched for years, names like Singha or San Miguel, Coca-Cola and Nescafé, or Express and Martell, alone represent their category in specific markets. This phenomenon, rarely seen in other parts of the world, can be explained by the collective orientation of the Asian culture.[8] Referring to Hofstede's dimension of power distance, dominating brands seem to radiate power and thus deserve respect. Having reached this position, the underlying assumption of consumers is that these brands are the best. They have no qualms in expressing their own trust of the product by going on to purchase it. Similarly, the purchase of a dominating brand that is bought by many others does not make the consumer stand out as an individualist. Such purchases are evidently acceptable within society as a whole. This sense of security is especially important for products that are consumed in the company of others, endowing them with immense brand 'equity'. However, this advantage is always limited to specific markets. Brewers from the Philippines and Thailand, and food companies such as Indofood in Indonesia or President in Taiwan, have found out to their cost that to dominate their own protected market is no guarantee of success when exporting the goodwill of their domestic brands into a regional, let alone global, marketplace.

Among those who are in the process of rolling out their brands internationally are fashion retailers like Giordano or Shanghai Tang from Hong

Kong. Both are well-known, clearly positioned retailers with integrated product development. Giordano is exploiting through its name the Italian country-of-origin benefit, while Shanghai Tang is creating an image of authentic, traditional, yet chic Chinese clothing and accessories. Other companies are attracted by the profit opportunities of international brands and invest heavily in distribution outlets without building their own brands. As a consequence, many big names in the world of fashion seem to be overworked and over-retailed in the centres of Hong Kong, Singapore, Jakarta or Bangkok. Any further strengthening of market-push strategies it seems, must lead either to insufficient profits for the numerous sales outlets or to the conversion of former luxury brands into mass-consumer items.

Some companies in Asia have, instead of building brands themselves, taken shortcuts by investing in brand-owning companies abroad. Hard Rock Café and Planet Hollywood both have Asian equity partners. The Japanese acquired a number of famous brands such as Aquascutum, while Dickson Poon from Hong Kong took over DuPont lighters as a product brand as well as such famous names in retailing as Harvey Nichols in the UK and Barney's in the USA. Samsung considered the well-known Rollei camera brand worth buying, while a state-owned Chinese bicycle manufacturer bought the famous American bicycle name Schwinn. In all of these cases, Asian investors take an active role in managing the brands either in their own region or on a global scale.

Differentiation

Positioning has been described above as the process of differentiating one's own product from those of others relative to the ideal offering that exists in the mind of the consumer. Consequently, US and European marketing textbooks emphasise the need to distinguish the product and to convert it into a brand with its own characteristics. The product's uniqueness is both its source of competitive advantage and the generator of profits. According to Western concepts, positioning helps to build a product's uniqueness or individuality from both the supply side, or the managers in charge, and the demand side, in other words the consumers.

In the Japanese market, however, this policy can rarely be seen, particularly among Japanese competitors. Companies do not want to differentiate themselves from their rivals and prefer instead to stick together in industry groups offering more or less the same products at more or less the same price. Competitive pressure and rivalry manifests itself through product churning, or the quick launch of almost identical products with minor modifications in reaction to competitors' launches or relaunches. This 'competitive parallelism' induces rapid incremental product improvements but shies away from the introduction of entirely new or unique products.[9]

Competitors in this environment consider that the risks are reduced as they assume that successful rivals are already close to the ideal point, which is the positioning that consumers see as ideally suiting their ideas. There is not much need to re-educate potential buyers, salesmen or retailers because they are already familiar with very similar products. In addition, sticking to product variants rather than introducing new models keeps investment in radically different machines and tools to a minimum, although flexibility and the speedy delivery of new product versions must be ensured to 'cover' the competition.

The clustering of companies with broadly the same product ranges, most visible in the consumer electronics and car industries, has always been accepted by the Japanese consumer, at least until now. The traditional consumer welcomes similarity and predictability, because the high market penetration of the standard product is reassuring. Cognitive dissonance, or the uncertainty of possibly taking a wrong decision, is reduced. The ideal offer is thus a new, slightly improved product from the same supplier.[10] Consequently, Japanese advertising stresses image creation and cultivation for the company rather than for individual product features or brands.

As Japanese society becomes less homogenous, and as more foreign firms enter the market playing by different rules, Japanese companies are expected to become more innovative and to place greater emphasis on differentiation in their positioning. More consumers, especially the younger ones, want to be unconventional and different. Their desire, however, is to be different not as individuals but as members of their own group compared with another group (or generation). They want to be different, but paradoxically in the same way.[11] Companies may therefore continue the policy of non-differentiation, although within more narrowly defined target groups or segments.

Marketing research in Asia

Marketing research across borders and cultures remains a difficult undertaking because of the problem of establishing equivalence in what there is to be explored and how it should be done. Depending on culture and other environmental influences, product concepts and functions have different meanings and thus evoke different reactions. The transfer of texts from one language into another often leads to misunderstandings and misinterpretations. Samples and measurements vary, and data collection and treatment are handled differently in different circumstances according to the requirements of the market and the sophistication of the researchers.[12] All of this raises fundamental questions about the comparability of marketing research results at a time when most larger companies are trying to manage their marketing activities either globally or at least at regionally, or simply want to use marketing research for new product launches and therefore need to select or prioritise markets.

Long-established companies such as Procter & Gamble and Nestlé in the Philippines, or Unilever in Indonesia, have for decades carried out intensive activities in the field to complement their desk research. They have developed elaborate internal information systems integrating inventories, logistics, distribution and sales, thereby utilising the opportunities that scanners, bar codes and computer networks can offer today. As long-established foreign firms with insider status, they have extensive intelligence-gathering capabilities. Their knowledge of the market, which is otherwise void of much reliable information, provides them with a strong competitive advantage over any newcomer.

The poor availability of information in the developing economies of Asia differs considerably from the situation in Japan, where the quality and accessibility of information is the best in Asia.[13] Spending on market research is far above that of the whole of the rest of Asia altogether and amounts to 9 per cent of worldwide expenditure. The competitive advantage in this, probably the most researched market in the world, is derived from the interpretation rather than the availability of data. Data interpretation is therefore often left to those ordering a market survey rather than to the agencies handling the research.

The high growth in consumer purchasing power in most of Asia has led to more diversified consumer needs. At the same time, the number of products and services on offer has risen enormously and, with it, the range of choice for customers. Consequently, customers have become more demanding and discriminating but also more fickle in their behaviour. As markets move from commodities to brands, preferences are becoming less dependent on price than on positioning factors. Lifestyle-orientated criteria have to complement, if not replace, demographic segmentation. These changes are most dramatic in urban China.

For companies in the region, all these changes have resulted in a vastly increased need to explore consumer behaviour through marketing research. Not surprisingly, research companies report a rapidly growing demand for their services, albeit mostly from multinational rather than

Asian companies.[14] Most market research conducted on behalf of multinational companies still consists of testing the suitability and acceptability of internationally existing products and services for Asian target groups, although the percentage of testing done on domestically developed goods is increasing. Local or regional companies seem to feel more 'at home' and are therefore better able to read the mind of the Asian consumer. Outside experts or agencies are less frequently asked to provide them with support.

Most of the full-service marketing research agencies are local, independent firms concentrating on their domestic market. Not all of them are able to undertake reliable research to an international standard, although most charge comparatively high fees for their services. The two largest regional firms, Survey Research Group (SRG) and Frank Small Associates, have been taken over by the internationally renowned companies AC Nielsen and SOFRES, respectively. They have thus become part of a global group, have exposure to the most advanced research techniques and are beginning to move towards some degree of specialisation. Other firms, such as Research International (which formerly belonged to Unilever), Gallup, or Dentsu Research Inc., are less evenly spread across the region. All of them conduct project-specific research, and some of them carry out syndicated and omnibus surveys for general usage and attitudinal studies.

The problems of funding research projects and of finding a reliable agency that does not already work for the competition have forced a number of multinational firms either to build up expertise in-house or to rely on their own salespeople to feed sufficiently good information back to their marketing or planning departments. Product tests or interviews in these cases are often improvised in showrooms or near demonstration vans or stalls in markets.

Japanese companies, in particular, feel a strong urge to carry out 'hands-on' market research that involves managers, rather than marketing research specialists, in talking to customers or distributors directly at the point of purchase. The underlying rationale for this method is of a cultural nature. Truth (and therefore data) is never absolute but depends on a given situation. Consequently, questions relating to customer preferences are best raised at the moment of a sales transaction or as close to it as possible. Sending out questionnaires or carrying out interviews on another date in a different environment will not shed much light on true behaviour. This is even more so because of the differentiating ways of expressing oneself in Japan. While *honne* represents the true desire of an individual, it will be expressed as *tatemae* and will thus largely conform to the expectations of the person making the inquiry. The result is that what consumers say they want may in fact be misleading.[15]

There are a number of other problems encountered in marketing research in Asia that are mainly culturally induced or reflect the stage of development of the economies involved. Some are obvious and largely practical in nature and can also be found in other multiracial and multilingual parts of the world. Others are more subtle difficulties that are specific to Asia or to some Asian countries. We shall list some of these issues, relating them to the four main stages in the process of carrying out marketing research: (1) definition of the problem and the research objective (the 'what'), (2) plans for the implementation of a research project (the 'how'), (3) the collection of data, and (4) the analysis, control and interpretation of data.

1. The desire to define clearly a problem and an objective can be seen as a typical outflow of the 'rational science' approach of Western marketing professionals. They will generate 'objective' market data and use quantitative techniques for data analysis in order to enable managers to take better decisions. This can be contrasted with the more intuitive, less specific, less systematic, 'hands-on' approach in Japan as we have explained above. This soft style of research is, however, combined with very elaborate environmental scanning, often consisting of piling up huge masses of hard data.[16] The obsession of Japanese companies with information-gathering worldwide is well known. Their ability to combine this with intuitive marketing research, however, must be limited to their own, homogenous society whose needs and wants can be relatively easily decoded by insiders. Outside their home country, Japanese companies and their agencies will also be forced to define their objectives more precisely.

2. Developing a research plan requires decisions on how to collect data. Observations, focus groups, surveys and experimental research are all used in the region, although it seems that quantitative methods are preferred over qualitative research such as focus groups and experiments. There appears to be mistrust in the opinions of a few participants expressed during in-depth discussions, in contrast to appreciation of the apparent certainty that large numbers of interviews bring in broader surveys in Asia.[17] Questionnaire surveys do not work in all countries in the region because of poor mail services or limited access to address material. In countries with low telephone ownership, telephone surveys are restricted to the upper segments of the population and the urban sector. In Japan, face-to-face interviews are much easier to carry out than telephone discussions, a cultural bias that contrasts sharply with the situation in the USA.[18]

Textbook-style probability sampling is most effective in countries that have strict registration requirements, such as China, Vietnam and Indonesia. These are the same countries where researchers are also either legally required or advised to obtain official permission from state authorities or local community leaders to carry out surveys. Especially in China, the distinction is not always clear between commercial data-gathering, political opinion polls and intelligence-gathering on state secrets. In China and Vietnam, market research was completely unknown until recently, although there already existed substantial know-how on conducting social and economic studies.

The multifamily households found in a number of countries in developing Asia presents a different set of challenges. The sampling unit, or the person to be interviewed, has to be identified, although it may not always be clear who in such a household is responsible for what or who influences purchasing decisions. In multiple-family households, face-to-face interviews can rarely be carried out in privacy. Touching on taboos will force the individual family member being interviewed to conform to certain expectations and role models.

3. The collection of data is, first, dependent on the availability and approachability of the persons in the sample. Hong Kong people tend not be at home and are always in a hurry. Consequently, the rate of refusal is relatively high. In China, on the other hand, one would naturally expect interviewees to be suspicious or reluctant to speak up. In fact, the response rate is reported to be good because of the excitement generated by being interviewed and asked for an opinion. Answers tend to be rich in quality, especially in rural areas where people are described as down to earth and less constrained than city dwellers.[19]

The courtesy of most Asians tends to bring a positive bias into most surveys, thus requiring very careful interpretation of respondents' answers. 'Would perhaps buy' in the West indicates that chances exist for sales but probably means 'definitely not interested' in an Asian context. This 'courtesy bias' is probably strongest in countries like Thailand, Indonesia or the Philippines. On the other hand, adherence to hierarchy in focus group discussions in Japan or Korea can lead to deference to the most senior member of the panel instead of the expression of independent opinions. Communication, comprehension and even racial problems can be expected in multicultural countries such as Malaysia or Indonesia if the profiles of the interviewers and the interviewees are not properly matched. A Chinese may not feel comfortable being interviewed by a Malay and vice versa.[20]

4. Analysis and control of the data depend on the level of sophistication of the researchers themselves, both in the field and in the back office. Good researchers are able to filter out some of the cultural biases in the results, especially when dealing with multinational companies less familiar with the specific environment. They will also know that, in markets with dominating brands, market research generates data on the market leader but not necessarily on consumer needs and wants. There is no indication that Asia sees a higher degree of dishonesty from those producing research results than is found elsewhere. The problem is universal. However, in some countries, the inexperience of people employed might suggest the need for a high degree of post-survey control and questioning of methodology.

The interpretation of the data relies on the division of labour between the firms (or departments in a firm if done in-house) ordering the piece of work and those carrying it out. As mentioned above, marketing research agencies in Japan tend to collect masses of detailed data, which they often deliver to their clients without much interpretation let alone a recommendation for action. This task is left to the ordering firm (not easy for a company newly arrived in the country or still looking at the market from outside). A similar constellation may also occur in other countries when the agency is relatively weak and inexperienced, and is therefore treated as a supplier of data rather than a partner in a decision process.

Bearing in mind some of the specific situations in individual countries and the cultural distance between Western markets and Asia, cross-cultural marketing research is bound to run into problems of comparability, especially when projects are carried out in several Asian countries simultaneously. Leading international agencies are already preparing to serve customers across the region through international co-ordination, specialisation and even the formation of regional virtual research teams.[21] Independent observers, on the other hand, consider the development of marketing research studies for all of Asia unwise. They recommend instead the sequence of pilot studies in the first country or countries, followed by some adaptation and a rollout thereafter.[22]

Notes

1. Schmitt, B. (1997) 'Who is the Chinese consumer? Segmentation in the People's Republic of China', *European Management Journal*, **15**(2): 191–4.
2. Roberto, E.L. (1987) *Applied Marketing Research*, Manila: Ateneo de Manila University Press, pp. 61–5.

3. Chai, J.C.H. (1992) 'Consumption and living standards in China', *China Quarterly,* pp. 721–49. See also Shaw, S.M. and Woetzel, J.R. (1992) 'A fresh look at China', *McKinsey Quarterly* (3): 37–51.

4. Ariga, M., Yasue, M. and Wen, G.X. (1997), 'China's generation III – viable target segment and implications for marketing communications', *Marketing and Research Today,* February: 17–24.

5. Kotler, P., Ang, S.H., Leong, S.M. and Tan, C.T. (1996) *Marketing Management: An Asian Perspective,* Singapore: Prentice-Hall, p. 565.

6. Scarry, J. (1996) 'Putting children first', *China Business Review,* May–June: 30–5.

7. Restall, C. and Gordon, W. (1993) 'Brands – the missing link; understanding the emotional relationship', *Marketing and Research Today,* **21**(2): 59–67.

8. Robinson, C. (1996) 'Asian culture: the marketing consequences', *Journal of the Marketing Society,* **38**(1): 55–62.

9. Johansson, J.K. and Nonaka, I. (1996) *Relentless – The Japanese Way of Marketing,* New York: Harper Business, pp. 81–2.

10. Hotaka, K. (1997) 'The two consumers: what's happening to Japanese marketing in the 90s?', *Journal of Japanese Trade and Industry* **16**(1): 12–17.

11. Johansson, J.K. and Nonaka, I. (1996) *Relentless – The Japanese Way of Marketing,* New York: Harper Business, p. 80.

12. For an overview of the flaws in cross-cultural marketing research, see Malhotra, N.K., Agarwal, J. and Peterson, M. (1996) 'Methodological issues in cross-cultural marketing research', *International Marketing Review,* **13**(5): 7–43. Also Cavusgil, S.T. and Das, A. (1997) 'Methodological issues in empirical cross-cultural research: a survey of the management literature and a framework', *Management International Review,* **37**(1): 71–96.

13. Lasserre, P. and Schütte, H. (1995) *Strategies for Asia Pacific,* Basingstoke: Macmillan, pp. 140–3.

14. Business Asia (1997) *Market Research in Asia,* 16 June: 5–6.

15. Johansson, J.K. and Nonaka, I. (1996) *Relentless – The Japanese Way of Marketing,* New York: Harper Business, pp. 36–56.

16. Johansson, J.K. and Nonaka, I. (1996) *Relentless – The Japanese Way of Marketing,* New York: Harper Business, pp. 36–56.

17. Kotler, P., Ang, S.H., Leong, S.M. and Tan, C.T. (1996) *Marketing Management: An Asian Perspective,* Singapore: Prentice-Hall, p. 158.

18. Naumann, E., Jackson, D.W. Jr and Wolfe, W.G. (1994) 'Examining the practices of United States and Japanese market research firms', *California Management Review,* Summer: 49–69.

19. Steele, H.C. (1990) 'Marketing research in China: the Hong Kong connection', *Marketing and Research Today,* August: 155–65.

20. Kushner, J.M. (1982) 'Market research in a non-Western context: the Asian example', *Journal of Market Research Society,* **24**(2): 116–22.

21. Banks, R. (1997) 'Is Asia different? Defining a strategy to serve multi-national clients in the region', *Marketing and Research Today,* February: 4–11.

22. Kotler, P., Ang, S.H., Leong, S.M. and Tan, C.T. (1996) *Marketing Management: An Asian Perspective,* Singapore: Prentice-Hall, p. 175.

7 The Marketing Mix

Product

Product standardisation and adaptation

Whenever a company expands across borders, it is faced with the issue of either sticking to its product without any change, adapting the product to the new market or developing an entirely new product. The decision taken will depend primarily on the preferences of consumers but is also closely linked with the cost of manufacturing and government regulations.

Multinational corporations tend to prefer the production of standardised goods in centralised plants, where they can achieve economies of scale, experience curve effects and exercise better control over quality. If this type of straight extension of product strategy is acceptable to the market, the company can in theory freely decide where to locate the plant. However, for mass-produced consumer goods in Asia, the option of importing the products from outside the country is severely constrained by two factors. On the one hand, government import regulations may either not allow them to be brought in at all, or make them very costly. On the other hand, and sometimes in addition, high transportation costs and long shipping and clearance periods may render the products uncompetitive in the local market.

These impediments matter less for luxury products destined for niche markets, for which price sensitivity is less of an issue and the country of origin is an important attribute of the product in the consumer's mind. Johnnie Walker Black Label whisky is the market leader in Thailand for almost no other reason than that it is a non-adapted, imported product. Similarly, Japanese OLs buy perfume in duty-free shops around the world because it is not made in Japan. No French manufacturer would consider producing perfume or other luxury items in Japan, even if it would lead to significant cost savings. Thus, while in theory suppliers of standardised products have a choice between imports and local assembly or manufacturing, the choice may in fact be restricted depending on the product category and the market situation.

The need for product adaptation and new product development is generated by five different factors:

1. *Consumer behaviour*
   Attitudes, familiarity with products, religious influence, local tastes and traditions, buying habits, taboos and so on.
2. *Physical environment*
   Climate, geographical spread, infrastructure for logistics, living space and so on.
3. *Market environment*
   Stage of economic development, purchasing power, size of market, availability of marketing instruments, structure of distribution channels and so on.
4. *Government regulations*
   Product and packaging rules, import restrictions, local content rules and so on.
5. *Competition*
   Degree of rivalry, existence of national champions, innovation and speed, areas of competition and so on.

Product adaptation can range from changes in pack sizes to major product reformulations, and from modifications of technical standards (for example, electricity supply) to up- or downgrading of quality levels in order to comply with existing local norms.

A large percentage of detergents in Indonesia, for example, are sold in small sachets rather than large cardboard boxes to cater to the limited purchasing power in a country where shopping is still done on a daily basis. Disposable diapers in Japan only became widely popular when they became smaller following the development of superabsorbent chemicals, which replaced bulky paper. Procter & Gamble had successfully pioneered Pampers in Japan, but then was forced to accept defeat when Japanese competitors entered the market with substantially smaller boxes that contained the same number of diapers as Procter & Gamble's own much larger containers. The Japanese product was simply better suited to fit the general lack of space in the country. This need for miniaturisation is a major stumbling block for many Western managers in Japan, particularly those from the USA used to abundant space at home, whether for appliances in the kitchen or for their cars in the streets.

High demands in terms of quality equally create a challenge for those trying to enter the Japanese market. Bananas with blemishes on their skins can basically not be sold in that market – an almost insurmountable barrier for traditional exporters from Southeast Asia. Garment producers add an extra seam to their jeans before exporting them to Japan. Quality assurance is also the reason for whisky importers into Thailand to add sophisticated caps to their bottles. These prove that the bottle has not been tampered with and the content replaced with cheap Thai spirit.

Product adaptation becomes more of a necessity when products cater to long-established tastes, habits and preferences. Producers of food, such as Nestlé, Unilever or General Foods, have all changed their products in one way or another. Others, such as Coca-Cola and McDonald's, have successfully added products not available in the USA to their product portfolio in Asia. Attitudes and feelings play an important role in other areas. Educational services provided by Western companies had to adjust to the learning-by-rote style in the region, while Mattel had to shrink the breasts and shorten the legs of Barbie dolls to make them acceptable to Japanese mothers.

Because of the specific nature of consumer behaviour in Japan and the physical separation of Japan from its neighbours, many of the product adaptations found there have been developed specifically for the domestic market. Local product adaptation is less frequently found in the other parts of Asia, where the limited size of the individual markets recommends a more regional approach to adaptation. This applies particularly to the ASEAN region, where a trend towards regional product adaptation and development is visible in the context of the first attempts to rationalise production across countries.

Depending on product and production technologies, the most pertinent way of supplying the local market with suitably adapted products is through local assembly. This approach allows some components and raw materials to be imported from places where similar products are manufactured. At the same time, at least some parts of the value chain can be carried out close to where the demand can be found. Figure 7.1 shows models of product/supply combinations.

Historically, European and American multinational corporations had a very strong market position in Asia, even in automobiles and consumer durables. Much of that advantage has been lost to Japanese competitors, in part because of the reluctance of Western companies to adapt their products to local market conditions. Being technologically advanced in comparison with Asian firms in the 1950s and 60s, their products catered only to the top segments. The resulting small volume did not justify local production. Japanese products, at that time much less sophisticated, were much better suited for a broader target audience, both in Japan and in developing Asia.

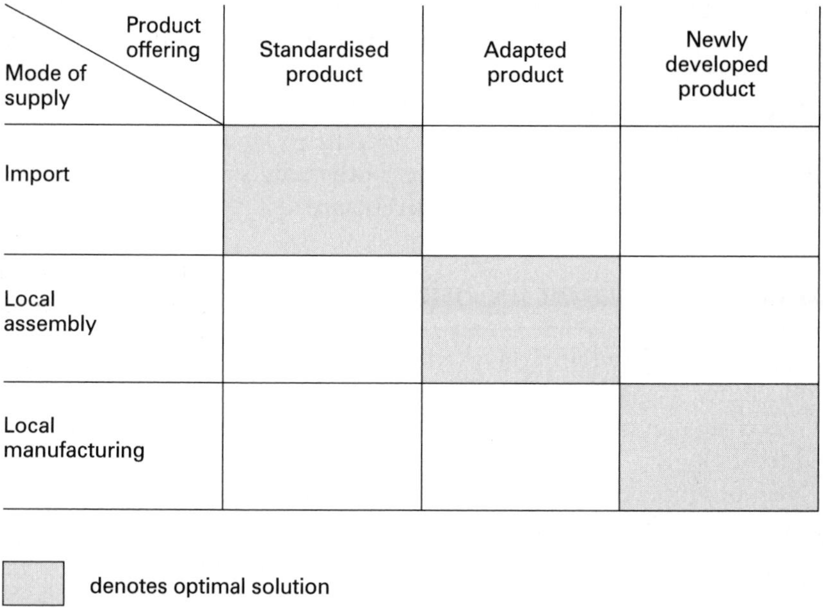

Mode of supply ╲ Product offering	Standardised product	Adapted product	Newly developed product
Import			
Local assembly			
Local manufacturing			

☐ denotes optimal solution

Figure 7.1 Models of product/supply combinations

While Western companies made few attempts to downgrade their offerings to achieve higher volume, Japanese companies in the following decades upgraded their products in line with improving market conditions throughout Asia and moved towards local assembly or manufacturing. When Western multinational companies made attempts to simplify products in order to bring down the price, consumers in Asia rejected them. Volkswagen's multipurpose car, a stripped-down version of a military type of vehicle, lost out in the 1960s against Toyota's pick-ups because it was seen as a second-class derivative of a real VW. In contrast, Toyota's offer was in line with the other models of the company's simple product range at that time.

Western companies fared much better with fast-moving consumer goods, especially in areas such as food, drinks, cigarettes and cosmetics. Here, the sheer volume of demand and the pressure to manufacture locally, from the point of view of both production costs and government regulations, facilitated the move to product adaptation. It is in many of these product categories that physical attributes such as size, weight, colour and so on can be changed relatively easily. Similarly, Western companies have adapted their offerings in the service industry, in which the process of the delivery naturally takes place in the presence of the consumer and thus mostly at the local level. Accor's highly standardised hotel chains, Novotel and Ibis, had to rise to a much more elaborate service level than they offer in Europe or the USA in order to meet the much higher expectations of their guests in Asia. Domino's pizza parlours in Japan added a guarantee for delivery within 30 minutes to their otherwise standard products and facilities in order to gain consumer acceptance.

Product development for Asia

The borderline between product adaptation and the development of new products for a specific market or region is blurred, especially when the products are part of one product family and are based on similar materials and technologies.

New product developments are undertaken when, first, a unique need has been identified that cannot be satisfied with existing or modified products, and second, when there exist within the company development capabilities and capacities that can be deployed. Anecdotal evidence suggests that few new products specifically developed for Asia have been launched by multinational corporations. There could be two reasons for this. The first relates to the mind-set in many successful multinational companies, which is geared towards globalisation. This thinking implies that similarities exist between markets and that these are greater than the differences. As a consequence, products from other parts of the world are imposed on Asian markets, in either standardised or adapted forms. Sufficient marketing muscle often ensures at least some success. In such circumstances, globally orientated managers rarely feel obliged to explore whether a product developed entirely for that market would have been more suitable and in the end more profitable.

The second reason lies in the often limited research and development (R&D) capabilities of multinationals in the region or for the region. R&D remains in most companies the least international function. People and activities are mainly concentrated at headquarters. In US multinationals, R&D may also be carried out in Europe, while European companies often have some R&D activities in the USA. Western companies rarely have R&D centres in Asia, and if they do they are primarily, although not exclusively, located in Japan. The capabilities of such units are mainly deployed for product adaptation rather than for the finding of new products. Where researchers are aiming to develop something new for Asia at headquarters, their success depends heavily on the link between the far-away markets and their technological work at home.

The alternative is that researchers draw on corporate experience in other parts of the world, especially those countries where there is expertise in dealing with less-developed markets. Volkswagen's Santana model was adapted to the Chinese market with the help of its Brazilian subsidiary. At headquarters, knowledge of the peculiarities of third-world markets was too limited to be reliable. Subsequent further development of the Santana 2000 model in the 1990s was again strongly influenced by input from the Brazilian operations. Similarly, Whirlpool drew on the expertise of its Brazilian operations to develop washing machines for the Indian market, where water and power supplies were less reliable than were required to operate its washing machines in Europe and the USA. When, in the 1970s, Unilever faced resistance in the Indonesian market to washing powder, it turned to its large Indian subsidiary for assistance. Housewives were sceptical about a washing process that did not require them to scrub clothes as forcefully as when hard soap was used. Unilever's Indian research laboratories fully understood the problem and developed an entirely new product, a detergent cream that had all the properties of a chemically advanced powder. In the physical form of a cream, the detergent could be used for scrubbing if consumers wanted to.

Leading multinational companies that have created entirely new products have often done so to complement an existing product range that consisted of either standardised or modified products. IBM, for example, undertook enormous efforts to develop and launch software in Japan, and later in other parts of Asia, based on Japanese, Chinese or Korean characters. This software was sold in parallel with software in English. Coca-Cola in Japan, as well as in China, developed a whole range of new soft drinks and canned coffees closely geared towards local tastes and traditions. Similarly, companies in the hair care business have all developed specific products suitable for the much thicker Asian hair. Cosmetic firms from the West had to learn that tanning products were of no value to Asians. The tendency of Asian women to avoid the sun as much as possible in order to have a white complexion contrasts sharply with the desire of many Westerners for a suntanned face that conveys the image of hedonistic indulgence on the beach or in the snow far away from the daily hassles of life. For Indonesians, as for many other Asians, a dark complexion indicates that a person is probably a peasant, construction worker or fisherman exposed to the sun in his or her daily outdoor work. Consequently, multinational companies such as L'Oreal and Procter & Gamble have invented whitening creams for Asian markets, which in turn meet no demand in the West.

Except for the Japanese, few Asian companies have developed entirely new products on their own. Any innovation that has taken place comes from Taiwanese, Korean or Singaporean firms engaged in industrial electronics. In consumer goods or services, companies from developing Asia have either imitated or adapted product ideas from abroad, or have brought indigenous product concepts up to international standards. The former route was taken by the Philippino firm Jollibee. It meticulously studied the operations of McDonald's before embarking on an almost identical fast-food idea but with products adapted to local tastes. Jollibee is now the market leader in the Philippines and is in the process of expanding rapidly into neighbouring countries. Instant noodle producers in Taiwan or *kretek* (clove cigarette) producers in Indonesia chose the second option, that of developing local products or concepts to world standards. The appeal of their products today matches that of international food and cigarette manufacturers.

Japanese companies have proved their product development capabilities in many product categories. From consumer electronics such as Sony's Walkman and an endless flow of creative video games from Bandai and Nintendo, to non-smearing lipsticks from Shiseido or condensed detergents from Kao, from ultra-light bicycles and digital cameras to 'dry' beer and energy drinks, there seems to be no end to innovation. At the peak of the bubble economy at the end of the 1980s, Japanese firms 'churned out' new products or product variants at breakneck speed to stop others from taking the lead. Where a company had been too slow in launching new products, it resorted to 'product covering', or introducing products equivalent to those of its competitors in order to avoid losing market share.[1]

Time-consuming marketing research was discarded, and inevitable market failures were very quickly corrected through a highly flexible manufacturing system that could adjust almost instantly to new product specifications. While the pace of change in Japan has slowed in the 1990s, competitive pressure has not. New product launches in many categories still far outnumber those in other developed markets, even if many are just derivatives of existing products.

Packaging

Packaging serves two purposes. On the one hand, it provides a container or wrapper that enables the manufacturer to move the product safely through the distribution channels to the final consumer. On the other hand, it serves as a marketing tool that promotes the product and creates awareness and preferences. Packaging decisions therefore deal with practical as well as with artistic aspects.

Japanese companies are far ahead of their Asian competitors on both accounts. This is due partly to their superior technology and partly to the advanced stage of development of distribution channels and logistics in Japan. In contrast, many producers of consumer goods in developing Asia still struggle with breakages, lack of good packaging material, the disappearance of returnable containers such as bottles (which are used by consumers for other purposes) or the need to adjust to the world of modern retailing, including self-service, scanners and bar codes.

The heightened sense of aesthetic sensibility in many Asian cultures has already been discussed. Depending on the specific culture and the circumstances of the use of the product, value is placed to a greater or lesser degree on complexity and decoration, harmony and naturalism. Products for daily use at home require less elaborate packaging than those to be consumed in public or offered as gifts. The pragmatic Chinese, for example, tend to value function over form for private-use purchases. Quality is considered to be more important than appearance. Gallup found that 51 per cent of Chinese surveyed buy for 'usefulness', while 26 per cent 'buy for design.' Compared with Americans, Chinese are almost twice as likely to purchase a product because of its function than for its beauty.[2] In similar circumstances, Japanese would still value the outer appearance more than the function.

In the context of the all-important gift-giving ritual, gifts are offered to create face for the receiver. Artistic values are evident in the great importance placed throughout Asia upon the packaging of consumer products, which is considered to be a reflection of the quality of the contents, which in turn enhances the standing of the receiver. In China, red is the preferred colour for packaging as it connotes happiness and good luck. In Japan, the packaging or wrapping technique adds ritual meaning to the object it encloses. To be able to wrap things properly is a measure of refinement and civilisation.[3] Gifts, even the smallest *omiyage* ('souvenir'), are wrapped assiduously. Towels are often given as gifts and therefore, except for the cheapest of towels, will always be packaged in attractive boxes. If intended to be presented to a guest, even the smallest cookie or rice cracker is individually wrapped. While the Japanese seem to outdo everybody else in this respect, Chinese buyers of expensive cognac equally appreciate the artistic value of extraordinary shapes and colours of bottles that will be offered exclusively as gifts. Although the bottle may contain the highest-quality cognac available, the cost of the container will often exceed that of the content.

The most extreme example of packaging involves the presentation of money in Japan, where it is often given as a gift for a birth, funeral, marriage, send-off for travel and so on. Special envelopes exist for each type of occasion. Anyone presenting money without using the appropriate envelope would be considered to be gravely lacking in manners.

Environmental concerns regarding excess packaging are beginning to surface, but the cultural meaning conveyed by packaging means that Japanese suppliers continue to spend more on packaging than their Western counterparts. For cultural reasons, waste disposal problems are not likely to affect the packaging industry in the foreseeable future.

Pricing

Price perceptions

Although many would regard price as an objective product attribute, its subjective evaluation is highly influenced by the cultural context. From the consumer's point of view, the concept of price contains both monetary and non-monetary aspects. The non-monetary price of items is related to the costs of the time it takes to effect a purchase, the costs of thinking and deciding what to buy and the costs of the physical effort to make the purchase and bring the product into use. Monetary and non-monetary costs are sacrifices in exchange for the satisfaction derived from the consumption experience. While monetary aspects of the price may be high in most of Asia in comparison with the higher income countries of the West and Japan, shopping, particularly in Asian urban areas, is often considered to be a major leisure activity and a principal means of relaxing and socialising. Therefore the opportunity costs of time can be low. Equally, the costs of elaboration of what to buy can be reduced in case of high brand or store loyalty. The physical effort, however, may be considered more costly as shopping by car is often impossible, either because consumers do not own one or because they cannot use it or park it in congested urban centres. Furthermore, carrying goods home or assembling and installing them at home (for example, IKEA furniture) may not be socially acceptable in certain groups of society and will therefore be seen as a costly barrier. Thus the perception of the real price of a consumer good may be lower or higher for the Asian consumer depending on the context.

Cultural context also influences the way in which a price is perceived as a surrogate indicator of quality. The dependence on price as a proxy for quality is especially strong when two conditions exist. First, consumers believe that differences between alternative product offerings exist. Second, consumers have little information or experience with the products concerned. The reliance on price as an indicator of quality is most critical in the case of purchases of products that affect the standing of the individual within the peer group. Thus the price–quality equation serves as a risk-reduction mechanism for the uninformed. In group-orientated Asia, such thinking is widespread and helps individuals to stay in line with the expectations of society. As the results of a survey by INSEAD's Euro-Asia Centre show, the perception that higher price means higher quality is found everywhere in the region, although the degree varies (Figure 7.2).[4]

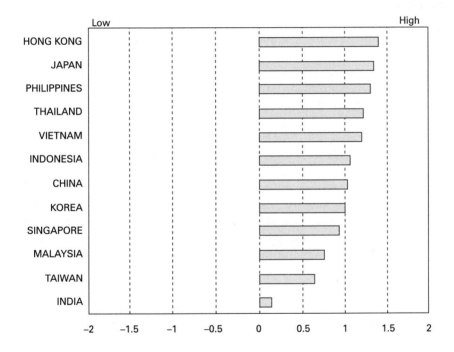

Figure 7.2 Customers' association of higher prices with higher quality

As a consequence of linking price with quality, high prices do not always deter people from consumption, even if their purchasing power is limited. Price-conscious, pragmatic Chinese, for example, are known to pay higher prices for durable goods. Their quality is difficult to evaluate, and individuals typically have limited experience with such products. Purchases of this kind involve the buyer in high monetary risk. Since price is correlated with quality, the purchase of a foreign-made product reduces the risk of product failure. This is especially important in a country in which many Chinese consumers have had bad experiences in the past with the quality of products made by state-owned companies. It means that foreign manufacturers of consumer durables, whose prices are nearly always higher than those of local producers, have some chance of selling at those higher prices. Chinese consumers also tend to prefer, and are willing to pay for, the latest technology and feel insulted if only older models are offered. The saying *xian ru wei ju* ('Whosoever comes first becomes the master') illustrates the benefit of being the first to offer the latest technology in China.[5]

Two caveats have to be entered here. First, despite their perception of the quality of foreign-made products and their interest in them, their lack of purchasing power often leads Chinese consumers only to window-shop for expensive, foreign-made goods, while finally buying locally made products at the cheaper state-run stores. Second, consumers will, over time, become more informed, and the quality of Chinese-made products will improve. As a result, the differences still perceived between imported products, products made locally by foreign affiliated firms and those made by local firms will fade away, and product quality will be judged primarily in terms of value-for-money considerations. This is already the case for many low-involvement goods for daily use, such as detergents, soaps, noodles and light bulbs. For non-durable, repeat purchase products such as these, Chinese consumers tend to prefer lower-priced domestic goods.

In the case of gift-giving or entertaining, high prices create positive perceptions, for the value of the item symbolises the value of the relationship between the giver and the receiver. This means that only expensive brands of cognac can be served in Chinese restaurants all over Asia in honour of the guest; even if the drink is consumed together with ice and Coca-Cola – making the taste or quality of the brand indistinguishable – this is still crucial. Asians are generally very sensitive to social risk, and the higher price of a gift is worth the psychological security it provides. Price is regarded not as a counterbalance to the product's advantages but as an additional product attribute. Too low a price may position the item outside the gift-giving realm and thus force the item to compete on price. For example, the popularity in Japan of Johnnie Walker Black Label whisky during the 1970s and 80s was largely due to the fact that everyone knew that it sold for exactly ¥10,000. If a ¥10,000 gift was required, Johnnie Walker Black Label was a likely choice. When the price of a bottle dropped below ¥10,000, it lost much of its appeal as a gift item.[6]

The heady 'bubble' years of the late 1980s in Japan encouraged foreign marketers to believe that the higher the price, the more success a product would automatically find with the status-obsessed Japanese consumer. While this situation may still be somewhat true today for those products intended for conspicuous consumption, the price level of imported products in Japan compared with the outside world became unsustainable when foreign exchange fluctuations hit the yen in the first half of the 1990s and Japanese consumers became increasingly price conscious. Companies such as Cartier had to lower their prices in order to remain trusted by a clientele aware of prices abroad.[7]

Japanese manufacturers that in the 1980s still had a firm grip on their distributors generally disliked competing on price and instead attempted to win consumers over by offering products of superior quality, with more advanced product features and a higher brand image. They also abhorred different prices being charged by different retailers for the same product and consequently tried to block the entry of discounters to the market, particularly those from abroad, such as Wal-Mart or Toys-R-Us.[8]

By now, discount stores are no longer perceived purely as sellers of low-quality miscellaneous goods. Consumers have become increasingly willing to accept the lesser attention given to service and elaborate wrapping in exchange for a more reasonable cost/benefit trade-off. These changes have helped to improve the perception of foreign goods, which can now be sold at lower prices and still be perceived as good-quality products. Isao Nakeuchi, the president and founder of Daiei, Japan's largest supermarket chain, commented in 1995, 'This is not just an outcome of the recession. Consumers are more sophisticated, knowledgeable and pragmatic than before... They understand fully what value means.'[9]

Skimming versus penetration

Assuming that a product offers some degree of innovation and can thus be differentiated from products already in the market, manufacturers have the option of pricing their brands either clearly above existing competing products or at a price level similar to theirs. In the first case, the demand will be limited to a selective group of consumers. This 'skimming' strategy works well when the products are highly visible and the price/quality equation supports the positioning of the new product as a premium brand. European-brand firms such as the German car manufacturers and the French lifestyle producers have often pursued such strategies. It has resulted in small market shares but also highly profitable operations.

By and large, Japanese firms have pursued the alternative strategy, that of market 'penetration'. Brands are priced at a level close to that of the competition, and attempts are made to gain market share by offering superior products. Profit is achieved by keeping prices stable while driving costs down by increasing volume through experience curve effects and target costing.[10]

Both 'skimming' and 'penetration' strategies seem to have worked in Asia. Firms pursuing one or the other, however, tend to be more success-ful than those applying both strategies at the same time, even for different products or different product categories. In the automobile industry, for example, the Europeans have made hardly any impact on the Asian mass market, which is dominated by the Japanese (except in South Korea). On the other hand, the Japanese manufacturers have not been successful in challenging the strong position of Mercedes-Benz or BMW in the upper segment despite the availability of comparable models in their portfolio. Even China, where a mass market does not yet exist, is dominated by Audi and VW's Santana, both representing the upper segment in the context of the market.

Regional pricing

Since the foundation of ASEAN decades ago, extensive discussions have taken place and some initial efforts have been undertaken to demolish some of the trade barriers between the countries of the region. While progress has so far not been great, there is a clear trend towards freer trade that extends beyond the boundaries of Southeast Asia and the deci-sions taken in the context of the ASEAN Free Trade Area (AFTA). This development forces companies in the region to question the validity of country-based price-setting and to consider moves towards a regional pricing policy.

At present, substantial price differentials exist between various markets for the same product. This does not disturb sales too much in cases where the markets are not in proximity to each other. However, it already distorts purchase patterns in many parts of Asia, particularly in the border zones between Singapore and Malaysia, Vietnam and China, and Hong Kong and China. Even in the case of geographically separated Japan, parallel imports by unauthorised traders[11] and tourists returning from shopping trips abroad have undermined consumer confidence in 'fair' pricing.

The reasons for price differentials are manifold. Government regula-tions, import barriers, foreign exchange rates, competitive rivalry, distribution systems and consumer demand vary from country to country and offer different opportunities for exploiting the market potential. In industries with high margins, such as in pharmaceuticals, the large difference between the sales price and the cost of production tempts companies to adjust in a flexible manner to a given market situation, in other words charging grossly different prices for identical products. When products flow easily across borders, any price differential that exceeds transaction costs will invite arbitrage. This leads to confusion in the market and to a downward pressure on prices in general.

Assuming that there will, over the next few years, be an integration of formerly separated markets into a more common market, transaction costs will fall. This is a not unrealistic assumption bearing in mind that, apart from timid announcements by ASEAN and the APEC (Asia Pacific Economic Cooperation) countries on the dismantling of trade barriers, the World Trade Organisation (WTO) is pursuing a policy towards freer trade on a worldwide basis. These attempts will undermine single-country marketing strategies, particularly in terms of pricing. Future developments in Asia will therefore resemble the changes in Europe during the past decade, although probably not to the extent of fully open internal borders and unified market regulations.

Faced with the increasing 'mobility' of products, companies can start to halt the flow of products into neighbouring markets by introducing different product versions in different countries. Such policy runs counter to the attempts of multinational corporations to establish truly global brands everywhere. It also reduces economies of scale and adds to the complexity of production and logistics. In addition, when only limited differentiation is introduced to keep the brand somewhat in line with its global appearance, products may still be shipped into other countries. This adds further uncertainties to the existing confusion over prices, particularly with regard to product identity, and suspicions that imported, differentiated products may not be authentic but fakes.

Alternatively, companies could move towards one single price (adjusted by administrative costs such as import duties, taxes and so on). This strategy is rarely recommendable in its purest form, as it normally implies adjusting to the lowest price level in the region and consequently lowers profits significantly. As experience with the unification of European markets has shown,[12] a middle way between the extremes of keeping high price differentials and lowering prices substantially in high-price countries has to be found as market integration proceeds. The compromise consists of shrinking price differentials to a rather narrow price 'corridor' that discourages arbitrage. This is done by increasing prices in the lowest-priced countries while also decreasing them in the highest-priced countries, but not to the extent that the price becomes uniform.

Optimising regional prices in this way is a difficult task as the analysis must be based on detailed country data, particularly price elasticities and marginal costs, which are not always readily available in companies operating in Asia. It is, however, important to go through such a detailed analysis since for manufacturers the objective is not to prevent parallel imports (although distributors may demand it) but to maximise profits in the region.

Trade-offs have therefore to be accepted, and some markets will be more affected than others. From a regional point of view, it may not hurt much if a high price in a small country such as Malaysia is affected by cheaper parallel imports. However, it will matter if a high and therefore profitable price level in a large country such as Indonesia is destroyed by an inflow of products from a small country with low prices. In other words, in a move towards regional pricing, prime attention has to be paid to the larger markets while the smaller ones have to follow.

Advertising

Content characteristics

Advertising is the most culture-bound element of the marketing mix because it is based on language and other communication instruments that are themselves very deeply rooted in a given culture of a society. Realising this, most advertisers take great pains to attune their message to the cultural environment. When designing advertising, the promotional message has to be consistent with the language, cultural norms, religious mores and perceptive capacities of the society for which it is intended, in order to avoid interpretations of the promotional message in unintended ways. Although this should be obvious, even the most successful marketers occasionally overlook the importance of understanding the intricacies of consumer perceptions. This point was illustrated by a Procter & Gamble commercial for Camay soap that featured a Japanese husband in the same room while his wife was bathing. While this scene might connote intimacy to a Western viewer, Japanese consumers found it a distasteful invasion of privacy. Once Procter & Gamble switched to a more abstract promotional image, sales of Camay soap improved significantly.

Language is one of the primary means of communication in advertising. Language differences require the translation of advertising language, product names and promotional phrases. Advertising language consists primarily of colloquial language – subtle yet precise – which is extremely difficult to translate since there is little literal equivalence and idiomatic expressions change from one language to another.[13] Even in the same language, word connotations can vary widely from culture to culture. Similarly, unintended meanings caused by careless translation are an invitation to disaster. In Thailand, for example, Exxon's 'Put a Tiger in Your Tank' campaign was completely ineffective as it translated into Thai as a cryptic message urging consumers to 'capture the tiger and put it in the bucket for high power'. The fact that Thais believe that the lion, rather than the tiger, is a symbol of strength was one problem. Another was that many Thais had difficulty understanding why there was any need for a tiger (or a lion) to be in the tank in the first place. Apparently, the tank (as opposed to the engine) is not universally perceived as the source of power for a car.

Some Western advertisers have tried to avoid potential difficulties with translation by leaving at least part of the copy in English, particularly in cases of products geared towards an up-market segment. While this may convey an image of foreignness and worldliness, communicating a message in English in Asia is problematic. As Hong Kong's Star TV discovered when it launched its first regional television channel, the number of people comfortable with English is small, and consumers generally prefer to be approached in their own native tongue, even in markets such as Hong Kong and Malaysia. In addition, in some countries such as Indonesia and Vietnam, the use of foreign languages in local advertising is restricted by the government.

As described in Chapter 3, the ideographic nature of many Asian writing systems, as well as the limited emphasis placed on verbal skills in most Asian education systems, leads to a stronger visual than aural orientation among Asian consumers. This difference is significant when designing advertising. Some experts have theorised that ideographic and phonetic characters are stored in different hemispheres of the brain and are therefore retained differently. As a result, the use of the superimposed writing of ideographic characters as a reinforcement of the advertising message is considerably more evident in Japanese commercials than in Western commercials, which rely more on aural emphasis.[14] Similarly, the Chinese consumer tends to be more responsive to visual than acoustic stimuli.[15]

The emphasis that most Asian educational systems place on rote memorisation in learning creates in individuals a superior capacity to absorb information and memorise detail, and this in turn has a significant effect on the rate of advertising message retention. Once a message is learned and comprehended, the retention rate is far higher for a Chinese than a Western viewer. Thus much less repetition of advertisements is necessary in order to reach a certain level of brand or product awareness than would be the case in the West.[16]

Advertising style

Cultural differences will also influence which style of communication is most effective. The choice is basically between informative, rational and reason-why messages and the creation of dream worlds that appeal to the emotions and make consumers feel different about themselves and their relationship with products. Neither style is exclusive, and overlaps exist. In comparing Japanese and American advertising, surveys show significant differences in style. Japanese advertisements indulge in creating a soft product image within a subtle frame of reference, while American commercials present hard facts to prove product superiority.[17]

Familiarity with the product advertised, however, also plays an important role in determining advertising style. Mainland Chinese, for example, reveal their pragmatism in their greater responsiveness to advertisements that emphasise concrete, functional and utilitarian product benefits rather than symbolic themes. They will read even the fine detail of product print advertisements.[18] Thus, at this stage of development, advertisements communicating image or lifestyle associations may be lost on a Chinese who wants to know what the product is, how it is used and what its benefits are. Part of the reason why mainland Chinese consumers regard advertising positively as being informative and helpful certainly lies in economics: for them, having a *choice* of consumer goods is still a relatively new phenomenon.

Chinese across the borders in Hong Kong have, on the other hand, been used to the trappings of mass consumerism for decades. They increasingly regard purely informational advertisements as dull, uninteresting and easy to forget as they become more sophisticated and knowledgeable about consumer products and advertising.[19] Hong Kong Chinese viewers find the most appeal in emotional advertisements that are interesting, entertaining and communicate a sense of personal relevance. Creative commercials utilising innovative visuals, portraying lively and dynamic scenes of people using the product and incorporating information on product benefits win the highest ratings by viewers. This is important because the likeability of an advertisement has been found to be the best predictor of its advertising effectiveness.[20] Thus, in the early stages of consumerism, an

explicit product focus is necessary, but as consumers become more sophisticated in their knowledge of consumer goods and more seasoned in
viewing and evaluating advertisements, they will be more attracted by
emotional and creative advertising.

The fact that most Asian cultures are high context (that is, diffuse)
allows advertising to be less explicit. Implicit meanings and context can be
relied upon for communicative power. A high context culture also provides
the right environment for highly symbolic advertising because individuals
are capable of understanding implicit messages and symbolism according
to the context. However, for individuals to be able to infer the same
meaning, there must be a high degree of homogeneity in society. This is
certainly the case for Japan but less so for countries in Southeast Asia and
China. Also, some Asian cultures are more positively influenced by
symbolic messages than others. As mentioned above, Chinese from the
mainland are at this stage more influenced by commercials in which
explicit conclusions are drawn than by those which feature symbolism and
require implications to be drawn.

The Japanese are well known for their preference for the oneiric, dream-
like style of advertising. The messages of many Japanese advertisements are
so elusive and esoteric that they often say nothing about the product. The
product may, in fact, be shown only at the very end or not at all. One
Kewpie mayonnaise commercial featured a shot of a skyscraper in which the
camera slowly moved down until, at the base of the skyscraper, sat a giant
head of lettuce. Such symbolism is deliberate: the viewer is being flattered
because the ability to 'read' the advertisement is an indication of sophistication.[21] This style enhances the fantasy of the consumer and allows the
consumer to imagine satisfaction and enjoyment, thus creating desire. A
succinct example is an advertisement by the department store Seibu, which
showed a picture of a 6-month-old baby swimming with his eyes wide open
in clear blue water. The caption read: 'Discovering Yourself'.[22]

The extensive use in Japan of short, 15-second television commercials
reveals culture-based variations in information-processing capabilities.
Although the Japanese do not necessarily process information more
quickly, they have learned from an early age actively to complete ideo-
graphs and sentences, and to fill in missing words in conversations. Thus
commercials can be left 'incomplete', omitting the 'successful application'
shots that conclude so many American commercials. The role of advertising in Japan seems to be much more of an image creator, a soft support for
contemplated or consummated purchases.[23]

The strong preference of Japanese advertisers for the emotional, image-
creating style has several reasons.[24] The first is based on cultural resistance

to hard selling. A seller too articulately and too strenuously exhorting the virtues of a product cannot be trusted. The second reason results from the market situation in Japan. As most industries feature a number of competitors with almost identical products, uniqueness can be, at best, only a temporary advantage. Thus the idea of a 'unique selling proposition' seems inappropriate. Third, while image-building is used to create differentiation and value added, detailed information about products in Japan is available from well-trained salespersons at the retail level. Where these do not exist, or are replaced by more depersonalised distribution channels, companies offer extremely detailed information material in addition to running image campaigns.[25]

Last, image-building in Japan is not limited to a brand but is in most cases linked with the corporate image. Advertising does not specifically focus on information about one specific product but instead creates a mood or dream that can be leveraged cost-efficiently across the whole spectrum of products. In the case of companies like Toshiba or Sony, their portfolio covers tens of thousands of products for both industrial and private use.

Asian and Western values

In these times of global marketing strategy, it is tempting to run identical advertising campaigns in different parts of the world. Marlboro's global campaign using cowboys has made it one of the largest brand names in the world. An example such as this is, however, misleading as for any one global campaign that has worked, there may be hundreds of unsuccessful attempts to impose advertising material on consumers living in a different cultural environment, who therefore fail to interpret the message in the desired way. Adaptation, if not re-creation, of Western advertising material is therefore often necessary. Ideally, this will consist of more than the translation of copy; in other words, it will transpose the message into the entirely different cultural setting of Asia.

One of the major differences in culture lies in the orientation towards individualism and collectivism.[26] Western societies are described as more individualistic and thus more prone to strive for self-actualisation, while Asians tend to be more collectivistic, thereby making constant reference to their peers. These attitudes argue for a more individualistic approach in advertising in the West, while for Asia a collectivistic style should be more persuasive. Studies have validated this relationship, which, however, appears to be stronger for products intended for social use rather than private use.[27] In consequence, advertising approaches in Asia that stress social norms and social acceptability will be favoured more than personal preferences and feelings.

In addition to this conceptual dichotomy in consumer behaviour, there are differences between Western and Asian advertising in the way in which campaigns are executed. One obvious example is the use of sex and sex symbols, but there are other, more subtle traps for Western firms. In many Asian cultures, it is inappropriate to show acts of physical intimacy such as kissing or hugging that are often featured in American soft drink and toothpaste commercials. The 'sex appeal' theme used by Ultra Brite toothpaste, for example, might very well be considered offensive in more conservative cultures.[28] While, among some Western cultures such as France, nudity in advertising may convey beauty, excellence and nature,[29] nudity would be perceived quite negatively in the Asian cultures most orientated towards traditional values. In general, sexual connotations in advertising are unsuitable when directed at the Asian consumer.

Advertising that advocates frivolous consumption too strongly and glorifies a luxurious lifestyle is equally bound to run into opposition. In Vietnam and in China, communist party officials may still consider such consumerism as politically incorrect. In Muslim countries such as Indonesia and Malaysia, Islamic leaders may object to any open or gross display of materialism and may argue for restraint on suggestive advertising approaches.

It is in this context that Western advertisers face the latent risk of being accused of importing not only Western products and advertising, but also Western values. This risk exists wherever opinion leaders believe that Asian values are fundamentally different from and morally superior to those from the West. In times of political tension, such thinking can easily lead to restrictions on advertising or the total blacklisting of products. Similarly, in periods of current account deficits, governments have an interest in clamping down on 'unnecessary' foreign products, imports in particular. To reduce such risks, Western advertisers also have to avoid campaigns that can be interpreted as Western arrogance or even 'imperialism'. An illustration of this would be a Caucasian seen to be talking down to or belittling an Asian person. With women's movements becoming stronger in Asia, a potentially even more troublesome advertisement would show an Asian woman in a subservient attitude to a Caucasian male.

The orientation towards traditional values in Asia also influences the degree of respect shown towards elders in advertisements. Research reveals that Japanese magazine advertisements show more respect towards elders than do their American counterparts.[30] Korean advertising also features the wisdom of elderly people far more frequently than does Western advertising.[31] In contrast to the Japanese, who find comic relief in advertisements showing adult silliness because it serves as a release from role propriety, Chinese perceive negatively the portrayal of adults conducting themselves in a silly or child-like manner.[32] In general, humour in Asian advertising arises from situations depicting two characters of unequal status.[33] In such cases, the characters act in a manner inappropriate to their individual status, which viewers find amusing because of the impossibility of such a situation in real life.

A result of the group orientation and familism common across Asian cultures is that an advertisement portraying a family setting is likely to be more effective than a solitary figure. As the display of individualistic values may be negatively perceived in the most traditional of Asian cultures, the number of characters featured in an Asian advertisement is generally higher than in the West. Characteristics in advertising likely to be effective with the Chinese consumer include family orientation, authority and age rather than the celebrity or sexy images frequently featured in the individualistic West. Commercials portraying the extended family reflect the reality of Asian family life and are therefore to likely be the most effective. Unilever has exploited this positive attitude towards family traditions in Indonesia in showing a household in commercials that uses the same Pepsodent toothpaste for three generations.[34]

Chinese people tend to respond well to advertisements that convey messages presenting symbols of Chinese culture, hence the success of Coca-Cola's publicity campaign specifically produced for China featuring popular images of family gatherings such as wedding ceremonies and the Chinese New Year. British-managed Cathay Pacific has identified itself as an Asian airline 'in the Heart of Asia'. The visual presentation of the campaign consists almost exclusively of brush strokes resembling Chinese calligraphy. This symbolism is highly appreciated in a period that covers the reunification of Cathay Pacific's home port, Hong Kong, with China and the end of British rule over the former colony. In the past, the airline has been less adept in choosing advertising themes. At one stage, Marco Polo, represented by a famous British actor, was brought back to life in a historical setting in its advertising campaign. For the Europeans, Marco Polo was a daring explorer beating the path to Asia. Parallels were thought to exist with Cathay Pacific linking the Occident with the Orient in modern times. For many Asians, however, Marco Polo was completely unknown. For others he was seen as an invader, depicted in the advertisements as an unshaven, sweaty adventurer, impressions not conveying the best image for Cathay Pacific.

In comparative advertising, specifically named or recognisable brands are compared with each other in terms of product attributes. While this method is used and appreciated in the USA, it is not widely accepted in Asia. Here the role of advertising is seen as praising one's own offerings but not as putting down those of competitors. This corresponds to the reluctance in Asia openly to criticise others and to avoid attacks on the 'face' of friends as well as enemies. Additionally, the Asian consumer may reject comparative advertisements as 'sour grapes' and sympathise with the 'attacked' brand.[35]

Although no law disallowed comparative advertising in Japan, it was not used at all until recently, probably out of fear of destroying harmonious relationships in a given market. It was left to a non-Asian firm, Pepsi, to break this taboo when it launched television commercials in which rap musician M.C. Hammer endorsed the product and at the same time rejected Coca-Cola. Following widespread protests, the films were withdrawn and replaced with a softer version. It is not evident that the Western, more aggressive approach of comparative advertising will gain popularity over time. Deep-seated social behaviour may continue to work against it, although a younger and information-hungry segment in society will probably be delighted to be exposed to more comparative advertising in future.

As is the case everywhere in the world, advertising has to stick to the rules. On the other hand, it is when rules are not obeyed and different routes are chosen that the greatest attention can be attracted. Cultural differences between Asian societies and those in the West generally demand adaptation or recreation of the message. However, advertisers can also underline and emphasise the differences. This is especially true for products purchased with status-seeking motivations. BMW has sought to set itself apart by stressing its foreignness and difference. The company accentuates its German origins and takes great pains to project the same kind of corporate image that it has in Europe and America. BMW's first advertisements in Japan were not the creation of a Japanese advertising agency but were literally translated from German to English and then to Japanese through the combined efforts of a German marketing manager and a British advertising agency. This produced an advertisement whose contents were incomprehensible but were something special, and BMW was able to draw attention because it was so un-Japanese.

Distribution

Channels and stages of development

Distribution represents the link between the manufacturer and the final consumer. It covers the whole aspect of channelling the products through the various layers of middlemen with the help of other agents such as transportation companies. The choice and the management of distribution channels affect all other marketing decisions. This is true even if they concern only the first stages in the distribution chain, which fall into the area of business-to-business marketing.

The very first step links the manufacturer with the importer and/or the wholesaler. The second step links the wholesaler with the retailer, while the third step then makes a direct connection between the retailer and the consumer. Shortcuts can be taken by the manufacturer dealing directly with the retailer. On the other hand, importers may sell to primary wholesalers, who in turn deal with secondary and even tertiary wholesalers before the products reach the retailers. This extended channel system is found in large countries such as China and Indonesia. However, it can still be observed in Japan, where the system relies on long-established relationships and frequent transactions because of the emphasis on trust and reliability and because of the lack of space. The selection of a certain distribution chain has an impact on logistics and pricing on the one hand, while on the other influencing the choice of retailers in terms of exclusivity, location and image.

Channel selection is dependent on a number of criteria such as the type of product offered, the segments and number of consumers targeted and the manufacturer's position in the market. The availability of trustworthy and capable distributors, and their willingness to finance and store inventory, is equally important. By and large, the greater the potential of the market in the long run, the more a manufacturer will want to be directly involved, and the more resources the company itself will allocate to handle certain aspects of the distribution.

Along with modernisation of the retail sector, the whole import and wholesale business in Asia is being streamlined. In the past, low entry and exit barriers in trade led to myriad middlemen selling to other middlemen before the products reached the retailers. The professionalisation of the import and wholesale trade, and the increased purchasing power of the larger retailers, has led to a decrease in the number of wholesalers.

Chinese distributors, who dominate the wholesale sector in Southeast Asia, have traditionally defined their business as the management of cash rather than the buying and selling of products. They obtain their goods from manufacturers against payment after 2 or 3 months. These goods are then sold to retailers against either cash or credit at very high interest rates. This very high asset turnover (assets/sales) allows them to add either a very low margin or no margin at all to the products they handle. Interest earned from granting credit, or the return on investment made with cash raised through wholesale activities in real estate or the stock markets, is enough to achieve an overall profit on activities. With one party interested in pursuing long-term marketing strategies and the other interested in raising funds, relationships between manufacturers and wholesalers are often difficult to manage.

Even though most countries have already taken steps towards the liberalisation of the distribution sector, foreign manufacturers operating in Asian countries other than Singapore and Hong Kong are usually prevented from going into the wholesale business. They are therefore often still forced to use local distributors and to limit themselves to promotional activities at the point of sale.

Relationships between a foreign manufacturer and its appointed importer are bound to run into trouble when products enter the latter's exclusive territory through parallel channels and are sold by unauthorised agents at a lower price. This happens rather frequently in the Asian region. As the official importers shoulder the costs for sales promotions and advertising, they cannot compete with parallel imports that are often bought from the cheapest sources worldwide and then brought through customs without, in some countries, paying full duty. Manufacturers have two options. They can try to stop these grey imports by checking their own order-processing procedures, keeping track of their products and limiting differential price policies in order to reduce or prevent arbitrage opportunities.[36] Alternatively, they can let the products flow uncontrolled into the specific country, thereby foregoing a systematic market policy. This can be observed in the case of hard liquor, cigarettes and other fast-moving consumer goods in China, Indonesia and Vietnam. The objective is to achieve a substantial market share and brand recognition with products that are sold relatively cheaply as a result of the non-payment of official customs duties, and at the same time to reap benefit from the image of an imported product that is thus perceived to be superior in quality. Such strategies seem to be feasible only during the first phase of the development of a market. Even then, however, they remain questionable tactics in terms of business ethics, as is the practice of using middlemen to implement them.

Retailing

Nowhere in Asia has change been as dramatic and as visible as in the retail sector. While in Europe and the USA retailing developed in a sequential pattern over a long period of time from 'mom-and-pop' stores via department stores to more specialised formats, the markets of the Asia Pacific region have experienced simultaneous investments in every conceivable retail format. Japanese department stores dominate the shopping areas of Singapore and Hong Kong, Bangkok and Kuala Lumpur, hypermarkets attract large crowds in Taipei, and shopping malls have become entertainment centres in Manila, boasting everything from ice-skating rinks to cinemas. The traditional retail sector, consisting of small family-run shops, market traders and itinerant vendors, has been in retreat for a number of years, at least in the urban centres.[37]

Growth in purchasing power, the increasing mobility of the consumer, and interest in a wider choice of products and services under one roof have been the driving forces behind this trend. Shopping has also become an important social and leisure activity. Shopping centres are combinations of department and speciality stores, restaurants and fast-food stalls, art galleries, discos and cinemas. Lack of capital and expertise has prevented the small traditional 'mom-and-pop' shops from competing with these new types of outlet. In this respect, family-run businesses fall short in terms of both scale and scope, especially when compared with large warehouse stores on the one hand and Internet traders on the other.

The concentrated buying power of chain stores and the increased use of information technology in their outlets make up for higher overheads. In suburban neighbourhoods and country villages, however, the new economics of distribution have not yet led to major changes. It is unlikely that these areas will experience modernisation in the near future. Here, as in Japan, the emphasis is on having a shop or street market close by where shoppers can buy fresh daily necessities in small quantities and carry them home easily. It is the personal relationship with the store owner that matters, as well as the credit one can enjoy without the need for a credit card.

Differences in the development of retailing between countries in the region and even within each country remain substantial. Vietnam, China, Indonesia and the Philippines are still dominated by traditional outlets, except in the major cities and the capital. In Thailand, Malaysia, South Korea and Taiwan, the retail sector is in transition towards the modern, sophisticated industry found in Singapore and Hong Kong. Japan stands apart, characterised by a highly sophisticated non-food sector, represented by department stores, and at the same time by a relatively antiquated food sector, represented by more than half a million family-owned neighbourhood stores. However, even this differentiation is insufficient. After deregulation and the relaxation of the Large Scale Retail Stores Law in the early 1990s, Japan was 'invaded' in the non-food sector by Toys-R-Us, while at the same time Japanese department stores continued their successful expansion into the Asia Pacific region. In the grocery sector, Japan's Ito-

Yokado developed the 7-Eleven franchise into an extremely efficient convenience store operation and ultimately acquired 7-Eleven's American parent company, Southland Corporation. Meanwhile, many small stores in Japan could no longer make ends meet and closed their doors.

Western retailers have moved into Asia with lightening speed. Where they faced legal restrictions, they tried to overcome them through franchising, licensing and joint venturing. Benetton (Italy), Esprit (USA) and Marks & Spencer (UK) sell garments in most ASEANIEs, just as Disney (USA) sells toys and memorabilia and Body Shop (UK) dispenses toiletries and cosmetics. IKEA (Sweden) and Habitat (UK) have started distributing their furniture in Singapore and Hong Kong, where the French *grands magasins* Galeries Lafayette and Printemps compete head on with Japanese department stores. Shops of luxury producers such as Gucci (Italy), Armani (Italy) and Louis Vuitton (France) are to be found in almost all capitals, the latter even in Hanoi. American fast-food chains such as McDonald's and Kentucky Fried Chicken count their Asian outlets among their most successful branches. Carrefour (France) introduced large supermarkets to Taiwan and has expanded from there into other countries. Makro (Netherlands) brought the cash-and-carry concept to Thailand before starting operations in other ASEANIEs.

Japanese department stores such as Daimaru and Sogo entered Asian markets as early as the 1970s and 80s. Japan's most aggressive 'internationaliser', Yaohan, saw its future in Asia and even moved its headquarters to Hong Kong. After setting itself the goal of opening 1,000 supermarkets in China alone by the year 2005, the company got into trouble in 1997 and had to switch from growth to retrenchment. It had, however, by then become a major player in a number of Asian markets. 7-Eleven's expansion of its convenience stores chain into the region has continued since Ito-Yokado took over operations from its former franchisee, Southland. The idea of modernising traditional neighbourhood stores through the transfer of know-how and the improvement of purchasing and control is appealing to many franchisees and customers of 7-Eleven. The stores' format represents arguably the best of East and West: emphasis on personal relationships combined with modern in-store information technology.

At the end of the 1990s, it is becoming apparent that many foreign retailers have not achieved their objectives. Many simply overestimated the opportunities in the region, particularly in China. Others underestimated the competitive pressure they would experience from both international retailers and the new Asian players. Neither did partnerships always result in mutual benefits. Those with fully integrated operations seem to do well. These 'concept retailers', such as Benetton, Body Shop, IKEA and Disney, bring with them their merchandising and marketing expertise, and remain in charge of product-sourcing and image-advertising. Franchisees, where they exist, are generally only responsible for site location and people management. They may also influence the product mix within the constraints of a given catalogue.

Unrealistic expectations and partnership problems are not the only reason for failure. Insufficient adaptation to a different environment and a different consumer has also led to disappointments. The giant American retailers Wal-Mart and Kmart both had to pull out of Hong Kong and Singapore when consumers did not feel comfortable in their large, cold and brightly lit outlets. As shoppers arrived at the stores mainly by public transport rather than in cars, American pack sizes were not appreciated either. Toys-R-Us similarly had to adjust its product portfolio to the space constraints in Asian households as well as to the higher percentage of educational toys bought in the region compared with all other parts of the world. Carrefour, unable to transfer its hypermarket concept to Taiwan, had to look for an alternative to the mass merchandising of a very wide variety of products. Instead, the retailer has concentrated on fresh food offered in large quantities at favourable prices in an atmosphere of a modern 'wet' market. The concept builds enough traffic for all other departments and has led to an operation that is profitable overall.[38]

Throughout Asia, department stores serve as arbiters of fashion, culture and social etiquette. In addition, a product's presence in a well-known department store assures the customer of the quality of that product. It is particularly crucial in introducing Western goods to Asian markets to utilise the department store's marketing expertise, up-market image and large volume of customers.

In China, department stores provide Chinese consumers with a means to educate themselves with respect to a product's features. The recent tendency is to 'window-shop' at the expensive joint-venture department stores, where salespeople are well trained and can provide extensive advice about product features and benefits, but actually to buy at the hectic state-run department stores, which are poor on service but have the advantage of cheaper prices.

In Japan, department stores are set apart from other retail establishments in their ability to offer customers not merely goods and services, but also status, prestige and respectability.[39] The generally higher quality of goods as well as superior attention to detail and service justify the department store's higher prices. The saleswoman does not merely fetch a customer's change, she literally *runs* to get the change. Department stores are therefore ideal outlets for manufacturers aiming at exclusive distribution and enhancement of the brand image. However, both the high service level of the store and its prestige orientate the loyalty of the consumer more to the store than to the brand and thus make the manufacturer highly dependent on the store. Luxury producers such as Cartier have tried to counterbalance this influence through high advertising spending and the establishment of independent, wholly owned flagship stores.

Department stores in Japan have traditionally played a very important role in a nation with an acute attention to proper form:

> The belief that there are appropriate forms of conduct for every occasion extends to the world of material goods... It is the department store's business to know everyone's proper place in society and to know the corresponding social conventions. If, for example, a gift-giving occasion is approaching, department stores must have consultants available to instruct consumers concerning to whom they are in debt, to what extent, and what gifts are expected as a result of that indebtedness.[40]

Although a person may purchase goods for personal use from a discount store or supermarket, respect for the recipient of the gift demands that it must be purchased from a prestigious department store. The wrapping of the gift will clearly indicate the store from which it came. Thus the correct department store automatically confers status and prestige on the gift offered. This is incredibly important in a nation where the status of the gift symbolises the status of the relationship and where the average family gives about 300 gifts a year. The department store relieves the individual of the psychological burden of much of the choosing and evaluating.

Although sales have stagnated during the 1990s, the department stores in Japan have kept their status as the nation's most prestigious retailers. They also continue to serve as the reinterpreter of Western customs and goods in a Japanese context. The introduction of foreign goods to Japan was made possible by the efforts of department stores to educate the public on topics ranging from table-setting and the use of cutlery to how to wear Western clothes and cook Western foods. Department stores continue to serve an educational function that does not really exist among Western department stores. This is exemplified in the art museums housed on the upper floors of many Japanese department stores and the offering of courses in cooking, languages, arts and crafts, theatre and sports. Seibu even introduced Seibu Community College on the eighth floor of one of its stores, offering courses that cater to the personal and recreational interests of its customers.

Department stores in Japan can take Western traditions, adapt them to the Japanese context and create uniquely Japanese traditions. Department stores have popularised Western holidays such as Christmas, Valentine's Day and birthdays as times for gift exchange that signify intimacy and affection. The related traditions surrounding each holiday are quite different from those in the West, however. On Valentine's Day, men, but not women, receive chocolate. On White Day, 1 month later, men return the compliment by giving women gifts of white chocolate. The Japanese have turned strawberry shortcake into a traditional 'Christmas cake'. The exchange of engagement rings provides another example. Traditionally in Japan, brides and grooms wore neither wedding rings nor engagement rings. A marriage was regarded more as a union between households than the romantic commitment of two individuals. Department stores utilised the tradition of *yuinouhin,* in which gifts are given from the groom's household to the bride's household, to fit the exchange of an engagement ring into the Japanese tradition. The engagement ring now serves not as a romantic gesture of affection but as an additional item to be included among the gifts bought in the department store.

Direct marketing

With the help of direct marketing, producers sell directly to the ultimate consumer without using intermediate distributors. It can therefore be considered to be an alternative distribution channel.

Direct marketing activities are carried out in two very different ways. Consumers are either approached through print and/or electronic media, as is the case with direct mail, or are visited by salespersons, for example at home. In the first case, sales incentives are provided in a *technocratic, anonymous* process, while in the second case, the personal relationship between seller and customer comes into play. In the collectivistic cultures of Asia, where interpersonal and social harmony are valued to the highest degree, it comes as no surprise that sales attempts through the media are less successful than those relying on buyer–seller relationships.

In Japan, domestic direct mail order houses such as Cecile and Senshuka have achieved substantial sales, as have foreign entrants like Otto Versand (Germany) in joint venture with Sumitomo. However, per capita catalogue sales are small compared with those in Australia, New Zealand[41] or the USA and Europe. Even the trend in the 1990s to place orders directly from Japan to mail order houses located in the USA in order to circumvent the local distributors has not greatly altered the situation. The popularity of the channel among the younger generation could, however, be taken as an indication of a growing business. Telemarketing, selling over the phone and electronic shopping have all been tried in Japan, although not yet in a sustained fashion.

Outside Japan, the concept of direct marketing in Asia is even less developed, although the new electronic channels have entered Hong Kong and Singapore. Dell Computers started in 1997 to sell tailor-made computers directly from its plant in Penang into the Malaysian market, thereby cutting out the middleman. This case is, however, a rare exception. The penetration of direct marketing in developing Asia remains limited partly because of insufficient infrastructure in terms of mailing lists or postal services, partly because of the lack of know-how in managing an information technology-intensive industry and partly because of generally lower income levels. There are a number of other reasons why this should be, both in Japan and in other Asian markets.

First, one of the major benefits that direct mail order houses provide to consumers in the West is convenience, in the shape of the opportunity to buy at home rather than having to leave home to go shopping. This benefit may not be appreciated by those many Asians who regard shopping as a form of entertainment or as a social event. Second, direct mail order houses are relatively new in the market, they are 'invisible', and their goods are 'untouchable'. They therefore face greater difficulties in establishing the trust of their customers. Risk-averse consumers may prefer to stay on the safe side in terms of knowing in advance about the quality of goods, having the opportunity to return the merchandise and being guaranteed an after-sales service. Third, a cultural bias towards personal relationships tends to value face-to-face contact with a salesperson more than an efficient transaction with an anonymous, faceless company. From the consumer's point of view, the salesperson is not merely a conduit through which to attain the desired good or service but a potentially valuable and important human relationship. The fact that most Asian cultures are characterised by a diffuse (versus specific) cultural orientation means that the customer and the salesperson tend to regard their relationship as more than merely fulfilling their role in a specific transaction. Just as business partners in Asia must take time to develop trust and understanding of one another, customers and salespeople often forge relationships over time. The Japanese cultural characteristics of empathy and dependence are reflected in the value placed upon a salesperson's ability to understand and anticipate the needs of the customer.

The importance of the cultural explanation is born out by the immense success of organisations selling directly through their sales representatives products ranging from cosmetics (Avon, Mary Kay) through household goods of a great variety (Amway, Tupperware) to vacuum cleaners (Electrolux). Most of these companies transferred their selling techniques directly from their home environment to Asia and found it easy to recruit capable and enthusiastic 'representatives' to work on commission, even in China. It is estimated that, in Japan, more than one million women in the cosmetics industry alone sell products to their relatives, friends, neighbours and others.[42] A well-functioning selling system has made Amway one of the most successful foreign investors in Japan. When the company entered the Korean market with its specialised selling method, thereby evading restrictions on distribution imposed on foreign firms, the government objected. It argued that, in a Confucian-based society such as Korea, the seniority of a representative could be misused in forcing a customer of more junior status to purchase unwanted goods. Amway continues to operate in Korea, but under close scrutiny of the authorities and competitors in the industry.

Sales and service

The role of the salesperson

Everywhere in the world, the relationship between the salesperson and the customer is a complex one. It seems to be very much a *vertical* one in Asia, as would be expected in a culture in which relationships are almost always hierarchical in nature. In the West, the sales situation is regarded as a *horizontal* exchange between like-minded, equal individuals, and the buyer–seller interaction is a negotiation that is often conceived of as a win–lose situation.[43] Consequently, a shopper in the West is greeted with the words 'May I help you?' or 'What can I do for you?'

In Japan, as in most other parts of Asia, the hierarchy implicit in the buyer–seller interaction is an acknowledgement that the customer holds all power. The seller is always ready to sell, while the buyer is not always prepared to purchase from that particular seller. As a consequence, a shopper in Japan is welcomed with the words 'Thank you for coming into our store.' Since there is no assumption of equality as in the West, the salesperson can concentrate more on serving the customer than on his sales pitch, thereby using his product knowledge to recommend the most suitable offering. The buyer's role as the superior in the relationship is to acknowledge advice and guidance. The salesperson is merely an assistant, or even a collaborator, to the customer and must therefore rely on the integrity of the products for sale rather than on presentation techniques.

Individual sales skill and the salesperson's ego are therefore less important than in the West, where a complaint about a product or the rejection of an offer may sometimes be taken personally by the seller.

Nevertheless, the salesperson is highly influential in directing the purchase decision. The risk-averse Asian consumer will rely on the opinion of a salesperson whom he has come to trust and respect. To ignore the advice of the person with whom one shares such a relationship would be insensitive, for it could potentially cause the counterpart loss of face. A study of Korean consumers revealed the most influential referents to be friends, family and the store salesperson, whereas for American consumers it is friends, family and boy/girlfriend.[44] Thus, owing to their influence in guiding the purchase decision, the proper training and incentivising of salespeople is particularly important in the Asian context. Once salespeople have established a bond of trust with the customer, they are far more influential in the retail environment than any point-of-purchase display can be.

In light of the norms of reciprocity present in the Asian cultural context, dealing with a particular salesperson on a repeated basis makes special sense. The salesperson in most Asian societies will often throw in a little something extra or do favours, for example extending credit without any formal agreement such as the signing of legal documents. He or she will refrain from exploiting the customer in a single transaction as the lifetime value of a satisfied customer is more important than any short-term gain. Car salesmen in Japan, for example, take care of all services required over the years. The salesperson offers to pick up the car at regular intervals, leaves another car behind for the use of the owner and delivers the serviced car back to the house of the customer. In exchange, the salesman expects the customer's loyalty. Such reciprocity of favours serves to deepen the human bond and fosters interpersonal harmony.

The importance placed upon and energy devoted to building a good buyer–seller relationship requires intensive training and incentivising of salespersons. Since aggressive behaviour is held in disfavour by the Chinese, salespeople are taught to let the customer know they are available to help but to keep a distance. An over-eager salesperson might make the customer feel uneasy and cause him to leave. Japanese salespeople are taught that they must show a cheerful, healthy appearance as well as willingness and enthusiasm. They must sell themselves before they can sell their products. Without patience and effort, salespeople cannot build personal relationships with customers.

Bargaining

In the modern world of the West, the prices of most consumer goods are clearly displayed on the shelves of supermarkets or in shop windows. Prices are therefore fixed, an outcome appreciated both by retailers interested in efficiency and control, and manufacturers of brands interested in the stability of sales and product positioning. In such an impersonal environment of mass marketing, the buyer is left with the alternative of 'take it or leave it'. Bargaining and relational exchange where price is supposed to be a friendly price, if not a friend's price, is practically impossible.[45] Exceptions are the purchases of expensive items such as furniture, cars or homes, in which a personal relationship between salesman and buyer is normally established, giving room to inject a human element of negotiation in the economic transaction.

This situation contrasts with most of Asia where, outside the modern retailing system, prices are not openly displayed and are thus negotiable. In the many 'wet' markets for fresh produce in the region or *pasars,* open markets for all kinds of household goods, bargaining is part of daily life. This applies even for low-value items, as their acquisition may still require an important amount of money for somebody with limited purchasing power. In most places, these markets with opportunities for bargaining exist in parallel with the depersonalised and efficient modern retail sector. This means that consumers obviously still find advantages in the more traditional way of doing their shopping.

On the one hand, consumers in Asia may perceive modern retail outlets as being more expensive or out of their own geographical reach. Both explanations are probably correct in countries such as Myanmar and Vietnam, but also in Indonesia and China, where supermarkets tend to cater to an up-market segment with higher value-added brands and are located in urban shopping centres far away from the high percentage of the population living in the countryside. The other explanation is not based on economic considerations but on the desire to use the occasion of shopping for social interaction with people outside the sphere of the family and the workplace. Bargaining involves the buyer in a role play that may be enjoyable. Time is not always pressing in Asia, or the sense that 'time is money' does not always apply. Succeeding in negotiations can boost the morale of the purchaser. He forms a bond with the seller, who has given away a special favour to someone whom he hopes will become a regular customer.

The great success of frequent flyer programmes in Asia, the attractiveness of buying a whole bottle of whisky or cognac in a bar at a special price that can be stored on the spot and emptied during the next visit, the struggle for survival of 'fair price' shops in Singapore and Hong Kong, and the continuing existence of plenty of camera and jewellery shops in the region without clearly marked prices all argue against the economic explanation that predicts a move over time towards more efficient retailing with fixed prices and thus without bargaining. The human longing for a more personalised exchange instead suggests that opportunities for bargaining will neither fade away soon nor ever disappear entirely from Asia.

The service dimension

The attributes that constitute service are similar across cultures. They may include advice, demonstrations, technical assistance, waiting time, delivery, warranties, ability to return merchandise and so on. However, the concept of exactly what constitutes 'good' service varies greatly according to cultural context and past experience. As most services are delivered in the presence of the customer – the time of delivery is called 'the moment of truth' – the role of the person involved on the seller's side is crucial. His or her behaviour is carefully observed and will often determine perceptions of the overall quality of the offering. The external appearance, communication skills and body language of the person will all influence those perceptions.

Service satisfaction can be defined as the result of comparing expectations with actual experience. Expectation is influenced by culture and past experience, and actual experience by the perception of the service delivered. As 'Asia is, by its very tradition, a service culture',[46] what would be considered mediocre service in an Asian hotel may still be judged superb in a hotel in New York or Paris. This is because the Asian consumer will consider the standard of service delivered to be lower than he is used to, compared with those living in New York or Paris. Superb service in Asia, on the other hand, is difficult to match anywhere else in the world. Singapore Airlines and Cathay Pacific among the airlines, and the Mandarin Oriental and the Shangri-La in the hotel business, are not by chance the leading service providers in their industries.

Whether a culture is 'doing' or 'being' orientated (that is, low context or high context) has a profound impact on how buyers and sellers interact. In 'doing' cultures, the focus is on the task at hand. Whether or not the stewardess on a Western airline takes the time to get to know the names of the passengers she is serving is irrelevant as long as the task is done quickly, accurately and courteously. On Singapore Airlines, on the other hand, courteous treatment for all passengers in business and first class includes being approached by name. In the USA, very much a 'doing' culture, it is neither uncommon nor considered rude for a customer simply to state his need or request to the salesperson, who will then focus on the task at hand. This contrasts with the Asian service concept in which the process of both sides getting to know each other represents the first step in the delivery.

The service dimension in Asia is thus more people orientated. It rates personal attention more highly than efficiency, and customisation higher than standardisation, even if the result is higher prices. The success of Singapore's Mount Elisabeth Hospital in attracting customers from abroad is at least in part because of its policy of treating patients as guests, thereby converting the hospital atmosphere into that of a first-class hotel. When the Seibu Group of Japan acquired the worldwide chain Intercontinental Hotels, one of the first improvements it introduced was to build up data files on guests showing their preferences in order to deliver an individualised service.

The 'Singapore Girl' of Singapore Airlines is the idealised version of a young, gracious and courteous Asian hostess, matched only by the role of the traditional, well-mannered and highly educated *geisha* in the classic world of Japanese entertainment. While routine tends to dominate in the modern world of services, it has a long tradition in Asia, where it often tends to be ritualised, particularly in Japan. In a sense, the *geisha* is the extreme case of ritualisation of services. Elevator girls still push the buttons in many office blocks as if visitors could not manage to find their own way up and down alone, and sales girls still use a higher-pitched voice when talking to a customer than to a colleague or friend. At gasoline stations, the serviceman will clean not only the windscreen, but also the footmats and ashtrays. Purchases, especially gifts, will be elaborately wrapped, even if the customer is in a great hurry.

Good service is also prompt service as customers should not be kept waiting. Trains are expected to arrive and depart exactly on time. Even in first-class French restaurants in Tokyo – run by Japanese chefs and staffed by Japanese waiters – the courses appear in rapid succession soon after the food is ordered. As a result, Japanese tend to regard the time spent over a meal in a restaurant in Europe as poor service rather than as a sign of a painstaking chef or an opportunity to relax.

The orientation of a culture towards 'doing' or 'being' also affects attitudes towards automated service. In the USA, where 'time is money', automated service has been quickly adopted and regarded as 'good' service in banking, travel, theatre ticket purchase, government services and so on. In 'being'-orientated societies, however, automated service removes one of the most fundamental components of 'good' service, that of personal contact. A customer may wonder how a machine can serve his needs better than a salesperson with whom he has established a relationship. Naturally, such attitudes are influenced by age, the level of education, international exposure and the kind of good to be purchased. A low-involvement product bought frequently, such as a can of soft drink, does not require personal service but should be available every time everywhere. As a consequence, and very much in line with the desire of providing good service, vending machines can be found all over Japan selling hot and cold drinks alike as well as related items.

The Western saying 'The customer is always right' stands in contrast to 'The customer is god' in Japan. The Japanese word for 'customer' is *o-kyaku-sama,* which translates as 'honourable guest'. Customers are regarded as divine guests whose patronage brings honour to a purveyor of goods or services. The mere presence of the customer on the premises is sufficient to elicit courteous greetings and bows of respect even if the customer declines to purchase anything. Japanese companies continually try to maintain and improve the quality of contact with and service to customers in exactly the same way as they work steadfastly to improve products and customer satisfaction.

Nevertheless, few Japanese companies in the service industry have been able to expand successfully abroad, probably because of the very special and demanding conditions in their home market. Exceptions can be found in retailing (Ito Yokado with 7-Eleven and the Japanese department stores). However, where services have been added to a product offering of a manufacturer, as in the case of Toyota's introduction of the Lexus to the American market, they have been an important aspect of a successful entry strategy.

Notes

1. Schütte, H. (1993) *Competing and Cooperating with Japanese Firms,* Working Paper No. 21, Fontainebleau: INSEAD-EAC, p. 13. See also Jones, K. and Ohbora, T. (1990) 'Managing the heretical company', *McKinsey Quarterly,* **3**: 20–45.
2. Levy, G.R. (1996) *Consumer Marketing in China: Chasing Billions, Catching Millions,* Hong Kong: Economist Intelligence Unit, p. 50.
3. Hendry, J. (1990) 'Lovely gifts... beautifully wrapped', *Japan Digest* **1**(1): 13.
4. Probert, J. and Lasserre, P. (1997) *The Asian Business Context: A Follow-up Survey,* Euro-Asia Centre Research Series No. 44, Fontainebleau: INSEAD-EAC, p. 23.
5. Baiyi, X. (1992) 'Reaching the Chinese consumer', *China Business Review,* **19**(6): 36–42.
6. Tobin, J.J. (1992) *Re-made in Japan,* New Haven, CT: Yale University Press, p. 47.
7. Probert, J. and Schütte, H. (1996) 'Cartier in Japan', Fontainebleau: INSEAD-EAC. The complete text of the case study can be found in Chapter 9.

8. Johansson, J.K. and Nonaka, I. (1996) *Relentless: The Japanese Way of Marketing,* New York: Harper Business, pp. 126–8.
9. 'Japan's consumers want a new deal', *Asian Wall Street Journal,* 28 March 1995: 8.
10. Johansson, J.K. and Nonaka, I. (1996) *Relentless: The Japanese Way of Marketing,* New York: Harper Business, pp. 129–33.
11. See also the section in this chapter on distribution channels.
12. Simon, H. and Kucher, E. (1992) 'The European pricing bomb: and how to cope with it', *European Mangement Journal,* 10(2): 136–44.
13. Usunier, J. (1996) *Marketing Across Cultures,* Hertfordshire: Prentice-Hall, p. 411.
14. Fields, G. (1983) *From Bonsai to Levi's,* New York: Macmillan, pp. 108–9.
15. Kindel, T.I. (1983) 'A partial theory of Chinese consumer behavior: marketing strategy implications', *Hong Kong Journal of Business Management,* 1: 104.
16. Kindel, T.I. (1983) 'A partial theory of Chinese consumer behavior: marketing strategy implications', *Hong Kong Journal of Business Management,* 1: 104.
17. Lin, C.A. (1993) 'Cultural differences in message strategies: a comparison between American and Japanese TV commercials', *Journal of Advertising Research,* 33(4): 40–8.
18. Tseng, C.S. (1996) 'Marketing in China: relevance of the Western model', unpublished paper, Fontainebleau: INSEAD.
19. Chan, K.K.W. (1996) 'Chinese viewers' perception of informative and emotional advertising', *International Journal of Advertising,* 15(2): 152–66.
20. Biel, A.L. and Bridgwater, C.A. (1990) 'Attributes of likeable television commercials', *Journal of Advertising Research,* 30(3): 38–44.
21. Clammer, J. (1995) *Difference and Modernity,* New York: Kegan Paul, pp. 38–40.
22. Seguela, J. (1994) *Pub Story: l'Histoire Mondiale de la Publicité en 65 Campagnes,* Paris: Hoebeke, pp. 169–76.
23. Johansson, J.K. (1986) 'Japanese consumers: what foreign marketers should know', *International Marketing Review,* 3(2): 37–43.
24. Johansson, J.K. and Nonaka, I. (1996) *Relentless: The Japanese Way of Marketing,* New York: Harper Business, pp. 133–40.
25. Club Med's 'dream holidays' are advertised through an image campaign. However, the Japanese tendency towards high uncertainty avoidance, the high opportunity cost involved in a disappointing vacation, as well as the limited experience of the travel agencies with this new concept, made the provision of detailed information essential. Club Med's brochures and videos provide extremely detailed explanations of the Club Med concept and the facilities in the resorts. For further details, see the 'Club Med Japan' case in Chapter 9.
26. Details have been discussed in Chapter 1 with reference to Hofstede's dimensions of cultural values.
27. Zhang, Y. and Neelankavil, J.P. (1997) 'The influence of culture on advertising effectiveness in China and the USA', *European Journal of Marketing,* 31(2): 134–49.

28. Onkvisit, S. and Shaw, J. (1985) 'A view of marketing and advertising practices in Asia and its meaning for marketing managers', *Journal of Consumer Marketing,* **2**(2): 5–17.
29. Usunier, J. (1996) *Marketing Across Cultures,* Hertfordshire: Prentice-Hall, p. 414.
30. Mueller, B. (1987) 'Reflections of culture: an analysis of Japanese and American advertising appeals', *Journal of Advertising Research,* **27**(3): 51–9.
31. Usunier, J. (1996) *Marketing Across Cultures,* Hertfordshire: Prentice-Hall, p. 417.
32. Kindel, T.I. (1983) 'A partial theory of Chinese consumer behavior: marketing strategy implications', *Hong Kong Journal of Business Management,* 1: 104.
33. Usunier, J. (1996) *Marketing Across Cultures,* Hertfordshire: Prentice-Hall, p. 417.
34. Kotler, P., Ang, S.H., Leong, S.M. and Tan, C.T. (1996) *Marketing Management: An Asian Perspective,* Singapore: Prentice-Hall, p. 800.
35. Ho, S.C. and Sin, Y.M. (1986) 'Comparative advertising in Hong Kong: issues and problems', *Hong Kong Journal of Business Management,* 4: 71–88.
36. Palia, A. and Keown, C. (1983) 'Combatting parallel importing: views of US exporters to the Asian countries', *Industrial Marketing Management,* **12**: 113–23.
37. Malayang, V. (1988) 'The distribution industry in Asian NIEs and ASEAN countries and the effects of the entry of Japanese retailers', *Management Japan,* **21**(2): 15–28.
38. Lasserre, P. and Courbon, P. (1994) 'Carrefour in Asia (A)', Fontainebleau: INSEAD-EAC.
39. Creighton, M.R. 'The Depato: merchandising the West while selling Japaneseness'. In Tobin, J.J. (1992) *Re–made in Japan,* New Haven, CT: Yale University Press, p. 44.
40. Creighton, M.R. 'The Depato: Merchandising the West while selling Japaneseness'. In Tobin, J.J. (1992) *Re-made in Japan,* New Haven, CT: Yale University Press, pp. 42–57.
41. Kotler, P., Ang, S.H., Leong, S.M. and Tan, C.T. (1996) *Marketing Management: An Asian Perspective,* Singapore: Prentice-Hall, p. 832.
42. Laidler N. and Quelch, J.A. (1993) *Mary Kay Cosmetics: Asian Market Entry,* Boston: Harvard Business School.
43. Johansson, J.K. and Nonaka, I. (1996) *Relentless: The Japanese Way of Marketing,* New York: Harper Business, pp. 14–24.
44. Lee, C. and Green, R.T. (1991) 'Cross-cultural examination of the Fishbein behavioural intentions model,' *Journal of International Business Studies,* **22**(2): 289–305.
45. Usunier, J. (1996) *Marketing Across Cultures,* Hertfordshire: Prentice-Hall, p. 312.
46. Kotler, P., Ang, S.H., Leong, S.M. and Tan, C.T. (1996) *Marketing Management: An Asian Perspective,* Singapore: Prentice-Hall, p. 605. Some of the examples given in this section are taken from this book.

8 Modernisation versus Westernisation of Asian Consumer Behaviour

Globalisation and consumer behaviour

The world economy is globalising. Time and distance are shrinking as efficiency and speed greatly improve communication, transportation and financial flows. The Internet alone has had an enormous effect in terms of international availability of information as well as the capacity for personal and professional communication. The media, too, have become internationalised; we can watch CNN in the vast majority of cities across the world. In entertainment, the film and music industries ensure the worldwide distribution of movies and music, communicating similar cultural values across the globe.

Today, we talk of 'global industries', 'global companies' and 'global products'. The intensifying of 'global competition' means that, in order to protect even their domestic market, companies must be able to compete on an international basis. Companies must organise their businesses to minimise the importance of national borders and allow capital to be raised, materials and components sourced, and manufacturing carried out wherever the job can best be done in terms of efficiency, effectiveness and cost. The global firm is able to be the most competitive because of its ability to plan, operate and co-ordinate its activities on a worldwide basis.

The danger, however, is to imagine that, as companies and competition globalise, consumers are globalising as well. It is our belief that this is not the case. The advent of the 'global product' is not a result of consumers' preferences for products available worldwide; the Japanese consumer who uses Colgate toothpaste simply does not care whether American consumers use the same Colgate toothpaste. Instead, 'global products' are being *pushed* upon consumers because of the desire of companies to capture savings through economies of scale and standardisation, rather than *pulled* by consumers.

It has been our argument throughout this book that culture ensures that *consumers are not the same*. They are fundamentally different in their tastes and preferences, perceptions, ordering of needs and motivations to consume. When cultures are widely divergent, the behaviour of consumers will be sufficiently different to require the adaptation of consumer behaviour theory. It is our strongly held belief that the fundamental differences underlying Asian and Western cultures make an alternative consumer behaviour theory specific to Asia a necessity.

Cultural bonds run deep where consumer goods are concerned. Particularly in the case of non-durable consumer goods such as food and clothing, the different tastes, habits and customs imparted by their culture prevent consumers from universally preferring the same product attributes, advertising messages, packaging and presentation. The relatively recent introduction of durable consumer goods such as electronics and cars to developing Asian markets means that there is less cultural meaning attached to the purchasing and consumption of these products. Thus durable consumer goods have far greater potential for offering on a global basis. However, even for these products, and even when economic and purchasing power differences are minimised, cultural differences are pervasive enough to call for different marketing strategies in different countries. This is perhaps less the case between Denmark and Sweden for example, but definitely the case between Asia and the West, and often among Asian countries themselves. The greater the cultural differences, the greater the necessity of designing a marketing mix specific to the cultural context.

Some commentators have suggested that the emergence of a global mass culture signals the homogenisation of cultures around the world. They fear that individual cultures are becoming impoverished, stunted and even eliminated by this homogenising process, which they otherwise refer to as 'Americanisation'. Consumer products such as Coca-Cola, Levi and Marlboro are regarded as the carriers of cultural meaning. The American origins and the images conveyed by these products through advertising provide them with the ability to communicate cultural values such as individualism and freedom. Many countries such as Malaysia and Singapore blame such Americanisation for the 'moral decay' that they see diminishing their traditional 'Asian values'.

Consumer goods do communicate cultural meaning, and in most cases it is Western products that are the most loaded with cultural meaning. While Japanese and Korean products are available worldwide, there is no talk of the 'Japanisation' or 'Koreanisation' of cultural values. Why is it that those products most likely to communicate strong cultural meanings are Western in origin? Why do Louis Vuitton and Fauchon communicate French luxury and romance, Burberry and Laura Ashley communicate English taste and class, but Japanese and Korean products simply communicate functional/utilitarian qualities and no cultural attributes? For example, millions of people drive Toyota cars or wear Seiko watches but, in doing so, they are hardly making a fashion or luxury statement.

There are several possible explanations for this lack of cultural attribution. As both Japan and Korea underwent late industrialisation, companies in these countries directed their energies to competing by providing goods with the best cost/quality ratio rather than by communicating emotions and cultural values. Their products were initially deemed to be of low quality and, for this reason, as well as to prevent nationalistic consumers elsewhere from avoiding their products, their country of origin was not emphasised. Finally, the reason may lie in the historically advanced level of development of international marketing practices in Western countries.

The increasing sophistication of Asian products and marketing techniques means that Asian consumer goods may soon also be communicating cultural meaning. Shiseido, for example, emphasises its Japanese origins and communicates an image of Japanese mystique, luxury and exoticism. It is able to do this because Japanese products now have an image of high quality and cutting-edge design. Consumer durables from Japan, such as those from Sony, are well known for their expert miniaturisation and innovative product features. Today, such attributes are considered to be distinctively 'Japanese'. Japanese fashion designers also emphasise the distinctively Japanese character of their designs.

As Asian economies continue to develop, the flow of influence is less and less from West to East and more and more in both directions. This can be seen in Western interest in Asian foods, arts, medicines, sports and so on. Also, global competition means that Western producers of products and services increasingly compete with Asian producers. The often higher level of service, more careful attention to customer satisfaction and insistence on quality forces Western producers to follow suit. Airlines and hotels provide examples of industries in which Asian competition has improved service levels across the industry. Combined with the pressure to standardise product lines globally, such pressures will lead to greater similarities of products across countries. However, the availability of similar products in different countries does not mean the same culture, consumers or consumer behaviour.

Modernisation versus Westernisation

At present, this process of 'globalisation' is, nevertheless, understood as being more Western in character than truly global. When we talk of a 'global consumer culture' in which people are united by common devotion to certain brands, movie stars and musical celebrities, what is actually meant is the global presence of Western culture. Western firms marketing products in Asian countries might be tempted to believe that, given time, consumers in Asia will become more like consumers in their home countries. Therefore, if we were to wait long enough, marketing strategies developed in the West would be perfectly appropriate to the Asian consumer. It has been our argument throughout these chapters that this will not be the case.

What Asian countries are experiencing is not 'Westernisation' or even 'globalisation'; they are experiencing modernisation. Modernisation may be interpreted as Westernisation because modernisation is a social change originally initiated by the West. Although modernisation was an organic process in the West, it was a process initiated by the West in Asian countries. Historians consider the beginning of modernisation in China to be the year the Opium War began – 1840 – and the modern period in Japanese history to have begun in 1868, the beginning of the Meiji Restoration. The external impact of the West created modern revolution. According to this view, modernisation could not have occurred without an element of Westernisation.

True 'Westernisation', however, would assume that non-Western countries become like the Western world. This cannot be the case because the non-Western world prior to modernisation had its own cultures that reacted to the process of modernisation in very different ways from the Western world. These cultures continue to react to and reinterpret the cultural values of the West, which are communicated through consumer goods, such that they suit the specific cultural context. Cultures are varied and dynamic, and cannot follow identical paths of development.

The fact that the process of modernisation itself proceeded in a very different manner in Asian countries compared with Western countries serves to reinforce the cultural differences between these two regions of the world. Modernisation in the West began with cultural modernisation in the form of the advancement of rational thinking through the progress of science, technology and education. This was followed by societal modernisation from a feudal to a more open society, political modernisation in the form of democracy and, finally, economic modernisation in the form of capitalism. These four modernisations occurred successively. Among Asian countries, modernisations have occurred both unequally in extent and relatively rapidly and simultaneously. In Japan, for example, they occurred in reverse order to the historical pattern followed by the West. The order has been economic, political, societal and cultural. Today, Japan remains most advanced in economic modernisation but is relatively slow to embrace the other three modernisations.[1] Arguably, the same can be said about a number of other Asian countries.

Huntington makes the argument that, even though the cultures of the world are moving from traditional to modern cultures, there is no reason to believe that they will resemble one another any more than they did when the majority of cultures were traditional.[2] The argument that modern societies will be more homogenous arises from the assumption that modern society must approximate to a single type – the Western type. Modern civilisation does not necessarily mean Western civilisation. The West was the first civilisation to modernise, but before modernisation it was still Western, and it remains so today. Even modern Asian cultures will remain profoundly Asian.

It is thus incorrect to assume that what is occurring in Asia is Westernisation, which will make Asian consumers identical to Western consumers. Since Asian countries have their own distinct cultural heritages and have followed a different path towards modernisation, they will never be replicas of the West. One hundred years or less of modernisation cannot erase thousands of years of cultural development.

Thus a 'globalisation' process that makes consumers around the world converge towards the same likes and preferences, habits and customs or motivations must remain either a fallacy or wishful thinking on the part of marketing gurus. The cultures of individual countries will continue to react to and reinterpret through their own cultural lenses the cultural values that may be communicated through consumer goods. The popularity of Western goods does not mean a 'Westernisation' of Asian consumers. The meanings that the goods hold for the consumers and the motivation to consume may be very different in different cultures.

The high level of consumption of Western goods is typically used as an argument for the loss of Asian culture in favour of Westernisation. The fact that such consumption stands out is testimony to the fact that it is not the norm throughout Asia, nor across all segments of Asian consumers. Even with the fame of McDonald's and Domino's pizza in Asia, 98 per cent of all restaurants in Asia serve the food indigenous to the local region. In Indonesia, the advent of *teh botol* (bottled tea) has been to the detriment of sales of Coca-Cola and Pepsi, and the consumption of *kretek* clove cigarettes has not declined in the least because of the success of the Marlboro man. A preference for Asian products persists.

Japan offers a prime example of the way in which cultures reinterpret consumer goods and their cultural meanings to suit their own context. The Japanese are a consumption-orientated society and consume many of the same products as Westerners. Media and entertainment are similarly influenced by the West. Japanese can watch American television dramas, listen to English-language radio stations, read European fashion magazines and attend rock concerts. Superficially, Japan does not look strikingly different from a Western country. Yet, the Japanese remain deeply distinctive in their cultural values and therefore in their patterns of consumer behaviour. Despite 50 years of a pervasive American influence in Japan, Japanese remain 'Japanese' in thought, behaviour and lifestyle. Although there is much talk about a societal move from *hitonami* ('alignment with society') towards *seikatsusha* ('designing one's own personal lifestyle to reflect one's values'), Japan remains a highly conformist society. The dyed brown shaggy hairstyles and grunge clothing worn by teenagers may look rebellious and individualistic, but we can see that the look is uniformly replicated. Furthermore, once a youngster enters the workforce, it is time for him or her to become a *shakaijin* ('society person') and conform to the behaviour deemed proper by society.

It is for this and the many other reasons we have described in this book that we do not believe that globalisation will obliterate cultural differences and standardise consumer behaviour around the world. Although consumers may superficially grow to look alike, cultural bonds in Asia run deep and ensure that the consumer behaviour of Asians remains distinctive from that of Westerners. Kipling's words remain as true today as when he originally wrote them: 'Asia is not going to be civilised after the methods of the West. There is too much of Asia and she is too old.'[3]

Notes

1. Tominaga, K. (1996) 'The spirit of capitalism: West vs East – the immaturity of modernization in Asia', paper presented at the International Symposium 'Community and Values in Asia and Western Society', Tokyo: International House.
2. Huntington, S. (1996) 'The West: unique, not universal', *Foreign Affairs*, 75(6): 28–46.
3. Kipling, R. (1891) 'The man who was', in *Life's Handicap*. First published at the end of the 19th century. It is today available as a Penguin Classics series paperback.

9 Appendix: Case Studies

CASE STUDY ONE: Cartier Japan

Hellmut Schütte and Jocelyn Probert (INSEAD-EAC, 1966)

It was December 1995, and the end-of-year shopping season well under way. Mr Guy Leymarie, President of Cartier Japan, was looking forward to the visit the next week of Mr Alain-Dominique Perrin, President of Cartier International, Mr Richard Lepeu, Managing Director of Cartier International, and their team. Perrin and Lepeu came to Tokyo every year in December to discuss the marketing plans put together by Leymarie and his team, and continued from there to visit other Cartier subsidiaries in Asia. His style of leadership was already familiar to Leymarie, who had been Secretary General of Cartier International in Paris until his posting to Japan in February 1992.

Leymarie knew that Perrin would have thoroughly read the documents he had already sent to Paris, and that the meeting would be more of a discussion than a presentation. He had made substantial changes to the operations of Cartier in Japan during the past four years, a period which had also seen a severe recession by Japanese standards, and he was confident that the company was now well attuned to Japanese consumer attitudes.

Background

Cartier was founded in 1847 in Paris and by the early years of the 20th century had established itself as 'the jeweller of kings and the king of jewellers'. Its jewels and watches were worn by the world's most famous people. Despite a difficult period in the postwar years of the 1940s and 1950s Cartier is once again one of the world's most renowned creators of 'haute joaillerie'. Many of the pieces offered to the discerning consumer of the modern day echo the designs and concepts created during Cartier's golden era, such as the range of 'Tank' and 'Pasha' watches. A more affordable line of products, 'les Must de Cartier', was launched in 1972 offering pens and cigarette lighters, and later leather goods and watches, for a younger age group.

Today, Cartier is an important element of the Vendôme Luxury Group, which also includes the wristwatch companies Baume & Mercier and Piaget, Montblanc pens and Dunhill leather goods, menswear and watches. Vendôme itself is part of the Swiss-based Richemont group, the luxury goods, tobacco and media conglomerate of South African origin which acquired Cartier in 1983. Vendôme's operating profits rose 15 per cent to £113.3m on turnover of £699.5m in the first half of the 1995/6 year (Exhibits 1 and 2). Cartier's contribution to group results is not revealed.

The name of Cartier was first introduced to Japan in the early 1970s through the Swiss trading company Liebermann Waelchli, which acted as agent for several prestigious names in the luxury goods sector. For the next 15 years Liebermann continued to represent Cartier in the Japanese market, and built a strong image of the company as a producer of quality leather goods, cigarette lighters and pens. A separate company, Sanki Shoji, handled watch distribution since Liebermann already represented Rolex.

By 1986 the decision had been taken at Cartier's headquarters in Paris to establish a more direct presence in Japan, which was rapidly emerging as an enormous market for luxury consumer goods. A joint venture was established between Cartier, Liebermann and Sanki Shoji, and management of the new entity was undertaken by Cartier's partners.

This arrangement was short-lived. In 1989, Cartier bought out its partners and established a wholly owned subsidiary. It also moved into a building next to the Okura Hotel, one of the best known hotels in Tokyo. Cartier Japan began with Japanese management and quickly developed into a very 'Japanese' company. Sales grew strongly during the period 1989–90 as the 'bubble' economy of the late 1980s reached its apogee, but mutual communication difficulties between the subsidiary in Tokyo and headquarters in Paris compounded misunderstandings over the changing economic environment of Japan. In February 1992 Guy Leymarie arrived in Tokyo to take over the management of Cartier Japan, and to establish a new strategy for development in the face of the bursting of the economic bubble.

The distribution system and consumer attitudes in Japan

Perhaps 90 per cent of Japan's 120 million people may fairly be described as middle class, and they enjoy high purchasing power. Shopping is a major pastime in a country where space and time for leisure is limited, and on any day of the week (but especially at weekends) consumers crowd the streets and stores. Department stores have developed into luxury emporia, offering enormous ranges of high quality goods and excellent service in addition to cultural events such as art exhibitions and lessons on *ikebana* [flower arrangement] and the tea ceremony. An important service for the very richest clients is offered by the department store's *gaisho* or external sales staff, who manage corporate accounts and – important for luxury goods manufacturers – the accounts of a select number of wealthy individuals. For these customers the *gaisho* select the most exquisite items to propose to clients in the comfort of their own home.

The role of the group in Japanese society is paramount, and has important implications for consumer behaviour. Membership of a group, whether it be family, university, or work related, requires conformity with its social values. Japanese consumers also demonstrate an extraordinary capacity to study and to learn about a product before acquiring it. They are trend followers, and the press has greater influence over consumer behaviour than in other countries, precisely because of the nature of society and pressure for conformity. The consequences of such group pressure are that every Japanese knows, for example, which jewel it is appropriate to wear on which occasion, or which gift, beautifully wrapped in the paper of a prestigious department store, to offer to whom under which circumstances. For producers of luxury goods, the homogeneity of demand creates the risk that their brands will lose their exclusive cachet.

The 1980s

The 1980s was the decade when Japanese people first began to really spend the money they had worked so hard since 1945 to accumulate. The 1985 Plaza Accord, which created the conditions for a substantial revaluation of the yen against the dollar, unleashed the start of a major asset boom in Japan. People began purchasing property, and stocks and bonds as never before. Young working women (known as office ladies, or OLs), unmarried but still living at home, had substantial disposable income to spend. They acquired a fascination for western luxury and designer products, and the brands that symbolised these desires – Louis Vuitton, Chanel, Dior – took an important place in the Japanese market. As the cost of buying a home rose to unattainable levels, some consumers turned to hedonistic purchases of luxury goods as substitutes (though strict social codes helped to avoid the worst potential excesses). Department stores vied to bring new western labels into their ground floor 'in-shop' boutiques. By the end of the decade Japan had become more important than the United States as a market for luxury goods. Some brands retailed in Japan at up to two times the price in their country of origin, and the foreign manufacturers enjoyed high profit margins.

During the late 1980s the strength of demand in Japan for luxury goods presented a challenge for traditional producers of such items: how to balance the desire to maintain a brand's exclusivity (for example, by limiting the amount available) while at the same time achieving sufficient volume to be the market leader. Success in this delicate balancing act would allow the marque to become the point of reference in the marketplace. Myths began to emerge. Perhaps the best known was the notice reputedly pinned on the door of the Louis Vuitton boutique in Paris saying 'No Japanese' once the daily quota of handbags and luggage had been sold, or the tale of students being paid to queue to buy extra bags for eager Japanese visitors to France. Amid the fever for designer goods, it became easy to establish a luxury marque in Japan, and Japanese companies themselves participated either by launching their own brands with European names, or by acquiring the Japanese production and distribution licence for a true European brand.

By the end of the 1980s Japanese consumers were sufficiently well travelled and knowledgeable to recognise the difference between a licensed product and 'the real thing'. They also knew that prices in Japan were substantially higher than those for the same goods in the west. This did not necessarily matter. Some sectors of society displayed a certain pride, not so much in the possession of a particular object but in the price they paid for it: it was a means of demonstrating their purchasing power. Epitomising this attitude was the owner of a Japanese paper company, who in 1990 paid a world record price of US$82.5m for Van Gogh's *Portrait of Dr Gachet*, with the intention of having it buried with him when he died.

The 1990s

The bursting of the asset bubble in 1991 and the onset of long-lasting recession ushered in new trends in consumer behaviour. Discount stores began to appear, often offering imported goods brought in through parallel channels at prices far below prevailing domestic levels. They were encouraged by the Ministry of International Trade and Industry, which regarded these upstarts both as a means of reducing Japan's trade surplus with the United States and of demonstrating to American trade negotiators the openness of the Japanese market. The strength of the yen further contributed to the flood of competitively priced imported goods onto the marketplace.

Department stores began to lose market share to discounters and super-markets. A second element in the restructuring of the market was a review of the Large Scale Retail Stores Law, effectively removing much of the power of local retailers to block consent for new supermarkets and depart-ment stores that had been given them twenty years earlier. The LSRSL revisions of the early 1990s led to many new store openings and intensi-fied competition within the supermarket sector and between department stores. The American toy chain Toys-R-Us also challenged the traditional distribution system by demanding direct dealings with Japanese toy manu-facturers, thus forcing a shift in Japan's traditional balance of power between manufacturer and retailer in favour of the latter.

For the first time, supermarkets began to challenge department stores in some product segments, particularly expensive cosmetics which had tradi-tionally been the domain of the department stores and their specialised sales staff. A ruling by Japan's Fair Trade Commission barred cosmetics manufacturers from setting retail prices, or from refusing to supply any retailer with goods, and this created the opportunity for supermarkets (and discount stores) to stock luxury domestic cosmetics at lower prices. Future abolition of a long-standing Japanese drugs law could permit parallel importers to legally sell foreign cosmetics and perfumes in Japan.

These changes in the retail market present both opportunities and threats to the western luxury goods manufacturers. On the one hand they have become hostages to the US–Japan trade conflict, since US demands for greater openness in the Japanese market threaten to prevent them continuing their exclusive distribution practices (note that within the European Union the right of selective distribution for luxury goods companies is a rare exception to the principle of the common market). On the other hand the restructuring of the Japanese distribution system has allowed the development of newcomers to the marketplace at a speed unthinkable in the 1980s. One European luxury goods company, for example, by 1995 had twenty boutiques within department stores compared with none in 1990.

In this environment Japanese consumers have become highly selective in their brand purchases. Some marques which appeared during the bubble economy have almost vanished from sight. Those which remain are being forced to justify the prices they charge. The product must correspond to the price: the myth of the brand has disappeared. People are still enthusi-astic purchasers of branded goods, but they must be well-known names and identifiable creations.

Reflecting these developments, branded goods prices began a down-ward adjustment. In instances where the adjustment was not sufficiently rapid, customers proved themselves prepared to negotiate a discount, based on their experience of prices abroad. On luxury items the discount could reach 40-50 per cent, bringing the ticket down to Paris levels or even lower. *'Le juste prix'* – the right market price – is the rule in Japan in the mid 1990s. 'It is very competitive, the price is controlled by the consumer', says Leymarie. Nevertheless, more and more well-established European luxury goods companies are establishing a presence in Japan.

Cartier Japan

When Guy Leymarie arrived in Tokyo in February 1992 the bubble era was over and 'the market was already heading downhill'. Leymarie identified a number of immediate challenges for Cartier Japan: to turn the company into a less Japanese organisation; to establish a new product strategy, including repositioning the brand; to redefine the distribution strategy; and to adjust the operations of Cartier to face economic change.

Management reorganisation

The Japanese managing director of Cartier Japan in 1989 had established a hierarchical organisation which functioned in typical Japanese fashion. It was difficult for people lower in the organisation to communicate with their seniors. At first, business was highly successful as Cartier Japan continued to ride the boom. At that time, the Cartier group's strategy department in Paris had relatively limited knowledge of the business environment in Japan. As the economic situation in Japan deteriorated in 1990 and 1991, communication between Tokyo and the headquarters in Paris became increasingly difficult, and an atmosphere of mistrust and mutual misunderstanding developed.

The decision to send a Frenchman to head the Japanese subsidiary ushered in a complete modification of management style. Reflecting the culture of Cartier as a marketing-driven group, Leymarie hired new managers from other firms with a strong marketing culture, such as Procter & Gamble. He intentionally hired older managers, being himself only in his mid-30s at the time and needing senior people to lend weight to his organisation.

Luxury goods companies traditionally work on the strategy that the product sells itself (*'le produit se vend'*). Leymarie wanted to add the essential human factor to this formula. He instituted a supervisor system to reevaluate the working methods of the sales staff, repositioning their status within the company, and emphasising training as well as their responsibilities to, and relationship with, Cartier.

It was also his idea to introduce an incentive sales programme among the staff, to further motivate them. This was rather a new concept for Japan, and an external Japanese company employed to conduct the feasibility study came to the conclusion that it would not work. Leymarie proceeded with the project anyway – although its implementation was delayed for three months by his failure to communicate properly its function to his staff.

The person selected by Leymarie to manage Cartier's wristwatch distribution was aged 61 and recruited directly from the wholesale industry. A key characteristic of the watch industry is the important role played by specialist wholesalers: intermediaries are critical. Cartier Japan needed someone with the range of contacts and experience of the Japanese market that can only be accumulated over 15 or 20 years, and which Cartier Japan itself sorely lacked.

Leymarie spends two days per week on internal meetings with his staff, building their confidence to communicate directly with him. Through a system of committees, by subject or by department, his goal is to break down the formal organisational structure created by his predecessor. The committees are non-hierarchical, and it took time for junior members of the team to participate actively in front of their seniors. However, the corporate culture is evolving in the right direction. 'We have to communicate as directly as possible between managers and staff,' says Leymarie. He attributes the progress of Cartier Japan in the last three years to the motivation of the retail sales staff through this system.

Repositioning of the brand

Under the auspices of the agent Cosa Liebermann, the Cartier brand in Japan had become synonymous during the 1970s and 1980s with high quality leather goods, rather than the distinctive jewellery and wristwatches for which it is famous elsewhere. This positioning did not significantly change during the first years of Cartier Japan's existence, despite the opening of a flagship boutique on Namiki-dori [see below] as a showcase for its fine jewellery pieces. A key task for Leymarie was to persuade Japanese consumers that Cartier is first and foremost a fine jeweller, not a competitor to Louis Vuitton handbags. His mission was to make it the leading jeweller in Japan.

The marketing of leather goods was radically reorganised. Somewhat to the concern of headquarters in Paris, three-quarters of the outlets retailing Cartier's leather goods were closed. The strategy was to limit the exposure of leather goods to the Japanese public, while nevertheless maintaining their sales.

For three years not a single advertisement featuring Cartier leatherware was issued. All publicity surrounding Cartier concentrated exclusively on its finely crafted jewellery and watches. Advertising was restricted to quality magazines whose target customer matched the Cartier profile. It appeared in magazines for the more mature sector, geared to company presidents and senior managers, or, like '*Kateigaho*' and '*Fujingaho*', to their wives; and in magazines, such as '*25 ans*', which are aimed at trendy, affluent, sophisticated consumers whose aspirations are high. (The French title of this magazine reflects the Japanese reverence for France as the home of the luxury goods industry.)

The staffing of Cartier boutiques was also deliberately conservative. Using an intermediary, Leymarie hired as manageress of the Namiki-dori boutique a Japanese lady some 60 years of age who had never worked before. Her manner reflected the style of presence that Cartier wished to create: the weight of tradition rooted in the image of the family, which plays such an important role in Japan.

Again reflecting the importance of the family in Japanese society, Cartier Japan finally prevailed upon headquarters in Paris to allow them to test market engagement rings. As 'le joaillier du roi', the jeweller of kings, Cartier had never been requested to create engagement rings (a piece of jewellery members of royal families never wear). The products created echoed the craftsmanship of Cartier's other rings: there was no intention to 'Japanise' the offerings for the Japanese market. The success with which the engagement rings were greeted in Japan persuaded Cartier to market the product worldwide.

Timely and effective new product launches contributed to the steady change in Cartier Japan's product portfolio. By 1995 approximately half of Cartier Japan's sales were of jewellery items. Watches accounted for a further one-third, and leather goods and others the remaining one-sixth.

Distribution

Cartier worldwide uses two separate distribution channels, and this system is replicated in Japan. Its boutiques retail Cartier products exclusively: jewellery, jewelled watches, pens, lighters, accessories, and so on. Like most of the best watch manufacturers, however, Cartier's timepieces are for the most part distributed through highly specialised wholesalers operating in a structured, conservative fashion. Japan is no different, and 'to seriously market watches we must enter that system', says Leymarie. Leatherware marketing is also traditionally conducted through a limited number of specialist wholesalers. More selective distribution became a key factor in the relaunch of Cartier Japan's image as a purveyor of fine jewellery and watches.

The wristwatch business

The problem was that when Leymarie arrived in Japan, the distinction between strategies for retail and wholesale trade was unclear – nor was it easy to clarify, because of special Japanese characteristics. The principal difficulty lay in the department store as a channel for distributing watches. Three different locations within a given department store could be selling Cartier timepieces: there could be a Cartier boutique on the ground floor, the traditional location for luxury goods shop-in-shops; on the fifth or sixth floor would be the department store's watch department, operated by specialist wholesaler/retailers; on the topmost floor would be the offices of the *gaisho*, who would market Cartier watches directly to their private clients. The competition between the different locations and the varied pricing strategies they employed caused confusion among consumers and sales staff alike.

As was the case for leather goods, Cartier Japan decided to reconcentrate its watch distribution radically. In early 1992 some 300 watch retailers were selling Cartier timepieces; by 1995 only 160 remained but they were all high quality retailers who could do justice to the company's products and had a sufficiently strong capital base to carry the stock. Cartier Japan also chose to grant exclusivity to a single distributor in some regions, in return for the distributor's commitment to attain a certain level of sales. 'We choose partners who choose us', says Leymarie. 'Our contracts are based on verbal understanding, thanks to the quality of our relationship with our distribution partners. This is the only way to do it in Japan.'

Watch retailers are visited by one of the company's eight salesmen, who advise them which models to take to ensure good stock rotation. As is the case for jewellery, Cartier Japan adopts a highly co-ordinated push and pull approach, ensuring that the timepieces it advertises nationally are already available in watch shops when customers begin to ask for them. The smallest retailers would stock 50 Cartier pieces (all purchased, not taken on consignment), compared with 70 to 80 pieces at the larger ones. The retailers are arranged in a pyramid according to the products they offer: the

Must range of watches and Cartier gold and steel watches are available in all 160 outlets. Gold watches and some jewellery watches are sold at the leading watch retailers, but the full range of exclusive jewellery and high jewellery watches are sold in Cartier boutiques only.

The boutiques

In 1995 Cartier Japan boasted a network of 22 exclusive boutiques (out of 160 Cartier boutiques worldwide), all displaying the full range of Cartier jewels, watches and accessories (Exhibit 3). Nineteen of these outlets are 'shop-in-shops' within department stores in the main cities of Japan, and two are in hotel shopping arcades: at the Imperial Hotel in Tokyo and at the Royal Hotel in Osaka. Cartier Japan's flagship, however, is a free-standing boutique on Namiki-dori, an exclusive shopping street in Tokyo's Ginza and the only one of its type in Japan. While Cartier is open to the possibility of adding new boutiques, there is no emphasis on expanding beyond the current number.

The Namiki-dori boutique was opened in 1989, the year Cartier Japan was established. Specialist retailers in the United States and Europe have traditionally occupied free-standing sites on luxury shopping streets, but this option is not open to companies like Cartier in Japan, owing to the dominant position of department stores with long and historic traditions which occupy the prime locations. Many of Cartier's present department store and hotel boutiques were opened in the period when Cartier was still represented by its agent or during the joint venture phase, but the scale of investment required to launch a free-standing outlet was too great and too long-term to interest Cartier's partners.

When Leymarie took over as managing director in 1992 he inherited a network of 27 boutiques in department stores and a smaller number of 'coins rouges' (red corners), which were mini-boutiques selling only part of the Cartier range. He closed seven boutiques in lesser department stores and all of the mini-boutiques. The quality of the host department store is carefully monitored. It is rare that Cartier would choose to close a boutique, but it can happen. In 1995 it withdrew from Seibu in Shibuya (Tokyo), which had remodelled its store to reflect a less upmarket customer target and less prestigious merchandising concept – one that no longer matched Cartier's product offering. Seibu itself is representative of the recent upstarts in the department store sector compared with Takashimaya and Mitsukoshi, which have several hundred years of tradition behind them: it was the epitome of the bubble era, and excelled at avant-garde displays.

As far as Leymarie is concerned, department stores remain unquestionably the primary distribution channel in Japan for Cartier jewellery. Hans-Peter Bichelmeier, Deputy Managing Director, concurs: 'Department stores have perhaps remained too stable, their business is being eaten away by the supermarkets and discount stores. They have lost the electronics business already and are losing some of their food business. Luxury consumer goods is the only potential growth area they have, and because of the advantages of their locations they will clearly survive and build this business.'

Adjustment to economic change

Between 1989 and 1991 Cartier Japan had increased its prices each year in order to maintain the traditional differential between prices in Japan and those overseas. The renewed appreciation of the yen against the dollar beginning in 1990, however, provoked a dampening of demand for foreign luxury goods among Japanese consumers. In March 1992 total aggregate sales at national department stores fell for the first month in what was eventually to prove a 45-month run of declines which ended only in November 1995. Cartier's products (which at that time were concentrated on leather goods and accessories, and watches but relatively little jewellery) had begun to experience weaker demand in 1991.

In 1993, as the yen continued to rise, Leymarie took an unprecedented decision: Cartier would align the Japanese prices of its jewellery and watches more closely with world levels. This was a potentially dangerous move in a country where received wisdom stated that retail prices cannot fall without destroying the reputation of the brand. On 15 May 1993 full page advertisements appeared in all the leading daily newspapers announcing the new strategy. They carefully explained that the more attractive pricing policy was to demonstrate Cartier's sense of good citizenship in Japan, in view of the strength of the yen.

Leymarie had visited in advance all the department stores with Cartier boutiques, to explain his actions. Customers who made a significant purchase during the preceding few days were allowed to pay the new prices. Distributors and consumers accepted the argument well. The price of a Cartier piece in Japan became demonstrably the same as the price in Paris. By taking direct action Cartier was able to avoid the negotiated discounting practices that competitors were facing from their customers, and which resulted sometimes in jewels being sold at prices that did not do justice to the product.

On 30 March 1994 Japan's leading financial newspaper, the *Nikkei Shimbun*, published an interview with the President of Mitsukoshi. Mr

Itakura stated that the department store would no longer market any imported branded product whose price in Japan was more than 50 per cent higher than in its country of origin, citing research undertaken in December 1993 which showed that 61.7 per cent of imported brands studied (75 brands and 569 references) had a price discrepancy of more than 1.5 times. His goal was also to encourage price reductions for domestic goods, which had been inflated unreasonably to match expensive imported items.

Three months later Rolex reduced the prices of its watches in Japan, using a similar explanation to the one used by Cartier. Thereafter the price reduction momentum increased rapidly among members of the industry association, and it was acknowledged that Cartier had been the initiator. Cartier Japan's market leadership was established.

Consumers' increasing expectations that the price of a product should reflect its value led Cartier Japan to another initiative, this time to establish a market reference price, and therefore price leadership, by issuing Gemstone Industry Association (GIA) certificates for jewellery with diamonds weighing only 0.5 carats. Normally the GIA certificate is given only with diamonds of 5 carats or more. Even so, a Cartier ring would still sell for four to five times the market average in recognition of its artistic and creative value, and the quality of the stones used.

Bringing the product to the customer

Mr Perrin, President of Cartier International, maintains strict control over the most important aspect of a luxury goods company: the product. Every item must receive his final authorisation for launch. 'There are very few luxury goods companies who retain this degree of control', says Bichelmeier. Some product ranges are modern interpretations of older designs created by Louis Cartier in the early 20th century, and themes continually reappear in new variations.

The marketing department is dominant at Cartier. At headquarters in Paris the product and marketing departments are combined, with one person responsible for a particular item from its development, through the launch phase, and into the final marketing programme. In Japan, marketing personnel are responsible for stock control and ordering, as well as marketing and promotion. A fundamentally important task is to ensure that enough of a product is available in Cartier boutiques in Japan when a promotional campaign is launched.

Cartier Japan works with all department stores, as long as they are the leader in any given area. Thus in the Shinjuku 3-chome district of Tokyo there is a Cartier boutique in Isetan, the undisputed doyenne of the area; in Osaka Cartier selected Hankyu and Takashimaya, each of which have their home base in the city; and Matsuzakaya in Nagoya is the city's most prestigious department store. In this respect Cartier differs from Tiffany, which is to be found exclusively in Mitsukoshi stores; from Louis Vuitton, whose outlets are normally in Mitsukoshi or Takashimaya; and from Hermès, which has a joint venture with Seibu. Like Chanel, which also used Cosa Liebermann as agent, Cartier prefers to remain independent.

The layout of the Cartier boutiques in Japan differs from that of boutiques in Europe and the United States, reflecting differences in shopping preferences. Customers in Japan enjoy browsing and seeing the full range of items on offer, even if they have a clear idea of the piece they wish to buy. Japanese outlets are therefore filled with showcases displaying Cartier watches and jewels, with sales staff available to offer advice as required. In the West, no items are on open display in Cartier shops, but sales staff will exhibit individual pieces on a velvet tray at the request of the customer. This may be a security issue, but even in Japan there is a guard inside the door of the flagship boutique.

Product launches or relaunches are accompanied by advertising campaigns in magazines, in POS (point-of-sales) material and in catalogues. Cartier Japan also uses film advertisements in selected Tokyo cinemas but, unlike in other parts of the world, it never advertises on television: the cost is too great to justify use of a medium which has broad appeal rather than the concentrated focus the company requires. 'People need awareness of our product, so we must concentrate our effort. They won't buy Cartier just because it is Cartier,' explains Bichelmeier.

Cartier Japan also draws upon the rich heritage of the company to substantiate its print media campaigns. The Cartier Collection in Geneva assembles a magnificent array of Cartier creations dating back to the turn of the century, which the company claims is unmatched even by the collections of such firms as Van Cleef & Arpels and Louis Vuitton. A major event in 1995 was the presence of the entire collection in Tokyo – only its third journey overseas – for a six-week exhibition at the Teien Museum, a former Japanese royal residence in the 1930s whose art deco architecture echoed the style of jewellery created by Louis Cartier in 1900–20. Cartier Japan held a gala reception at the Teien Museum, to which the press was invited as well as the cream of Japanese society. More than 200,000 people visited the Teien exhibition from all over Japan.

Although the Cartier Collection in its entirety rarely travels abroad (for obvious reasons of security) individual items are frequently used to promote the launch of new Cartier ranges. Every month or two, part of the collection is in Tokyo: perhaps some pens from the early 20th century, or an evening bag, or wristwatch. When a new engagement and wedding ring collection is being presented, for example, Cartier Japan may invite young men and women from good families to a party, where the young ladies would be persuaded to try on a tiara from the Cartier Collection. The aura that surrounds the collection is a constant magnet for quality press journalists.

Client interest is also maintained through the launch of limited edition jewellery and watches. In 1995, for example, Cartier produced a limited edition Tank watch for the relatively inexpensive Must range. Cartier Japan was allocated 100 men's and 100 women's watches out of the 1,000 pieces available worldwide, at a price of ¥200,000 – very reasonable by Japanese standards.

Pricing policy remains a challenge. The across-the-board price cuts in 1993 resulted in a number of pricing anomalies, some of which were rectified later through product relaunches. Having peaked in April 1995 at US$1 = ¥80, the yen rapidly depreciated thereafter by over 25 per cent versus the dollar and the Swiss franc. In late 1995, Cartier Japan raised its prices generally to take account of the weaker yen. Price alignments are calculated as a combination of manufacturing costs (Swiss francs since its watches are made in Switzerland and French francs for the jewellery which is created in French workshops) and exchange rates to the yen.

The competition

Cartier recognises that it was relatively late in establishing a direct presence in Japan. Nevertheless, it was one of the few foreign luxury goods company to invest heavily in the early 1990s while the market was changing. Some key competitors were undergoing a difficult transition phase while others were not yet properly established in the market, and this allowed Cartier Japan to capture some of the business of its rivals. On the other hand, companies like Tiffany were consistently strong competitors. Since 1994 other jewellers have become more active investors, including some which were well established in their home market but had not yet entered the Japanese market.

■ *Harry Winston* – the world's most exclusive fine jeweller has established its only boutique in the Hotel Seiyu Ginza, itself Japan's most exclusive hotel.

■ *Van Cleef & Arpels* – Cartier's traditional competitor, offering high quality jewels and enjoying a strong home base in Paris. Its distribution agreement with Seibu department stores was highly successful during the bubble years of the 1980s but proved somewhat less so in the sober 1990s. The jeweller nevertheless retained its links with Seibu, which has been reducing stocks and putting its own house in order.

■ *Bulgari* – a recognised competitor in the medium-priced, ¥300,000 – ¥1,000,000 segment designated 'affordable' (compared with Cartier's, Harry Winston's and Van Cleef & Arpels' expensive pieces). Its designs are simple and are identifiably Bulgari, and its home base in Italy is strong. In 1993 the Italian company established its first boutique in the New Otani hotel and office complex in Tokyo, and two years later opened outlets in Kyoto (Takashimaya), Osaka (Takashimaya), the Osaka Hilton Hotel and the Fukuoka New Otani Hotel. These are all cities where Cartier is already present.

■ *Boucheron* – a strong competitor in Paris thanks to its designs and creations, but less known internationally. Its entrée to the Tokyo market is through Bluebell, a privately owned company of French origin which specialises in the import and distribution of luxury items.

■ *Chaumet* – headquartered like Cartier in the Place Vendôme in Paris. Its Japanese boutiques are in Mitsukoshi stores.

■ *Tiffany* – altered the legal and financial nature of its partnership with Mitsukoshi, which had been highly successful during the 1980s, and established its own company in 1994. Its department store boutiques are all still in Mitsukoshi stores, but a free-standing boutique has been opened in Osaka. Tiffany competes with Cartier at the lower end of the spectrum, in the ¥100,000 – ¥500,000 range, and enjoys a particularly high reputation for its engagement rings and wedding rings. Its overall image in Japan, however, has suffered since it attracts a young clientele by selling jewellery made of silver costing as little as ¥30,000.

Coping with growth

In spite of the new pricing policy and the changes in corporate strategy instituted by Cartier Japan, the company experienced sales growth of 40 per cent in value terms during 1993–5. Although in volume terms sales grew more slowly the average price of products sold remained stable in 1994 and increased by 20 per cent in 1995, reflecting the repositioning of the brand and the consequent higher demand for more expensive jewellery and watches.

The personnel numbered 200 as of December 1995, compared with 220 in February 1992 – an indication of the purges of the system which took place following the change in management style. By March 1996 Leymarie expected to employ 260 people, reflecting the strength of growth.

An operations department now helps the marketing and sales teams meet their strategies and objectives. Another mission is to facilitate stock management, for example by developing specialised computer programmes or instituting a new system for stock deployment in the 22 boutiques. Products are now categorised into best-sellers (specific references within a product range which receive national press and advertising coverage) and harmonics (product references which are representative of the brand but are complementary items, in the sense that they may help customers choose the best-seller in the end). Best-seller items must be available in all boutiques. Since the price of Cartier products is very high, significant sums of money are tied up in inventory at any one time.

The pace of growth at Cartier Japan has placed substantial burdens on the retailers at store level. A current project for the operations department is to simplify the administrative tasks boutique staff must undertake, to allow them to spend more time with their customers. Another project is to improve the after-sales service so that '[we] surprise customers positively and they walk out of here more happy', says Bichelmeier. The company expects to differentiate itself further from competitors by investing substantially in a new service centre in the Ginza, in the same building as its flagship boutique. The new centre, which opens in May 1996, will double the number of watchmakers and jewellers available to attend to customers' needs.

Challenges for the future

Cartier Japan has undergone substantial change in the last four years, and has reached the point where it is the acknowledged market leader among quality jewellers. One of the results of this achievement is that headquarters in Paris has for the past year been using Japan, together with the French market, as a test ground for new products. The knowledge base about Japan at headquarters has also improved immeasurably, thanks to a steady stream of visitors from there to Tokyo.

The strategy now is to consolidate the Cartier Japan position, while facing an internal and an external challenge.

The internal challenge is to continue to react correctly to market demands and trends, and stronger competition, by properly adjusting the company's internal structure to meet growth. Cartier must develop a service dimension to differentiate itself through customer services, and must inspire the loyalty of its staff. Also at issue is whether the organisation should continue along functional lines rather than concentrate on product categories.

The external challenge is to adapt to continuing change in the Japanese marketplace. Competition from other quality jewellers is stronger than at the start of the 1990s. Further, as Japan's rapidly ageing population would suggest, the proportion of office ladies 'who spend their lives away' is in decline. Should there be a repositioning of Cartier to take into account such democratic change?

Thinking long term, what would be the implications of a shift from a consumer society towards a leisure society? Would this require a shift by Cartier towards a new segment of the population, a repositioning, or an extension of the existing product portfolio?

Exhibit 1   Vendôme luxury group results*
(in millions of Swiss francs)

	1993	1994	1995
Turnover	2462,9	2596,0	2652,9
Cost of sales	993,8	1024,4	1038,3
Gross profit	1469,1	1571,6	1614,6
Operating profit	398,9	377,8	453,6
Profit before taxation	455,0	431,5	482,8
Net profit	340,2	336,7	394,3
Earnings per share (Sfr.) (excl. exceptional items)	0,488	0,552	0,565

* The Vendôme Luxury Group was listed in London and Luxembourg for the first time in 1993.

Source: Annual Reports.

Exhibit 2 Vendôme luxury group sales to third parties
(in millions of Swiss francs)

	1993	1994	1995
Europe	1077,7	1103,3	1098,8
Far East	827,2	888,5	981,7
Americas	480,4	528,3	499,3
Other	77,6	75,9	73,1
Total	**2462,9**	**2596**	**2652,9**

Note: The Vendôme Luxury Group does not provide a segmental
analysis of profitability and net assets by geographical region.

Source: Annual Reports.

Exhibit 3 Cartier boutiques in Japan

CASE STUDY TWO: Goal! Japan scores in soccer

Hellmut Schütte and Jocelyn Probert (INSEAD-EAC, 1997)

Mr Kawabuchi was a man with a vision. Passionately fond of soccer himself, he had played in Japan's epic bronze medal-winning team at the 1968 Mexico Olympics, and dreamed of making the Japanese as soccer-crazy as the Europeans and Latin Americans. He wanted football to appeal to everyone in Japan, and he wanted the national team to play in the World Cup for which Japan had never qualified. He knew that unless the game was rooted in the hearts and minds of the people, the national team would never be truly world class. To breed players of international standing, Kawabuchi had to make Japan's brand new professional soccer league, the J.League, a success.

As chairman of the J.League, Kawabuchi's task was to professionalise soccer. That meant getting the backing of the corporate world, and the support of the civic authorities and the general public. The civic authorities would have to provide the playing facilities, and ordinary people would have to pay to come and watch the games, as they did for professional base-ball. Kawabuchi thought there were a lot of latent soccer-lovers in Japan who would come to matches as long as they were packaged properly.

The J.League concept

Back in 1988, Kawabuchi and other members of the Football Association of Japan (JFA) had started to talk about revitalising soccer in Japan. The JFA wanted to turn Japan into a great soccer-playing nation. It was a high profile sport internationally, and Japan was hungry for respect and a better national image. Ordinary people worldwide seemed more impressed by sporting achievements than economic success, and Japanese international sports stars rarely won global acclaim.

Some members of the JFA thought Japan stood a better chance of winning soccer world championships than any other team ball game. 'All the best soccer players have the same physique as us,' said one. 'Think of Pele, think of Maradonna, think of Eusebio or Keegan. We are not big enough to be the best at rugby, nor tall enough to play basketball.'

The JFA was aware that the major soccer countries had the backing of a strong professional league while in Japan soccer was only an amateur game. 'We concluded that if Japan continued with just its non-professional league, it would never be able to compete successfully internationally and would never get to the World Cup.' South Korea, which was always keen to rival Japan at everything, had set up a professional soccer league in 1983 and already had a record of participation in four World Cup tournaments.

Kawabuchi and the JFA strongly supported the idea of Japan hosting the World Cup in 2002 – and a professional league looked like the only way of making sure Japan had the necessary facilities for it. In 1988, there were only three stadiums in Japan which could hold 40,000 people, and there weren't many even able to hold 20,000. Japan would need 12 new stadiums for 40,000 people by 2002, and that was going to cost US$16 billion. Where would the money come from?

The launch

On 15 May 1993, Japan's first professional soccer matches kicked off around the country amid tremendous fanfare. National awareness of soccer was buzzing after successes in various championships in Asia during 1991 and 1992: in the Kirin Cup (a club tournament), in the Dynasty Cup (which determines the national champion of East Asia), and, the crowning glory, the Asian Cup (when Japan beat Kuwait, the United Arab Emirates and North and South Korea, all of which had previously qualified for the World Cup).

There had been a steady build up of publicity for the league over the preceding months, beginning with the televising of the 1992 Yamazaki Nabisco Cup, which attracted a record 9.9 per cent TV spectator rating. Streams of people began heading for the football stadiums. Professional soccer turned into an overnight success and a hugely fashionable spectator sport.

Soccer in Japan: the background

People only began playing sports beyond school age during the late 1940s and 1950s, when companies started to organise sports teams and cultural activities as part of their workforce welfare programmes. Amateur inter-company and inter-university competitions created a regional tournament mentality, but national competitions didn't really exist. Baseball was the big sport in Japan, thanks to American influence, and it was the only team sport played professionally. It was also the only team game where talented youngsters could make money from a sporting career. The only other professional sports in Japan were golf and sumo.

Playing sports became much more popular in Japan after the 1964 Olympic Games were held in Tokyo, and the first national leagues for ice hockey, volleyball, baseball, soccer and so on were formed in 1965, all based on 'amateur' company teams. In fact, companies began hiring some youngsters specifically for their prowess at a particular sport, to boost the performance of the company team. Some companies had already realised that they could improve their corporate image through sports activities. Eight company-sponsored teams from all over the country played in the Japan Football League's first national soccer championship in 1965.

When Japan's national soccer team won the bronze medal at the 1968 Mexico Olympic Games, the country went crazy. This was the first time a Japanese football team had ever achieved such success in any international tournament. All at once, football was the game to watch and play. Four of the ten sporting events drawing the largest audiences to the Tokyo national stadium that year were football matches. Voluntary soccer schools organised by parents sprang up all over the country.

But the fashion faded away. After Mexico, sports gradually became more professionalised within the company system and it was harder to be a part-time sportsman. Companies gave their sporting staff plenty of time off from their jobs for training, but it was tough for players not to get into the squad of 16 for the next match and to have to go back to their regular work alongside diligent colleagues. Young people who had been the stars of their university teams lost heart if they weren't selected to play in the company team. Parents of skilled high school soccer players discouraged them from thoughts of playing beyond graduation because there was no chance of making a career of it. Players' motivation withered and spectatorship fell.

At junior schools, though, soccer remained popular. The Ministry of Education had endorsed the game during the 1960s as part of the sports curriculum in preference to baseball, because it didn't involve hard bats and balls and the physical exercise in playing soccer was greater. In high schools, though, baseball was a serious sport and the high school baseball championship held in July and August was a national sporting event attracting massive crowds to the Koshien stadium as well as huge TV spectatorship. Any youngster with 'played at Koshien' on his CV was sure to get a good job.

Soccer struggled on as a minority sport in Japan throughout the 1970s and 1980s. Kids playing in the street or park practised pitching baseballs, not kicking a football around. Japan Football League matches still only attracted a few thousand spectators from the companies whose teams were playing. There was no nationwide support for individual teams and there were no players who reached international standards.

Getting the J.League started

It was in 1989 that Mr Kawabuchi and his friends formally recommended the creation of a professional soccer league to the board of the Football Association of Japan (JFA). They then set up a Professional League Study Committee and between June 1989 and January 1991, they investigated the way that national sports were organised in other countries and looked into methods of financing the new league's development. There seemed to be four main issues: the organisational structure of the new league; the participating clubs; the sponsors; and the 'facilitators', or companies that would handle the non-game aspects of the league.

The organisational structure

The Japan Professional Football League was formally established in November 1991 as a non-profit making association. Kawabuchi was chairman. Mr Mori, brother of one of the other players in the team that had won the 1968 Olympic medal and a long-time member of the JFA, became vice-chairman. The managing director was Mr Kinomoto, another major contributor to the game of soccer in Japan. All the other board members were either directors of the JFA or were elected from among the presidents of the participating soccer clubs.

The new league was quickly dubbed the J.League, a snappier name than its formal title and one that would be much easier to market. The league would operate under the umbrella of the JFA, like all soccer clubs in Japan, and the JFA would represent its interests in dealings with FIFA, football's international governing body. Clubs aspiring to join the J.League would have to work their way up the pyramid of prefectural and regional soccer associations into the amateur Japan Soccer League (JSL), and then become associate members of the J.League by registering their interest and paying a fee. To actually graduate to the J.League, though, a team would have to finish first or second in the annual JSL championship.

The soccer clubs

Choosing the right teams to participate at the start of the J.League was important.

Kawabuchi and his fellow directors strongly believed that the only way to get the general public support which the league needed was to create a true 'home town' system with a close mutual commitment between the soccer club and the local people. They wanted to create the sort of atmosphere found in Manchester or Rome or München-Gladbach, where local people are passionately involved in the fortunes of the home club. Above all, they wanted to avoid the sort of franchise system used by the American football league, where a team's home depends on the preference of the legal owner. They knew that local communities in Japan were looking for ways to create their own identity. Japanese society is traditionally focused on group membership and the family remains an important social unit, but many people had left their birthplaces for the cities during the industrialisation of Japan in the 1950s and 1960s, and in the countryside, new urban environments had grown up around industrial plants where the inhabitants' loyalties lay with their employer. So the concept of local community feeling in Japan was quite recent.

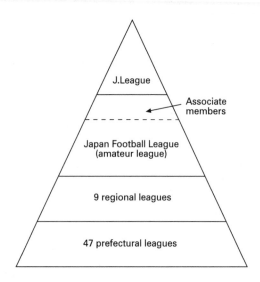

A home town soccer team had to excite the emotional support of the majority of the local population, not just the few who already enjoyed watching football. The support had to be sustainable too. A club could become a symbol of the town's identity and a measure of its civic pride – there were plenty of clubs in Europe to take as examples. A successful football side could also contribute towards a healthy local economy and a local 'feel-good' factor. Perhaps later, some soccer clubs would be able to excite a national following, like Liverpool in the UK, Ajax in the Netherlands or Flamengo in Brazil.

The J.League management believed that only towns of more than 100,000 people (designated as cities in Japan) would be able to generate enough sustainable support for a professional soccer team. Even so, not just any club from the cities could join the J.League. Clubs had to become independent entities, separately established from their original corporate backers.

They also had to make a commitment to developing youth teams (under-18s, under-15s and under-12s) in addition to the normal first team and reserve team: long term development of the game was a key point in the J.League's planning. Of course, they needed adequate facilities too: regular access to a stadium that could seat at least 15,000 people and which was equipped with floodlights for evening matches, as well as proper practice facilities for the youth teams.

Ten teams seemed the right number to play in the J.League's first season. Nine of the company teams playing in the amateur Japan Soccer League (JSL) were city-based and had met the other criteria, so they were obvious choices. The question was, which would be the tenth (see box, Creating a Home Town Team). The list of teams was announced on 14 February 1991, giving the clubs sufficient time to prepare themselves for professional soccer. Exhibits 1 and 2 show the teams, their corporate backers, the slogans they chose to promote themselves with fans, and their location. Verdy Kawasaki and Yokohama Marinos, playing as the company teams of Yomiuri and Nissan, had for several years been the strongest and the most popular in the amateur JSL. Two new teams joined the J.League from the JSL in 1994 and another two in 1995. When the ten founder clubs of the J.League became independent, they received up to ¥1.5 billion in capital from their shareholders, who were mostly either individual corporations or small groups of companies.

Creating a Home Town Team: a Profile of Kashima Antlers

In early 1990, a year before the announcement of the first ten teams to play in the professional soccer league, a small town of 45,000 people in Ibaraki prefecture, north-east of Tokyo began an extraordinary attempt to win the backing of the league selection committee for its football team.

Traditionally a small farming town, Kashima participated in the wave of industrialisation that swept Japan in the 1960s and 1970s. Sumitomo Kinzoku (commonly known as Sumikin), Asahi Glass and Mitsubishi Yuka established a plant in the area. As in other prefectures, Ibaraki prefecture offered no entertainment facilities for its inhabitants. The town was also isolated, approximately two hours away from Tokyo, and Sumikin found it increasingly difficult to persuade people to work there. Resorting to desperate measures, Sumikin even began funding half the cost of a night out in Tokyo for its workers.

cont'd

In the 1980s, the prefectural authorities began searching for ideas to reinvigorate the area, with two aims in mind: to integrate the original farming community more closely with the 'outsiders' who had come to work in the industrial plants, and to create an environment where young people would be happy to live.

The debates in Ibaraki prefecture coincided with preparations for the J.League. Sumikin approached the prefectural office with a new idea: its corporate football team, which played in the JSL from its base at the Kashima plant (rather than near Osaka, where the company's main operations were located), should join the professional league. The notion was welcomed by the prefectural office. Ibaraki prefecture already had a fairly large soccer-playing population, and the relatively low rainfall had created a climate attractive to teams from outside the prefecture, which had come regularly to the area for training camps and high school tournaments.

Mr Kawabuchi was less impressed with the idea. "He told us we were 99.9999 per cent certain not to be accepted," laughs Mr Kitahata, who was MITI adviser to the governor of Ibaraki prefecture at the time. Kawabuchi was highly sceptical, since the Sumikin team was by no means a star in the JSL and, what was more important, he strongly believed that only places large enough to have city status would be able to give a team the type of support he envisaged.

Kashima set out to prove the strength of its local support. Of the seventy companies with factories in the area, 42 finally agreed to become shareholders in the football club. With such a broad shareholding, the theory was that there should be no problem in ensuring enough tickets would be sold for each match. Even Mitsubishi Yuka, in neighbouring Kamisu, finally agreed to lend support although it had refused initially on the grounds that the Mitsubishi Motors football team also expected to join the J.League as the Urawa Reds. Kashima representatives also elicited the support of the local labour unions for the club as a welfare activity for the workers. Kashima town also took a stake in the new football club. The effort went further. The head of education for Ibaraki prefecture agreed that junior high and high school children be allowed to attend matches as an extra-curricular activity, their tickets paid for by the education department.

Kawabuchi, impressed though he was by these efforts, imposed another precondition to his support for the Kashima bid: the town needed a proper football stadium. Although Japan has many multi-purpose stadiums, few places exclusively for playing football existed. The governor of Ibaraki prefecture quickly agreed to public funding for a new, US$100 million stadium on the outskirts of Kashima town.

In February 1991, the J.League committee's selection of the 10 teams was announced on the 9 p.m. national news. Nine teams were a foregone conclusion, since they all held city status in Japan. Competition for the tenth place lay between Kashima, Iwata, Hiratsuka and Kashiwa, all relatively small towns. Kashima won the place, and the fame arising from the two-minute interview on the national news accorded to the mayor of the town was sufficient to make him a fervent football supporter.

(cont'd)

> Since winning the bid, Kashima continues to involve its residents in many ways. For example, whereas other football clubs use outside firms at matches for security duties, ticket collection, and so on, many of Kashima Antlers' ticket collectors and ushers are local people known as 'sports volunteers'. Thanks to such high identification of the townspeople with the football team, the 15,000 seater stadium is filled to capacity for every match – which suggests that roughly one in three people in the town is there.

The players

A primary aim of the J.League was to raise the standard of football in Japan to international levels. That meant bringing in outside talent. Judging by the number of Brazilians playing in the J.League, the Japanese equate success in soccer with Brazil (and a couple of teams have even adopted Portuguese slogans to prove it – see Exhibit 1). The strength of the yen in 1992–93 no doubt also encouraged world class foreign players to consider a career in Japan. Zico, and several players in the Brazilian 1994 World Cup-winning team (Jorginho, Dunga, Leonardo and others), Argentina's Medina Bello and Bisconti, Germany's Littbarski, England's Lineker, Italy's Schillaci... all have made their mark with J.League clubs. Respected players also play for the associate members of the J.League (those clubs hoping to soon join from the JSL).

The newness of the J.League means that many Japanese club players are in their late teens or early twenties, much younger than in the long-established overseas leagues. At first, they stood in awe of the great foreign players and struggled to overcome feelings of veneration and deference at the prospect of tackling, for example, the captain of the Brazilian national team (Dunga). Nevertheless, apparent success and the adulation of thousands of young fans have gone to the heads of some Japanese players. Their aspirations have changed from the desire purely to be a good footballer, to wanting to drive a Mercedes and enjoy the trappings of the rich and famous – not normally available to the young in seniority-conscious Japan.

The paradox is that although soccer is essentially a team game, it provides a theatre for individualistic performances. The opportunity for a player to stand out from the rest of the team is what makes football so exciting for the spectators and the players themselves. Their biggest motivation is to play for the national team in the World Cup and in international matches overseas, not just to be a star in Japan.

The Japanese footballer closest to attaining national hero status is Kazu Miura, who plays for Verdy and the Japan national team. He spent six months in 1993 with Genoa Football Club in Italy, which raised the considerable interest of fans at home, before returning to Japan. Other teams have local heroes, like Masahiro Fukuda of the Urawa Reds, who can fill the home stadium for every game.

In a repeat of history, foreign managers, particularly Brazilians and some Europeans, were taken on to train the teams to international standards of play. Back in the 1960s, a West German had coached the Japan national team to its bronze medal success in Mexico. However, managers don't always have the same degree of control over their teams as they do in their home countries. Club general managers tend to interfere in the footballing affairs of the team. One manager, for example, returned from a holiday to find that a player had been signed during his absence and others have been fired despite a series of successful seasons with a club for 'not following the Japanese way'. A foreign manager coached the national team to various regional successes in the early 1990s, but he was removed in 1996 in favour of a Japanese to prepare the team for the 1998 World Cup qualifying rounds.

The sponsors

Sponsorship was a key element in Kawabuchi's plans. An official sponsor would lend its name to the league championship, in return for substantial sums of money. In the professional soccer world this is actually quite rare, even though it is very common in other sports. In Europe, only the English teams play in sponsored leagues.

The J.League was trying to find sponsors in 1991–92, just at the end of Japan's bubble era. Still, Kawabuchi and his team didn't expect problems in finding corporate backing because of the appeal of soccer as an international sport, unlike professional baseball in Japan which was basically sponsored only by the companies owning the teams. Having the J.League handle all sponsorship contracts centrally, rather than letting individual clubs cut their own deals, would help them raise the money. The J.League also insisted that firms sponsoring the league had national brand coverage. Around 120 companies became involved in league sponsorship (see Exhibit 3 for the main categories), raising some ¥2,000 million for 1995.

Clubs could arrange their own sponsorship contracts over and above the overall J.League deals, but the limits of what they can do are defined centrally. Up to three companies, for example, can contract to display their logo on players' shirts (front, back and sleeve). Nestlé paid several hundred million yen per year for the right to display various brand names (Nestlé,

Buitoni, Kitcat) on Jubilo Iwata shirts. The main corporate owner of a club may pay a sponsorship fee to put its name on the teams' shirtfronts.

Individual clubs keep the money they raise from their own sponsorship contracts but J.League sponsorship fees are portioned out equally between the clubs.

The second round of contracts (1996–98) was negotiated in 1995. Some of the original sponsoring teams renewed their contracts for a second term, beginning with the 1996 season, but the complete list of sponsors now (Exhibit 4) is substantially different from the opening season. Potential financial backers were better placed to evaluate J.League sponsorships in 1995, based on the league's ability during its first couple of seasons to attract spectators to live games and generate TV audiences. The second period of sponsorship contracts was expected to raise revenue of ¥4,160 million for the J.League.

The facilitators

The J.League didn't want to adopt the team franchise system used in the United States, but it was very interested in the way that the American sports associations organise their marketing. European soccer leagues don't have centrally organised marketing machines, and in Japan, professional baseball teams do their own individual team promotion. Kawabuchi reasoned that if the soccer clubs were to act individually, the promotional scope of the game as a whole would be limited – but it could be limitless if done on a national basis. Kawabuchi and his colleagues decided to copy the American pattern and create a coherent, focused strategy to market soccer in Japan. It wouldn't only involve advertising the matches, though, it would be a full package including associated product marketing.

The J.League's thinking on centralised merchandising neatly matched the ideas of Sony Creative Products (Sony CP), a subsidiary of Sony Music Entertainment. Sony CP approached the J.League to propose a marketing plan covering the design, manufacturing, distribution and licensing of products to develop the image of the J.League and its constituent members. Sony CP would also design team mascots and logos, and create an overall J.League logo to appear on a range of products. Such a marketing concept was practically unheard of in the world of soccer, especially among the 'old' footballing nations.

The J.League management team also wanted to try another idea new to Japan: the mass marketing of replica kits (shirts, shorts, socks and so on). Among professional baseball teams, only the Yomiuri Giants and the Seibu Lions made any attempt to reach the mass market, although other teams sold uniforms to spectators at the stadiums. (The potential for kit sales for sumo is rather limited and the only merchandising effort is at tournament events.) Team strips for the soccer clubs were chosen by a J.League committee, and the colours were deliberately jazzy in order to appeal to supporters: bright orange for S-Pulse, lime green and yellow for Bellmare, pink and pale blue for Cerezo, and so on. Japanese baseball uniforms were dull in comparison. The effort put into developing J.League team colours was part of the drive to encourage fans to identify with their teams.

Agreement between the J.League and Sony CP was reached in September 1991 and the two parties signed an exclusive five-year contract in February 1992. Mizuno, competing fiercely against other sports goods makers, won a contract to manufacture and supply all team uniforms and replica kits for the first two seasons. Later, it renewed its contract for another two years.

The unified marketing system allowed 'consistent pricing, design and quality, ensuring responsible trademark management and equal exposure for each club'. One of Kawabuchi's fundamental principles was that all teams should have an equal chance of exposure and an equal share of the merchandising revenue.

Several affiliates of the J.League were created to handle other activities, including J.League Pictures (which controls the rights to video recordings of J.League matches and supplies publicity videos of the league) and J.League Photos (which maintains a library of still photographs of matches).

Marketing the J.League

Positioning

During the planning phase of the J.League, the management fully expected their main audience to be soccer fans. That meant mostly people who played and enjoyed football in their schooldays – the oldest of them would be in their late thirties by now – and children who were still playing or had been playing until very recently. Because of smaller family sizes in Japan, children were usually indulged by their parents. If soccer promotion was focused clearly at the youth market, the J.League could become a hit.

Spectators at the average baseball game were very different from the J.League's target market. Baseball was a very male-oriented game, and most people in the crowd were men over 40 years old who liked to go along and relax with beers and their business friends. Watching the game itself didn't always seem to be the main reason for going. Kawabuchi and his colleagues didn't expect to convert baseball fans into soccer fans, they were going for a different market altogether.

When the league was launched, he seemed to be right. The crowds became passionately involved in the action on the field. It was real family entertainment. Mums and grandmas were just as keen to come and watch as dads and grandpas. Going to soccer matches quickly became a new leisure time amusement in a country where there weren't many other possibilities for family recreation.

What really surprised Kawabuchi and the rest of the J.League management was the huge number of young women (office ladies, or OLs) at matches. For them it was a new craze. They represented the 'fashion' aspect of the J.League, enthusiastically getting tickets for all the matches and buying the accompanying merchandise. They didn't mind paying up to ¥5,000 for the best seats, or shelling out ¥11,000 for a shirt in their team's colours. It didn't matter that they didn't know much about soccer itself, they came along to cheer the cute young men chasing the ball around. Teenage girls came to cheer individual players, often boys they had been at high school with. Alongside these women were the families: there's not a hint of the hooligan tendency that keeps young women and children away from European football matches.

So where were the real football fans, the young men who had played soccer at junior school? Kawabuchi figured there must be grassroots support out there somewhere. The J.League needed them, it couldn't survive on the whims of the OL crowd. The problem was the relatively small capacity of the stadiums and the OLs' single-minded pursuit of the available tickets. The more laid-back serious fans were simply squeezed out in the rush. By the second and third seasons, the fashion aspect of the J.League was beginning to fade and there were more male fans in the audience. Spectators were more knowledgeable about football by then as well, and could recognise and applaud skilful play by the opposing team, rather than simply react to a good move by a player on their own team.

The delivery

Some sports in Japan are content to rely on income from televised events, but Kawabuchi and his colleagues actually wanted spectators to go to soccer matches. Still, the J.League knew how important TV is to consumers in Japan. They also had to market a lot of goods associated with the J.League.

The match: a live event

An early decision had been taken to organise the season from the point of view of the spectators, to maximise live match spectatorship – a key factor in the desire to create close connections between the teams and their home towns. Television viewers also needed the visual appeal of fresh grass instead of mud baths. That meant reducing to a minimum the number of matches played in the coldest, dampest part of the year and allowing games to be played during the evening in the heat of the summer. The season would therefore begin in March and continue, with a mid-season break, until early December.

Also to maintain spectator interest, every game would have a clear result. At the end of the normal 90 minutes of play, if the scores were level, the teams would play up to 30 minutes of extra time and whichever side scored the first goal would win the match; if neither side scored, a penalty shoot-out would decide the result. This system is not used by the leagues of other footballing nations.

The J.League wasn't interested in knowing how many tickets were sold for each match (the critical measure at other sports events); they wanted to know how many people were actually present. A problem had emerged because some soccer club sponsors were buying large numbers of tickets and giving them away as promotional incentives to their customers. People who weren't interested in soccer ended up with these tickets but didn't use them, while true supporters were left frustrated and ticketless outside the ground. All the J.League could do to curb sponsors' promotional use of tickets was point out that for the long term good of the league, it was better for clubs to sell tickets to their fans. Now the no-show problem is largely restricted to the VIP boxes. In the second half of every match, the size of the crowd was announced. Exhibit 5 shows spectator numbers for the first three seasons.

The televised event

Japanese consumers are avid trend followers, so TV coverage was crucial to the success of the J.League. The general feeling is that 'if it's on TV, it must be good'. Knowing that a particular game will be televised is likely to boost live spectatorship – exactly the reverse of the European experience, where football clubs now don't allow live broadcasts of their matches because they are afraid all their fans will stay at home to watch.

Dentsu, Japan's leading advertising agency, was the sponsor of the main soccer events in Japan before the launch of the J.League, including the Toyota Cup (played between the best South American team and the best European team) and the national high school soccer championship. The latter didn't win much interest among spectators until Dentsu persuaded the NTV television channel to broadcast it. But Dentsu gave the thumbs down to the idea of professional soccer in Japan, and at first refused to become involved in the J.League. That opened the way for Hakuhodo, another advertising giant in Japan, to seize its chance. The immediate success of the J.League in its first season soon had Dentsu regretting its decision. By 1995, it had managed to claw back 30 per cent of the J.League advertising spend from Hakuhodo, by handling negotiations for TV broadcasting rights on behalf of the J.League. European soccer leagues also normally negotiate the TV rights for their clubs. J.League clubs, though, could arrange their own regional TV contracts.

During the 1993 and 1994 seasons, televised matches were rationed by the J.League among the five national networks. All teams were guaranteed a minimum of two games broadcast nationwide. The huge popularity of the league in its first year meant that TV companies were keen even to televise matches between sides that were playing poorly. By the second season, national TV companies preferred to show only the more popular teams and TV spectatorship declined. There was, however, extensive television coverage of the 1994 World Cup.

In 1995, it was decided to restrict national TV coverage to one game per match day, to be shown in prime time. The J.League asked TV companies to indicate in advance the matches they were interested in showing, and made selections from the submissions to allow even distribution of airtime among the teams and an equal share of matches for the TV networks. Local TV stations submitted their choices directly to their local clubs.

True football fans would be frustrated by the Japanese way of televising matches. Advertisement breaks happen at regular intervals, whatever might be happening in the game, and because the games don't necessarily end after 90 minutes (if the scores are equal) the final result might not even be shown.

Associated products

Target groups and product range

Children's parents are by far the biggest purchasers of J.League merchandise, splashing out for themselves as well as for their offspring. The OLs have also been big buyers, especially in the first couple of seasons. Many spectators at matches wear at least one piece of J.League merchandise, and some entire families are kitted from head to toe in their team's colours.

Each J.League soccer club could choose up to ten Sony CP-designed products to be manufactured with its team colours and logo. The selection ranged from mascot puppets, hats and scarves through flags, towels, calendars and pens to kit bags, knapsacks and signed footballs. Clubs choose which products they want, depending on the profile of their fans: the average Urawa Reds supporter is relatively old, and likes to buy suitcases and sweaters with the team logo; Kashima Antlers fans range in age from small children to grandmothers, and hats with antlers are popular.

The range of items of replica kit and the selling prices are the same for all teams, for example ¥11,000 for a shirt with team name and logo and ¥4,800-5,200 for shorts in the team colours. A windbreaker jacket with matching trousers costs more than ¥30,000.

Sony CP also took care of the licensing of many other products, most of which had nothing to do with football: bicycles, walkmans, batteries, underwear, socks, food (potato chips, candy) and drinks (J-Water – an isotonic drink – and beer in a special J.League can). Fuji Bank, one of Japan's largest retail banks, even issued a J.League passbook.

Distribution

By autumn 1992, Sony CP was ready to begin selling to the general public club mascots and individual team products as well as J.League-badged merchandise. To keep control and coordinate the marketplace, products would be sold through an independent distribution network rather than through established retail channels.

'Category-1' outlets sold only items related to the J.League and its member clubs, including replica kits. The first shop opened in October 1992 in Kobe and by the end of 1995, 120 Category-1 stores were in place. Most of the shops were franchises, but five are owned by Sony CP. Twenty Category-1s are in Tokyo, either in the form of free-standing shops or as boutiques inside department stores such as Mitsukoshi in Shinjuku.

A second distribution channel for J.League merchandise is the 'J-Station' chain of outlets, which is Mizuno's responsibility. J-Stations sell replica kits made by Mizuno but they also stock some Sony CP-devised goods. There are around 700 of them dotted throughout the country, mostly within existing independent sports shops although Mizuno operates 20 itself (ten in Tokyo and ten in Osaka).

The third channel for J.League goods is the exclusive team shop: clubs are allowed a maximum of five shops, but most have only one or two, at the home ground and perhaps in the town centre. Revenue from team shops naturally belongs directly to the team concerned. A subsidiary channel is the mail order system available to official supporters clubs. These fan clubs have been able to buy merchandise by mail order since 1993, but from the 1996 season the general public have been able to send off for goods. Initially clubs didn't think team merchandise would be popular with their fans, and so didn't focus on that side of their activity. Later they put in much more effort.

Approximate sales (wholesale value) of J.League merchandise in the first three years ranged from ¥20–30 million.

Mizuno sold 600,000 pieces of replica kit to fans in 1993–95. As a 'serious' (rather than fashion) sports goods company, Mizuno only targeted soccer players at first, and was amazed to find teenage girls and children buying soccer uniforms. In the first three years, 90 per cent of sales went to supporters (and only 50 per cent of these to men) and just 10 per cent to soccer players. Even people who didn't like soccer were attracted by the bright colours of the kit – nothing like it had been seen before in Japan. Although the first flush of enthusiasm is wearing off among OLs, who bought the kit as a trendy outfit to wear on their fashionable outings to soccer matches, Mizuno sees a steady and reassuring 5 per cent growth in purchases by the true player market.

Mizuno's soccer division now represents 7–8 per cent of its total sales, from practically zero at the start of the 1990s. It was much more familiar with selling baseball items, but the popularity of baseball was hit by the launch of the J.League in 1993. Baseball staged a comeback in 1995, when Hideo Nomo shot to stardom as the Los Angeles Dodgers' pitcher after an undistinguished career in Japan, while a youngster called Ichiro playing for the Orix Blue Wave was topping the Japanese batting averages. Although absolute yen figures are not available, an index of Mizuno's football-related sales gives an idea of growth:

	Soccer Division Sales	Non-J.League Soccer Items	Baseball DivisionSales
1992	100	100	100
1993	300	120	95
1994	250	125	100
1995	200	128	110

A significant outcome for both Sony CP and Mizuno of their experience with the J.League has been the high profile they have gained in the world marketplace. Sony CP was selected by ISL, the marketing arm of FIFA, to handle the worldwide merchandising rights for the 1998 World Cup in France, thanks to the success of its J.League campaign. It beat off competition from such giants as Disney Products for the contract. An office will be established in Paris for Sony CP (handling the business in Japan, Asia and Africa) and its Los Angeles-based sister company Sony Signatures (for the American and European side). The corporate image of Mizuno has been raised worldwide by the exposure of the J.League teams to international TV audiences, and the company is moving into football markets in Latin America and the UK to challenge the dominance of companies like Adidas. It has also been contacted by Japanese non-soccer teams for uniform designs.

The finances

The J.League itself is a non-profit association. It covers running costs by taking a percentage of sponsorship fees and collecting membership dues from clubs and fees from candidate (associate) members. It receives no share of merchandising royalties or TV rights.

Three per cent of what Sony CP and Mizuno make in merchandise sales goes to the J.League as royalties, which are then distributed to individual clubs according to their share of the total. Royalties on merchandise carrying the J.League logo are split evenly between the teams.

Clubs have three principal sources of income: ticket sales; revenue from their own merchandising and the sale of regional TV broadcast rights; and a share of the sponsorship, national television rights and merchandise sales distributed through the central J.League system. Discussions about a football lottery to raise more revenue for clubs and finance new stadiums came to nothing.

At the start, there was no great difference in the wealth of the various teams because of the J.League policy on equal distribution, but over the long term, a club's financial fortunes will be determined by its income from ticket sales – itself a factor of the home ground's seating capacity and the ability of the team to keep its fans loyal. Clubs are working with their local governments to increase the size of their stadiums to accommodate the demand for tickets. Jubilo Iwata, for example, began with a ground capacity of 17,500, raised it to 19,000 by 1995 and plans to have 23–24,000 seats in 1996. Ticket prices (controlled by the J.League) range from ¥2,000 to ¥5,000.

Exhibit 6 shows the budget for the J.League in 1996, agreed shortly before the 1996 season began.

The local community effect

There is no doubt that the smaller towns – Kashima, Iwata, Urawa – are the best at inspiring their fans, whatever the match results. In any case, the impact of 20,000 supporters in little towns like Kashima or Iwata is far greater than 60,000 Verdy supporters in Kawasaki, a city of over a million people. Jubilo Iwata has a supporters club of 25,000 people, even though its stadium holds fewer than 20,000 spectators, and they turn out in their thousands even for end-of-season matches against non-J.League teams. Forget any ideas of supporters only following successful teams: 'the Urawa Reds have amazing support, the best in the league, even though they finished bottom in the first four series', says one observer. At Urawa, the crowds are reputed for their singing; at Verdy Kawasaki matches the fans prefer samba-rhythm drumming – and 70 per cent of the spectators are young women, attracted by the strong Brazilian influence of the team. (The Yomiuri media group, which is Verdy's main shareholder, doesn't hesitate to promote the team, and that helps to explain its popularity with the OLs.)

Tokyo doesn't have its own team, partly because there's no overall identity to the city, but also because there aren't the necessary facilities. Only one stadium in Tokyo meets the minimum J.League requirements, but it's too close to a hospital for floodlights to be used for evening matches. Verdy Kawasaki was rumoured to be planning to cross the Tamagawa River and build a new stadium in Yoga in the Tokyo district of Setagaya, but its plans were blocked by the Kawasaki municipal council which had already agreed to pay for the rebuilding of its existing stadium.

In Osaka, support for the city's two teams (Gamba and Cerezo) is less fanatical than in the smaller towns. Gamba's support base is rather weak, which some say is because the team is too strongly identified with a single company (Panasonic). It's also the only team whose home ground (the Expo '70 commemorative stadium) isn't financed by the local community. The J.League tries to insist on the 'home town' concept by refusing to allow the names of the companies owning the clubs to appear in team names, but some have tested the limits. JEF United Ichihara, for example, is jointly owned by Japan East (Railways) and Furukawa, and Verdy Kawasaki, the Yokohama Marinos and Gamba Osaka all feature the names of their corporate backers in their logos.

The two essential elements of previous sports booms, according to the J.League, are TV coverage and heroes. Psychologically, Japanese seem to need to find a hero even more than others do. In the run-up to the J.League and during the first season or two, Japanese soccer had to rely on the drawing power of imported foreign heroes in the absence of any real domestic stars. There weren't even any Japanese playing for European soccer clubs like there were in the late 1980s, when Japanese TV coverage of foreign football matches was switched from the UK to Germany because Okudera began playing for a West German team.

Japanese players who join overseas clubs have huge fan clubs – because fans think the status of foreign leagues is much higher than the domestic league, and because they want to see Japan internationally famous. It's the same for baseball in Japan. Unfortunately for the Japanese, there's been a real shortage of national soccer heroes playing overseas in the 1990s – none at all in 1995. If Japan had gone to play in the 1994 World Cup in the United States, instead of losing as they did in the last seconds of the final qualifying match, several players would probably have been signed to play for European teams and would instantly have earned hero status.

The results... and the challenge

In 1992, before the J.League was launched, the Japanese national soccer team was ranked #62 in the world according to FIFA. Three years later it was ranked #33. Since 32 teams now qualify for the World Cup championships, up from 24 previously, Japan stands a fair chance of participating in forthcoming tournaments. It knows it won't be a serious contender to win the cup until it ranks among the world's top ten teams.

As time passes, Japan's pool of skilled professional players will broaden. It expects to be clearly the #1 team in Asia within ten years, compared with being roughly equal now with several others. The performance of its youth teams in the World Cups played in 1995 was encouraging.

Popular enthusiasm for soccer in Japan is still tied to the success of the national team. The national team will be good if the local teams are good, the local teams will be good if they are well supported locally, and local support will be strong if the national team does well. Kawabuchi and the J.League hope local teams will win the fervent support of local supporters, come what may. How much would a failure to qualify for the World Cup in France in 1998 affect the popularity of the J.League?

The J.League has to keep its matches interesting to maintain support, or the mass media might abandon soccer. What would happen then to sponsorships and advertisers? Is the expansion of the league – to 16 teams in 1996, rising to 20 by 1998 – a threat to the overall quality of soccer in Japan? Another potentially serious issue for the long term standing of the J.League is the standard of refereeing of matches. Foreign match officials have been brought in to raise standards but Japanese referees have to be more authoritative and stand up to the 'heroes', and the linesmen must learn to disagree with the referee's decisions if necessary.

The J.League board believes a split in the J.League into first and second divisions would motivate the clubs (the winners of the lower league would be promoted to the upper one, and the worst performers in the upper league would be demoted). Professional soccer leagues elsewhere in the world operate on this principle, but is it a good idea for Japan? No decision has been made on the timing of such a split. What are the advantages and disadvantages?

The merchandising campaign was directed very successfully at children during the opening seasons, and through them their parents became soccer supporters as well. Japan is a rapidly ageing society and the percentage of children in the overall population will decline. Also the profile of soccer supporters is shifting from the young females, who are fans of individual players, towards true lovers of the game. What impact could these changes have on the way that soccer is marketed in Japan?

In the 1995 season, baseball produced two new heroes for Japan, Nomo in the United States and Ichiro at home. Would Japan revert to baseball as its favourite game?

The United States, meanwhile, was preparing to launch its own professional soccer league, following the national team's strong showing in the 1994 World Cup. Inaugural matches between the ten teams of Major League Soccer (MLS) kicked off in April 1996, backed by a unified marketing effort, licensed merchandise, and sponsorship deals worth over US$50 million to give the league the financial security which earlier attempts at professional soccer had lacked. This time the stars would be home-grown: even the participation of stars like Pele, Cruyff and Beckenbauer hadn't been able to prevent the North American Soccer League, MLS's predecessor, from going bankrupt. Average attendance during the MLS's first season was predicted to be 12,000 per game, mostly children and their parents, but the key to success was seen to be television coverage and audiences.

In 1995, Japan launched its formal bid to host the 2002 World Cup after several years of preparation and unofficial lobbying. Advertising giant Dentsu acted as campaign manager and a parliamentary committee, including former premier, Miyazawa, actively engaged in the process. The only other contender to stage the championships was South Korea, which had already qualified four times to play in the World Cup. Both countries became locked in bitter and expensive rivalry to court FIFA officials, with national honour at stake. In June 1996, FIFA decided that the two countries should co-host the 2002 tournament. In July 1996, the whole of Japan went beserk when its national team beat Brazil in an opening round of the 1996 Olympic Games in Atlanta, its first appearance at the Games in nearly 30 years.

Exhibit 1   Teams in the J.League (1995 season)

Teams	Principal Ownership	Slogan
Kashima Antlers	Sumitomo Kinzoku	Dashing beauty
JEF United Ichihara	JR East (50%), Furukawa Denko (50%)	The mighty front
Kashiwa Reysol**	Hitachi	Heat it up
Urawa Red Diamonds	Mitsubishi Motors	Red in Urawa
Verdy Kawasaki	Yomiuri	Com a bola no pé
Yokohama Marinos	Nissan	Sail on to victory
Yokohama Flügels	ANA, Sato Kogyo	Take to the skies
Bellmare Hiratsuka*	Fujita	Winning waves
Shimizu S-Pulse	TV Shizuoka (8%) plus many local companies	Pulsing with excitement
Júbilo Iwata*	Yamaha	Fleet elite
Nagoya Grampus Eight	Toyota	Here we go
Gamba Osaka	Panasonic	The swift attack
Cerezo Osaka**	Yanmar Diesel, Nippon Ham, Capcom	Los lobos victoriosos
Sanfrecce Hiroshima	Mazda, Ford	Pour the heat on

Avispa Fukuoka and Kyoto Purple Sanga joined the J.League in 1996
* joined the J.League in its second season (1994)
** joined the J.League in its third season (1995)

Source: J.League documents

Exhibit 2   Geographical dispersion of J.League teams

Urawa Red Diamonds
Bellmare Hiratsuka
Shimizu S-Pulse
Júbilo Iwata
Nagoya Grampus Eight
Kyoto Purple Sanga*
Gamba Osaka
Cerezo Osaka

Kashima Antlers
Kashiwa Reysol
JEF United Ichihara
Verdy Kawasaki
Yokohama Marinos
Yokohama Flügels

Sanfrecce Hiroshima
Avispa Fukuoka*

* new to the J.League in 1996

Source: J.League

Exhibit 3   J.League supporting companies (1992–95)

Capacity	Company	Content
Series Sponsors	Suntory Nippon Shinpan	Leading sponsor for official league matches. Can erect advertising placards at all official league matches and use the series sponsorship mark
Official Sponsors	NTT Mobile Communications Network Okasan Securities Calbee Foods Shiseido Shogakukan Japan Energy Corporation Nissin Food Products Nippon Life Insurance Bobson Mizuno Daiei Convenience Systems	Can erect advertising placards at all official league matches and use the official sponsorship mark
Licensed Advertising and Public Relations Sponsors Japan	Citizen Watch Sekisui Chemical Kentucky Fried Chicken Japan Fuji Bank	Can use J.League approved campaign mark and campaign slogan (- is a part of the 'We love J.League' campaign) in advertising and public relations
J.League Data Center Sponsor	Dai Nippon Printing	Company name included on records of official J.League matches and other bulletins. Credit is given in advertisements and when data is used for secondary purposes
Man-of-the-Match Sponsor	Suntory Match')	Company or product name included in the phrase, J.League – 'Man-of-the-
Official Suppliers	Suntory Kodak Japan Mizuno Menicon	Supplier of official sports drink (J. Water) Supplier of film for records of official matches Supplier of team kit for league matches Supplier of contact lenses for J.League players, managers and coaches
Other suppliers	Crix Yasuda Cosa Liebermann Hit Union Seiko	Supplier of corner posts and flags, and lines-men's flags for official J.League matches Supplier of boots for referees of official J.League matches Supplier of kit for referees of official J.League matches Supplier of wristwatches for referees of official J.League matches

Exhibit 3 *(cont.)*

Capacity	Company	Content
	Molten	Supplier of official balls for official J.League matches
Merchandise Licences	Sony Creative Products	Production and sale of goods using team names, logos, mascots, etc. and J.League designs and commercial marks
	Cemic	Production and sale of TV game software using team names, logos, mascots, and so on and J.League designs and commercial marks
	Daichi Display	Production and sale of medals and accessories using teams names, logos, mascots, and so on and J.League designs and commercial marks
	Mizuno	Production and sale of kit and other sports goods using teams names, logos, mascots, and so on and J. League designs and commercial marks
Others	Nippon Broadcasting System	Radio broadcasting of official J.League matches on AM, FM, short-wave and satellite audio services

Exhibit 4   1996 J.League sponsors

Capacity	Company	Content
Official Sponsors	Calbee Foods Canon Sales/Canon Daiei Convenience Systems Daiichi Kangyo Bank Japan Energy Corporation Nippon Shinpan Nippon Life Insurance Suntory	The top category of sponsors, contributing to the J.League through the sponsorship of league matches
Fair Play Campaign	Citizen Trading/Citizen Sekisui Chemical	Support the J.League's efforts to promote the spirit of fair play. May use the slogan 'J.League Fair Play Campaign'
Official Suppliers	Dai Nippon Printing Kodak Japan Mizuno Suntory	Support the J.League through the provision of products or services
League Cup Sponsor	Yamazaki Nabisco	Contributes to the development of the J.League through the sponsorship of league cup matches

Source: J.League

Exhibit 5   J.League attendance

	Full Season Attendance	
	Total	**Average**
1993	3,235,750	17,976
1994	5,173,817	19,597
1995	6,159,691	16,922

Note: In the 1993 season 10 teams each played 18 games
in the first half season and 18 in the second half; in 1994
12 teams played 22 games in each half; and in 1995 14
teams played 26 games in each half.

Source: J.League

Exhibit 6   The J.League budget 1996

Income		
Sponsorship	¥4,500 million	(+ ¥1,500 million)
Merchandising royalties	¥1,330 million	(– 50%)
TV broadcasting rights	¥1,120 million	(– ¥500 million)
Entry fees and club memberships	*¥2,031 million*	
Total	¥8,981 million	(broadly unchanged)
Expenditure	¥8,954 million	(broadly unchanged)
Balance		
Surplus	**¥27 million**	

Source: Nikkei Shinbun, 21 February, 1996

CASE STUDY THREE: Club Med Japan

Hellmut Schütte and Eriko Ishada, INSEAD-EAC (1990)

Introduction

In the winter of 1988/89, Alexis Agnello, Chairman of Club Mediterranée Asia-Pacific-Indian Ocean was sipping a glass of wine at the Club's ski resort in Sahoro, Hokkaido. He was content with the progress Club Med was making in Japan. Sahoro, the first vacation village opened there, was running at nearly full capacity. The membership growth rate had been far greater than the rapidly increasing industrial average. However, maintaining or enhancing Club Med's position in Japan required various long-term strategic decisions, as many large Japanese companies were entering the leisure industry and expected to offer Club Med-style holidays. The unofficial target for Club Med members in Japan by 1999 was ambitious: 200,000 members, rising from 49,300 members in fiscal year 1989. In order to achieve such an ambitious goal, Club Med had to establish more villages, either in Japan or in other parts of Asia. Other possible sources of growth were new types of Club Med products catering to the manifold aspects of the booming Japanese leisure market and new target groups beyond the young, urban, cosmopolitan clientele Club Med dealt with everywhere in the world.

Background

Club Mediterranée was founded as a non-profit sports association in France in 1950 by Gerard Blitz, a former member of the Belgian Olympic Team, along with some of his friends. As the association grew, running it as an informal, loosely organised group became increasingly difficult. In 1954, Blitz invited his close friend Gilbert Trigano to join the association on a full-time basis. Trigano, who saw commercial potential in the concept, became managing director and transformed it into a profitable organisation.

As Club Mediterranée grew in size, it became necessary to structure the geographical expansion more formally. In 1972, Club Med Inc. was formed as a US subsidiary which would sell package tours and operate resorts in areas outside the Europe/Africa zone. Over a short period of time, North America became the second largest market for Club Mediterranée. Exhibit 1 depicts the composition of members by nationality. In 1982, in order to manage, market and develop more effectively, the Club established four completely autonomous geographical zones. Club

Méditerranée S.A. headed European and African operations out of Paris, and South American activities were run from a base in Rio de Janeiro. Club Med Inc. managed the group's North American operations from offices in New York and directed the business in Asia, the South Pacific and the Indian Ocean out of Tokyo and Hong Kong. Club Méditerranée regards the European market as mature, the U.S. market as close to mature, and the Japanese and other Asian markets as growing (hence the importance of the Japanese market).

By 31 October 1988 (the end of the fiscal year), Club Méditerranée ran operations in a total of 243 locations with 120,837 beds. In addition to traditional Club Med villages the group manages various forms of holiday villages and residences under different names, some of them acquired over the years. Valtur is aimed at the Italian market. OCCAJ operates and markets vacation villages and rental packages in France. Maeva handles rentals of leisure properties for Clubhotel, Utoring and Locarev. Club Méditerranée's villas are traditional hotels enhanced by the Club's own special savoir-faire. City Club combines hotel accommodation in or near a downtown area with conventional premises and fully-equipped sports and leisure complexes. There are 96 Club Med villages, 15 Valtur villages, 29 OCCAJ villages and residences, 88 Maeva vacation residences, 12 villas, and one City Club. Club Med is by far the world's largest operator of holiday resorts and in 1987/88 catered to over 1.6 million holiday-makers. It is the leading tour operator in France and ranks third in Europe in terms of both clients and revenue. Club Méditerranée is also Europe's fourth largest hotel chain and holds twelfth place worldwide.

Club Méditerranée's philosophy and club formula

The Club Méditerranée's main concept has been 'back to nature': escape from everyday pressures and urban hassles. In advance, the guests pay one price for their holiday, which includes room, air fares, transfers from airports, meals and sports. In order to eliminate the need for carrying or worrying about money, guests wear prepaid necklaces of beads used as currency to cover any spending within the village. Until recently, there were no phones, locks, or TVs in the rooms. Telephones were considered as a means to connect guests with the hassles of the outside world.

What makes the Club unique are the staff called 'GOs', 'gentils organisateurs' or 'nice organisers', who run the villages. Guests are referred to as 'GMs', meaning 'gentils membres' or 'nice people'. The GOs, one for every eight GMs, mix with the GMs, teach them sports and present entertainment every night after dinner. The presence of the GOs creates a special atmosphere in the village. GOs are enthusiastic young people who work long hours and are available for GMs most of the day. There are currently 6,400 GOs in the world; because of the nature of the work, there is a high turnover. Still, every year more than 30,000 people apply for 2,000 openings. GOs have to be above all good communicators. They also need to have special skills such as music or sports. Knowing the importance of GOs, Club Med spends substantial resources on training them. To keep GOs motivated, they are moved from one village to another every six months.

Each village is designed to maximise social interaction. The bar is centrally located in order to be a meeting place. GMs and GOs are randomly seated together at meals in groups of six or eight, and single rooms are not usually available. Shy guests will be encouraged, but not obliged, to participate in the various sports and social activities of the Club during the day and may be asked by a GO for a dance in the discotheque at night.

History of Club Méditerranée in Japan

The Japanese market was identified as being attractive as early as 1964, when Gilbert Trigano visited Japan for the Tokyo Olympic Games.

In 1973, the large trading house C. Itoh became the sales representative for Club Méditerranée in Japan. However, this relationship was ended as Club Méditerranée was not satisfied with C. Itoh's commitment to marketing and village development. In 1979, Club Méditerranée K.K. (Japan) was established to market Club Med's products. In 1984, an association was announced with Seiyo Ltd, the leisure branch of the Seibu Saison Group, a major Japanese distributor. Trigano had known Seibu Saison Group Chairman Seiji Tsutsumi for twenty years or so. During an interview about the joint venture, Mr. Tsutsumi said that his Group had perfected its retail business and would like to concentrate efforts on leisure activities. The Group hoped to gain expertise from Club Méditerranée in resort facility management and the 'art of entertaining', even though Seibu already had substantial expertise in this kind of business. Mr. Tsutsumi felt that through this alliance Seibu Saison would be one step ahead of other Japanese competitors, for whom leisure development meant just building nice facilities. The agreement between the two partners foresees, among other items, the marketing of Club Med holidays in Seibu Saison's stores and the opening of vacation villages in Japan.

The relationship is not exclusive for either side and Seibu Saison has numerous joint ventures with other foreign companies, including one with

Accor, a French hotel group to introduce 'sea therapy'. It also has an investment in St. Andrew's golf course in the U.K. Although Club Med has considered various projects with other Japanese companies, the collaboration with Seibu Saison remains a very special one. Not only do Club Med and Seibu Saison cooperate in Japan, but Seibu Saison owns 3 per cent of Club Mediterranée S.A.'s registered shares in France. Mr. Tsutsumi is a member of the Board of Directors of Club Med S.A. and his sister, who lives in Paris, was invited to join Club Med's President's Special Advisory Committee.

Another large shareholder is Nippon Life Insurance, the largest Japanese life insurance company, which acquired 4.9 per cent of Club Mediterranée S.A.'s registered shares. The role of Nippon Life Insurance is limited to a financial arrangement for the time being.

In December 1987, Club Med opened its first Club Med village in Japan at the ski resort of Sahoro 140 km east of Sapporo as a 'showroom' village in Japan. There Japanese clients can experience first hand what Club Med has to offer. The village operates out of a hotel which was acquired by a subsidiary of Seibu Saison in 1985 but suffered from a low rate of occupancy, especially during the summer season. The village is managed by a joint-venture company 50 per cent of which is owned by Club Med Inc. and 50 per cent by Seibu Saison. Club Med's first major move was to transform the interior of the hotel.

Membership has increased substantially since the opening of Sahoro, as Exhibit 2 shows. One year after the village opened the rate of occupancy had doubled: during the winter it reached 96 per cent and in summer 56 per cent. Nevertheless, the opening of other villages has been delayed due to difficulties in finding other suitable sites and the very high land prices.

Other than the Sahoro ski village, Club Med in Japan has been pioneering new ideas. In the winter of 1989/90, Club Med chartered the cruise vessel Fuji Maru to create a 'floating Club Med Village' in cooperation with Mitsui OSK, the Japanese liner operator which owns the ship. For 26 days a total of 1,000 Japanese were entertained by GOs brought in from other villages and Club Med's reserve staff. Most of the guests were married couples between 40-60 years of age who had been on cruises before. Hardly any of them stayed on board for the whole trip to Hong Kong, Singapore and Bangkok, but the ship was fully booked at prices ranging from US$1,800 for six days to US$8,000 for 26 days.

Another project currently under consideration in Japan is the construction of a City Club with strong emphasis on corporate use. Several real estate developers have approached Club Med already in connection with such an undertaking located close to Tokyo or Osaka.

Recent trends of Japanese overseas travel

Demand for overseas travel among the Japanese is growing rapidly, and the recent sharp appreciation of the yen has made it economically feasible. In fact, some overseas tours have become cheaper than domestic tours. For example, a five-day package tour from Tokyo to Guam costs somewhere around 90,000 yen, while a similar trip to Okinawa, Japan's southernmost island, is closer to 110,000 yen. The number of Japanese travelling abroad has risen from 5.5 million in 1985 to 8.4 million in 1988 and could well reach 10 million in 1989 (Exhibit 3). It seems that the so-called "10 million programme", established by the Ministry of Transport, in September 1987 to increase the number of Japanese travelling overseas by 1991 will be attained way ahead of schedule. The figure still indicates that fewer than one in ten Japanese leave the country even once a year. In comparison with other industrialised nations this number is low, and the potential for growth is immense. In the UK, for example, 44 per cent of the total population went abroad in 1986. In the US, 15 per cent of the population travelled abroad in 1987.

Most Japanese go overseas on pleasure trips. In 1987, approximately 83 per cent of overseas travel was categorised as pleasure trips and 15 per cent as business trips.

Exhibit 4 shows the breakdown of overseas travellers by age and sex. A recent phenomenon is the rapid increase of young women travelling abroad. In 1988, 1.3 million of the total 8.4 million travellers were women between 20 and 30 years old. The majority of them are so-called 'OLs', Office Ladies. They usually work for big companies and live with their parents, so they have few financial and family obligations. These young women like to travel as often as possible before getting married. Honeymooners, although they are not classified separately in the statistics, constitute an important segment. The other growing sector is people over 60 years old.

The use of package tours is popular. Some 90 per cent of Japan's honeymooners use them, as do approximately 78 per cent of total sightseeing tourists. The use of well-known brand package tours such as JALPAK, which offer better service but consequently have higher prices, has remained constant. Less well-known, cheaper package tours have been gaining popularity, and all Japanese tour organisers have introduced what they call 'second brand' tours to meet this growing market demand. More and more people are asking their agencies only to arrange round trip air tickets and hotel reservations for the first and last days in destination countries. They prefer to decide itineraries and programmes for the intervening days on their own. An increasing number of young people, among them university students, prefer this type of travel.

The favourite Japanese destinations are also changing, shifting from Southeast Asia to North America, Australia and other more distant regions. The change in destination is somewhat in line with the changing expectations for a vacation. According to a survey carried out by Mainichi Newspaper, most tourists spent their time shopping, sightseeing, and eating (Exhibit 5). In this sense, Hong Kong and Singapore were the most popular destinations. On the other hand, the answers to a question about what type of overseas travel people like to do were quite different. Both men and women chose leisure-stay tours first and sight-seeing tours second (Exhibit 6). Places like Australia and the South Pacific Islands were closely associated with leisure-stay tours.

The growth in overseas travel is expected to continue as long as there is no drastic economic change. Airport capacities represent one limiting factor for further growth. Japanese overseas travelling is extremely seasonal, with peak seasons in March and July–August and at the end of the year (Exhibit 7). Although there are other international airports, Narita and Osaka airports bear heavy burdens and are close to full capacity. The new Kansai Airport will only open in 1993.

Japanese attitude towards leisure

The Japanese are regarded by Westerners as workaholics whose work days are seldom interrupted by holidays. However, according to a recent survey for the Prime Minister's Office, more than half those polled now prefer to have more free time rather than extra payment. They also prefer to spend more money on leisure activities than on consumer durables. Both leisure and work are important in the lives of 39 per cent of the respondents, and only 33 per cent answered that work is more important for them and leisure time is to prepare themselves for work. However, 8 per cent said that leisure is more important than work (Exhibit 8). The survey also demonstrates the fact that there is a considerable difference in attitudes towards work among different age groups. For example, 45 per cent of people in their fifties answered that work is more important than leisure, but only 21 per cent of those in their twenties think that way.

Generally speaking, the younger generation, especially the so-called 'shin-jinrui' ('rebellious youth'), with their more individualistic, Western attitude towards corporate life and work, tend to take longer holidays. The young people's attitude towards work is frowned upon by older generations because the former prefer to spend money rather than save and have fun rather than work long hours. Within the same age group women tend to take more holidays than men, as they do not see corporate life as a life-long commitment.

Nevertheless, compared with other societies the Japanese work a lot. The average annual holiday taken by workers was only 7.5 days in 1986. It actually decreased from an average of 8.8 days in 1980, although workers are given 14.9 days annual paid holiday on average.

There are several reasons why the Japanese do not take holidays. First of all, there is a lack of leisure infrastructure in Japan. The long journey to airports, road congestion and the high cost of transport and lodging make all trips very difficult. Secondly, the Japanese are not used to having 'active' leisure activities such as sports. Exhibit 9 shows the breakdown of leisure hours by activity for different age groups and the two sexes. It shows that only 20 to 30 per cent of leisure time is spent on 'active' leisure such as sports, with the rest of the time spent on 'passive' activities such as reading magazines and watching TV. Thirdly, most Japanese feel guilty when they take a long holiday because it means that their colleagues have to do additional work. Instead of causing friction with their colleagues, they prefer not to take long holidays.

The Japanese government now encourages more holiday taking. The government's new five-year economic plan approved in May 1988 calls for reducing Japan's annual working hours from an average of 2,111 hours in 1987 to about 1,800 hours by 1993. By comparison, French and German workers only worked 1,650 hours in 1986. Up until recently, only 30 per cent of the total workforce worked a five-day week. In February 1989, the five-day work week went into effect in financial institutions. The government and industries are expected to follow. If the percentage of employees working a 5-day week grows by 10 per cent per annum, it will reach 70 per cent, the current level in the U.S. and Europe, in 1992. Coupled with increased propensity to spend on leisure activities, all of this will create a great demand for leisure industries. The Economic Planning Agency estimates that extending the five-day work week to the remainder of the workforce would boost consumer spending substantially. If salaried Japanese used all of their paid leave, leisure consumption would be even higher.

Bearing these trends in mind, the market opportunities for companies such as Club Med seem to be endless.

Marketing Club Med in Japan

Segmentation strategy

When Club Med was first marketed in Japan, nearly 100 per cent of its customers were honeymooners. The price, the romantic image, the destination (New Caledonia), and the length of stay (two weeks) appealed only to honeymooners.

As overseas travel patterns changed and the number of experienced travellers increased, other customer segments became important. Exhibit 10 shows the breakdown of Club Med members in Japan in 1987/88 as compared with 1984/85 and the average stay for each segment. The ratio for honeymooners has come down to 40 per cent. The average length of stay has not increased, mostly due to a rise in short stay package tours to destinations near Japan.

The current major target group is the so-called OL segment, now accounting for 35 per cent. The Club Med's image as a young, international, fun-loving organisation appeals to most OLs. They are frequent travellers but tend to be quite price sensitive, and their budgets are lower than those of honeymooners. The budget of an average sightseeing tourist is estimated to be around 274 thousand yen and that of honeymooners is 387 thousand yen. Club Med hopes unmarried young women will become repeat clients as they come back for their honeymoons and then again several years later with their families.

In 1987/88 families with children comprised 15 per cent of the GM population in Japan. Club Med was surprised to find that so many Japanese families travel with their children. Now most of its villages in the region are equipped with Mini Clubs, where children are taken care of by GOs and participate in various activities whilst their parents enjoy themselves off on their own. Club Med Sahoro opened a Mini Club in summer 1989.

Although corporate business still represents only a small proportion (7 per cent in 1987/88), it is expected to grow rapidly. Club Méditerranée provides conference or training packages in exotic locations in the Club Med ambiance. It also provides meeting facilities and even office equipment. Big companies such as Sony and Toshiba use these facilities. A new village at Opio on the French Riviera opened in 1989 is specially designed for such purposes and is strongly marketed towards Japanese corporate clients. This sector will certainly become more important, as the government has extended tax-deductible company trips from two nights to three. Company trips are a common way of rewarding employees and increasing their loyalty. The change from two to three nights means that company trips can take place further afield or even overseas. Club Med Sahoro is focusing its marketing efforts towards corporate clients in the summer season. In summer 1989 corporate clients accounted for 40 per cent of GMs.

Product strategy

In general, Club Méditerranée believes that since the Club Med concept appeals to the French it will also appeal to other nationalities once the language barrier is removed.

In Japan, however, a more flexible approach was introduced by Mr. Trigano. He has stated that 'We have tried very hard to improve products for the Japanese. It seems they need an alibi to go on holiday, so we offer them courses on how to use the computer, or speak French or English or whatever they want.'

In order to cater to Japanese demand, Club Med shortened the length of stay as a first step. Club Med's standard packages have been designed on a European basis where four or five weeks of holiday is the norm and a week or more of public holiday can be added. Instead of two week packages, which are common for the European market, one week tours were developed for the Japanese market. Recently, three night package tours to Club Med villages have been launched aiming at the OL segment. The average stay of the Japanese GM is 5 to 5.5 days, whereas the average stay in France is 15 days. This takes into account the fact that long vacations will not take root in Japan even in the long run, as the Japanese prefer to take holidays of three to four days in each season.

Secondly, the utmost care has been taken to arrange the most convenient departure schedule. For example, being able to depart on Monday is essential for honeymooners, as wedding ceremonies are usually held on Sunday.

Thirdly, villages in Asia/Pacific zones were designed to be more luxurious compared with Mediterranean villages, which means there is a telephone in every room and rooms are airconditioned. Nevertheless, the quality of the accommodation still does not fully meet Japanese requirements. Instead of sleeping under thatched roofs in rooms decorated with bamboo and other local materials, they prefer a more neutral and hotel-like environment verging on the antiseptic. All announcements and signs in the villages are in English, French and Japanese.

Club Med has been successful in recruiting Japanese GOs who speak two or three languages and are prepared to work long hours for the standard salary of US$600 per month. There are now almost 200 Japanese GOs, most of them female, who facilitate communication with Japanese GMs and help them to settle into the Club's atmosphere. However, some Japanese guests find Japanese GOs too Westernised, while the Japanese

GOs want to be assigned not only to villages with large numbers of their countrymen but also to Europe and the US/Caribbean.

Club Med is known for good eating. Both local food and French cuisine are served in buffet-style restaurants. Japanese dishes are added to the menus in villages catering to Japanese tourists. For those who would like to eat in quieter surroundings, such as honeymooners, there are separate dining rooms.

Club Med makes extensive use of comment cards filled out by GMs. They are well analysed and fed back to product development and operational management.

Promotion

Club Med's advertising expenses in Japan account for 8 per cent of sales. About 40 per cent of this goes to the printing and mailing of brochures containing detailed information, as the Japanese like to have extensive knowledge about a tour before departure. Club Med has achieved high awareness in the mind of Japanese tourists, as shown in Exhibit 11. A poll of Japanese holidaymakers by AB Road magazine awarded Club Med top marks as the tour operator they were 'most willing to try'.

The present rate of repeat business in Japan is only 20 per cent. This compares with Club Med's worldwide average of 70 per cent. It is partly due to the high number of additional members joining during the year who have not had an opportunity to consider a return visit to Club Med. It is, however, also due to the high percentage of honeymooners for whom their time in Club Med is a very special occasion and not a standard holiday. A regular newsletter and invitations to parties and events given by the Club are designed to promote a Club spirit among GMs and increase the number of repeat holidaymakers. In order to encourage word-of-mouth communication, Club Med is considering offering a free one-day stay at a village for those who successfully introduce a new GM to the Club.

In Japan, Club Med makes extensive use of a 'European' image in its advertising, with photos of beautifully tanned, smiling Westerners on the beach. Even for Sahoro, the first Japanese village, the brochure shows a number of Westerners, although currently only 8 per cent of Sahoro's GMs are from outside Japan, mainly from nearby Asia. About half the GOs there are non-Japanese. Club Med rarely uses TV advertising, mainly due to its cost in Japan.

Distribution

As Club Med's holidays appeal to urban dwellers, distribution is concentrated in Tokyo and Osaka. There are about 700 travel agents with 7,000 sales outlets throughout Japan. Approximately 90 per cent of overseas travellers book their trips through these agents. Major tour operators sell their products through either their own sales outlets, independent outlets or their competitors' outlets. In the beginning, Club Med depended entirely on other agents. In order to promote sales more aggressively, it has built up its own direct sales channels. Direct sales in Japan now account for 15 to 17 per cent of total sales.

Club Med's products require a fairly detailed explanation, as they are different from other tour packages. In order to help people understand and to lure them, beautiful video films on Club Med village life are shown at the Club Med sales counters and video tapes are available for home viewing as well. There are Club Med sales points in Tokyo, Osaka, Nagoya, Sapporo and Fukuoka. In addition, there are eight sales points in Seibu Department Stores, which are staffed by Japanese GOs. Out of the 700 travel agencies 500 deal with Club Med, and 3,000 of the 7,000 outlets sell Club Med packages.

Price

In general, the price is not really considered of prime importance by the Japanese because of the high opportunity cost in the case of vacation failure. They prefer to go for well-proven products.

Although Club Med is a 'European product' with an upmarket image, prices are competitive compared with other well-known Japanese package tours such as JALPAK. The price is determined by the length of stay, departure date/season, and destination. The price of competitors' products and Club Med's internal price structures are carefully taken into consideration in pricing. Usually the price of tours departing from Japan is higher than tours leaving from other parts of the world. According to internal statistics, the average Japanese GM pays US$380 for a day of vacation. This compares with US$140, which the average Australian pays per day, and US$70 paid in Malaysia (these figures include transportation costs). In the case of Sahoro, the price is much higher than average ski package tours offered by Japanese competitors. One night at Sahoro costs about US$200. GMs are still satisfied because this sum includes high quality ski lessons following the methods of the Ecole de Ski Francaise and unlimited access to the lifts and gondola with no waiting time, which is rare at Japanese ski resorts.

The future

While it had taken Club Med many years to penetrate the Japanese market, Alexis Agnello felt very pleased with the recent progress the company had made. He believed that the 'Club Med magic' – the close interaction between GOs and GMs in an informal, pleasant environment cut off from everyday life – had finally been accepted by the Japanese. Moreover, it could not be imitated by others. Sahoro worked well, and so did the other villages in the region such as Bali or Phuket. Club Med did not have any problem finding enough multilingual GOs who accepted to work very long hours for a very low salary. Management was increasingly able to squeeze very favourable terms out of airlines due to Club Med's growing traffic volume. The business was carried forward almost automatically by the leisure and travel boom in Japan.

Nevertheless, 49,300 GMs per annum made up only 0.04 per cent of Japan's population. This hardly compared with the 0.66 per cent of all French people going on holiday with the Club. Was it right to stick to a concept different from anything else in Japan, where virtually every local government was drawing up plans to develop resort complexes in accordance with the Law for Development of Comprehensive Resort Areas enacted in 1987? Seventy projects were already underway within Japan. Major private companies were entering the leisure industry in search of growth. Companies in heavy manufacturing, which had gone through rigid restructuring, had started to convert their closed factories into leisure sites and thus utilise their excess employees. Club Méditerranée K.K. (Japan) was taking part in this development, though on a limited scale. Some time ago the firm announced that it was taking a 5 per cent share in a newly formed company called Asahi Kaiyo, which will convert former shipyards into marinas and leisure centres. Other partners were Seibu Saison (35 per cent) and Japan Air Lines, Mitsui and Nippon Steel (5 per cent each).

The overseas travel boom had also accelerated resort development overseas, where land prices and labour costs were comparatively low and government approval came fast. Large-scale leisure facilities such as golf courses and resort condominiums were under construction by various Japanese consortia in Hawaii, Guam, Saipan, Australia, and on the West Coast of the United States. In Australia, some twenty major projects were underway with Japanese capital.

In order to cope with such development, Club Med would have to open up more villages inside and outside Japan rapidly and try to broaden the product range to reach a more general Japanese public. Possible sites were along the sea somewhere in Japan, on Okinawa, in Tokyo, Osaka, the Philippines and Australia. Being unique may be good, Mr. Agnello thought, but is it enough to be attractive? Perhaps we should start a Club without international flavour, without informality, without too much activity – a Club exclusively for the Japanese. This would be a Club in which learning and shopping would be of major concern, a Club which would move around, a Club whose purpose would be to get to know five countries in three days, with a duty free shop in the centre of the resort...

Mr Agnello knew that he was dreaming. Back in Paris, they would never allow him to modify Club Med's recipe for success, the pride of everyone in the organisation. And even if he were to be allowed, would he have 200,000 Japanese GMs in 10 years?

Exhibit 1 Composition of members by nationality

	1986/87	%	1987/88	%
EUROPE/AFRICA				
France	382,200	38.52%	391,100	35.88%
Italy	59,100	5.96%	76,800	7.05%
West Germany	57,400	5.79%	66,400	6.09%
Belgium	45,400	4.58%	53,300	4.89%
Israel	23,000	2.32%	33,500	3.07%
Switzerland	26,800	2.70%	29,700	2.73%
UK	14,600	1.47%	15,800	1.45%
other	44,600	4.50%	40,400	3.71%
sub total	653,100	65.82%	707,000	64.87%
SOUTH AMERICA				
sub total	26,000	2.62%	33,200	3.05%
NORTH AMERICA				
USA/Canada	215,700	21.74%	228,900	21.00%
other	16,800	1.69%	17,000	1.56%
sub total	232,500	23.43%	245,900	22.56%
ASIA/PACIFIC/INDIA				
Japan	25,100	2.53%	37,100	3.40%
Australia	21,200	2.14%	23,000	2.11%
other	34,300	3.46%	43,700	4.01%
sub total	80,600	8.12%	103,800	9.52%
TOTAL	992,200	100.00%	1,089,900	100.00%

Source: Club Med annual report

Exhibit 2   Growth of membership in Japan

1980/81	6,706	38%
1981/82	9,300	39%
1982/83	12,100	30%
1983/84	11,700	– 3%
1984/85	17,200	47%
1985/86	21,100	23%
1986/87	25,100	19%
1987/88	37,100	48%
1988/89	49,300	33%

Source: Club Med

Exhibit 3   Growth of Japanese tourists overseas

1964	128,000
1970	663,000
1974	2,336,000
1980	3,909,000
1984	4,659,000
1985	4,948,000
1986	5,516,000
1987	6,829,000
1988	8,430,000

Source: Ministry of Justice

Exhibit 4   Composition of Japanese overseas travellers by age,
by sex (1988)

1. Male   over 50   16.0%
2. Female   20s   15.9%
3. Male   40s   15.6%
4. Male   30s   15.2%
5. Male   20s   12.0%

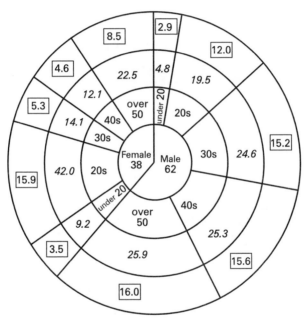

* Outer circle figures are percentages against total.
** Inner circle figures indicate percentages against total by sex.
Source: Ministry of Justice

Exhibit 5 What was done during overseas travel

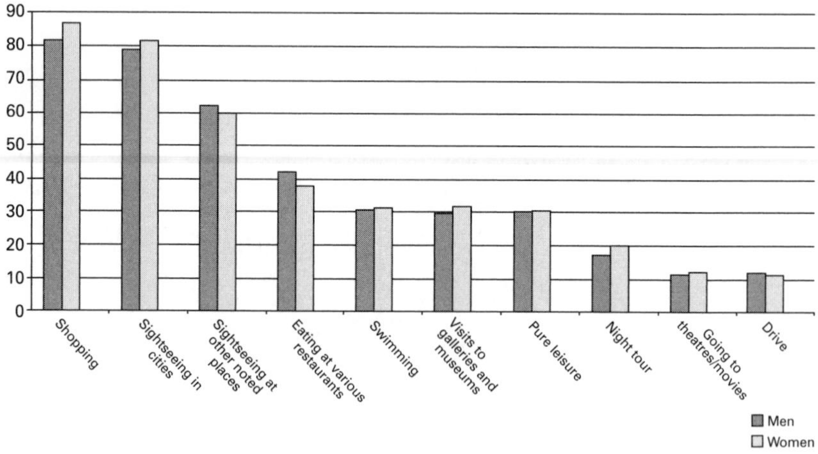
90
80
70
60
50
40
30
20
10
0
Shopping
Sightseeing in cities
Sightseeing at other noted places
Eating at various restaurants
Swimming
Visits to galleries and museums
Pure leisure
Night tour
Going to theatres/movies
Drive
Men
Women

Source: A survey by Mainichi Newspaper (on Japanese overseas air travellers)

Exhibit 6 Overseas travel one would like to make

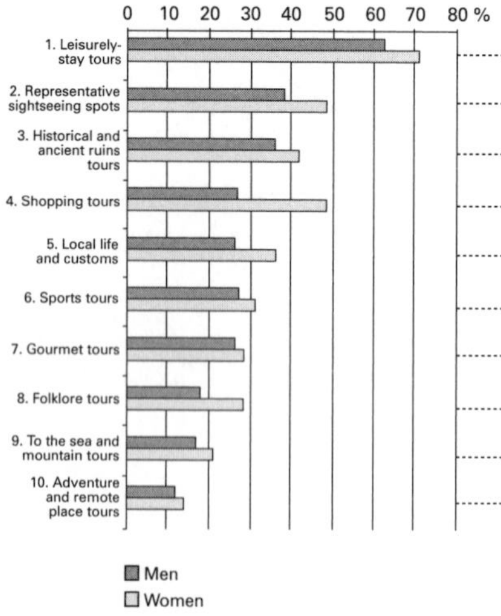
0 10 20 30 40 50 60 70 80 %
1. Leisurely-stay tours
2. Representative sightseeing spots
3. Historical and ancient ruins tours
4. Shopping tours
5. Local life and customs
6. Sports tours
7. Gourmet tours
8. Folklore tours
9. To the sea and mountain tours
10. Adventure and remote place tours
Men
Women

No. 1	No. 2	No. 3	No. 4	No. 5
Hawaii	Australia	USA, West coast	Switzerland	South Pacific Islands
Australia	France	Switzerland	England	W. Germany/ Italy
China	Greece	Italy	Spain	France
Hong Kong	Singapore	France	Hawaii	Italy
China	Australia	Spain	England	USA, West coast
Hawaii	Australia	Guam	Canada	South Pacific Islands
Hong Kong	France	Taiwan	China	Italy
France	Austria	Italy	West Germany	Spain
Hawaii	Switzerland	Australia	South Pacific Islands	Canada
Other Latin America	China	North Africa	East Africa	Brazil

Source: A survey by Mainichi Newspaper (on Japanese overseas air travellers) 1988

Exhibit 7   Number of Japanese overseas travellers by month

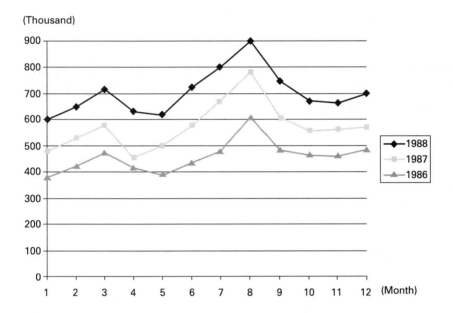

(Thousand)

Source: Ministry of Justice

Exhibit 8 Attitude towards work and leisure

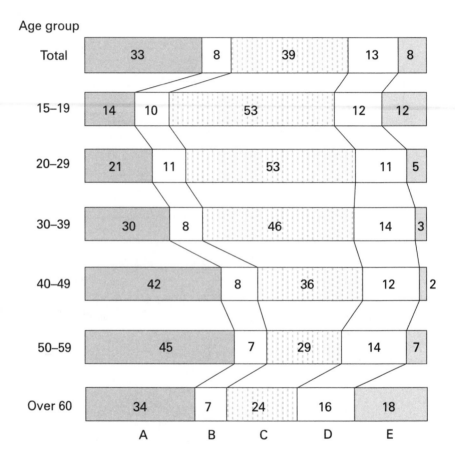

Age group

	A	B	C	D	E
Total	33	8	39	13	8
15–19	14	10	53	12	12
20–29	21	11	53	11	5
30–39	30	8	46	14	3
40–49	42	8	36	12	2
50–59	45	7	29	14	7
Over 60	34	7	24	16	18

Source: Prime Minister's Office, Public Relations Section, *Opinion Poll on Leisure Time and Travelling*, January 1986.

Exhibit 9   Breakdown of leisure hours by activity

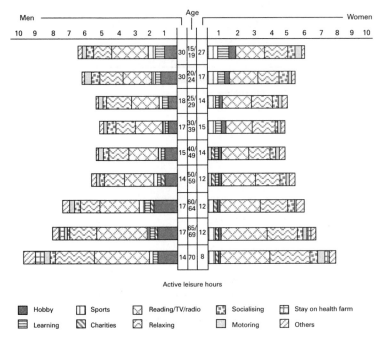

Active leisure hours

| | Hobby | | Sports | | Reading/TV/radio | | Socialising | | Stay on health farm |
| | Learning | | Charities | | Relaxing | | Motoring | | Others |

Source: Somucho, *Basic Survey on Social Life* (Interim report), October 1987.

Exhibit 10   Japanese members by segments

	1984/85	1987/88	Average stay
Honeymooners	72%	40%	7 days
OLs	16%	35%	4.5 days
Families	10%	15%	7 days
Corporate clients	0%	7%	2.5 days
Others	2%	3%	n.a.

Source: Club Méditerranée

Exhibit 11a   List of most well-known Japanese package tours*

LOOK	98.8%
JALPAK	97.5%
HOLIDAY TOURS	90.1%
CLUB MED	82.2%

* percentage of respondents who recognised
the brand name

Exhibit 11b   List of most popular Japanese package tours*

CLUB MED	62.9%
JALPAK	51.7%
LOOK	51.5%
HOLIDAY TOURS	25.5%

* respondents are asked to name three
package tours they would like to try

Source: A survey by AB Road Magazine

References

Ajzen, I. and Fishbein, M. (1980) *Understanding Attitude and Predicting Social Behavior*, Englewood Cliffs, NJ: Prentice-Hall.

Alatas, S.H. (1972) *Modernization and Social Change*, Sydney: Angus & Robertson.

Ariga, M., Yasue, M. and Wen, G.X. (1997) 'China's generation III – viable target segment and implications for marketing communications', *Marketing and Research Today*, February: 17–24.

Arunthanes, W., Tansuhaj, P. and Lemak, D.J. (1994) 'Cross-cultural business gift-giving', *International Marketing Review*, 11(4): 44–55.

Asia Letter Group (1991) *Insider's Guide to the Japanese Market*, Hong Kong: Asia Letter Group.

Asia Times (1996) 'All of a sudden the customer is king in South Korea', 19 September: 1–2.

Asia Travel Trade (1989) 'Here come the Koreans', July/August: 38–9.

Asian Business (1990) 'The impending tourist tide', February: 56–8.

Asian Business (1992) 'Tricks of the Japan trade', February: 20.

Asian Business (1996) 'Shopping till they drop', May: 14.

Asian Wall Street Journal (1994) 'Japanese shopper power', 10 August: 6.

Asian Wall Street Journal (1995) 'Japan's consumers want a new deal', 28 March, Japan advertising supplement.

Asian Wall Street Journal (1995) 'Market shifts, study finds', 27 April: 1.

Asian Wall Street Journal (1996) 'Teens may be linked by malls, TV, and Nike, but they're far apart on hopes and values', 24 June: 21.

Asian Wall Street Journal (1996) 'Cracking the market: Korean consumers snap up previously shunned imports', 12 September: 1.

Asian Wall Street Journal (1996) 'Custom-made', 30 September: 24.

Asian Wall Street Journal (1996) 'For the price of a designer bag, Japanese school-girls offer sex', 2 October: 1.

Asiaweek (1993) 'A controversial gamble', 10 February: 25.

Asiaweek (1993) 'It's only rock'n'roll', 28 April: 34–8.

Asiaweek (1993) 'Coping with kids', 8 September: 36–9.

Asiaweek (1993) 'To drink or not to drink', 20 October: 30.

Asiaweek (1994) 'The rich way to pedal', 30 June: 33.

Asiaweek (1995) 'Camping with a difference', 15 September: 42.

Asiaweek (1995) 'A TV extravaganza', 20 October: 32.

Asiaweek (1995) 'Getting serious about fun', 10 November: 37.

Asiaweek (1995) 'Little emperors', 1 December: 44–50.

Asiaweek (1997) 'Billion dollar ideas', 10 January: 41.

Asiaweek (1997) 'In a cold sweat', 24 January: 36.

Baiyi, X. (1992) 'Reaching the Chinese consumer', *China Business Review*, 19(6): 36–42.

Banks, R. (1997) 'Is Asia different? Defining a strategy to serve multi-national clients in the region', *Marketing and Research Today*, February: 4–11.

Baron, R.A. and Byrne, D. (1987) *Social Psychology: Understanding Human Interaction*, 5th edn, Boston: Allyn & Bacon.

Beijing Review (1993) 'Local versus foreign food', March: 15–21.

Biel, A.L. and Bridgwater, C.A. (1990) 'Attributes of likeable television commercials', *Journal of Advertising Research*, **30**(3): 38–44.

Bond, M.H. (1991) *Beyond the Chinese Face*, Oxford: Oxford University Press.

Brown, D.L. (1996) 'The changing Japanese consumer: new attitudes, purchasing habits on quality, value, and imports', *East Asian Executive Reports*, **18**(5): 8–16.

Brunner, J.A., Chen, J., Sun, C. and Zhou, N. (1989) 'The role of *guanxi* in negotiations in the Pacific Basin', *Journal of Global Marketing*, **3**(2): 7–23.

Business Asia (1996) 'More than a scoop', 23 September: 12.

Business Asia (1997) 'Market research in Asia', 16 June: 5–6.

Business Beijing (1996) 'Kids hold important vote in family spending decision', November: 42–4.

Business Week (1993) 'They've got their feet in the door', 31 May: 20.

Cavusgil, S.T. and Das, A. (1997) 'Methodological issues in empirical cross-cultural research: a survey of the management literature and a framework', *Management International Review*, **37**(1): 71–96.

Chai, J.C.H. (1992) 'Consumption and living standards in China', *China Quarterly*: 721–49.

Chan, K.K.W. (1996) 'Chinese viewers' perception of informative and emotional advertising', *International Journal of Advertising*, **15**(2): 152–66.

Clammer, J. (1995) *Difference and Modernity*, New York: Kegan Paul.

Creighton, M.R. 'The Depato: merchandising the West while selling Japaneseness'. In Tobin, J.J. (1992) *Re-made in Japan*, New Haven, CT: Yale University Press, pp. 42–57.

De Mente, B. Lafayette (1993) *Behind the Japanese Bow*, Chicago: NTC Publishing Group.

Dong, W. (1993) 'Generational differences and political development in South Korea', *Korea Studies*, **17**: 1–16.

Economist (1993) 'For God and growth in Malaysia', 27 November: 67.

Economist (1994) 'Fings ain't wot they used to be', 18 May: 59–62.

Economist (1997) 'Window shopping in Shanghai', 25 January: 71.

Economist (1997) 'Who's top?', 29 March: 21–5.

Far Eastern Economic Review (1990) 'Asian affluents': 82.

Far Eastern Economic Review (1993) 'A losing gamble', 2 December: 28.

Far Eastern Economic Review (1994) 'Asia lifestyles', 11 August: 35–47.

Far Eastern Economic Review (1994) 'Snobs like us', 27 October: 80.

Far Eastern Economic Review (1994) 'The hard sell', 24 November: 101.

Far Eastern Economic Review (1994) 'Tee masters', 29 December: 80–2.

Far Eastern Economic Review (1996) 'Chanel surfing in Tokyo', 11 January: 80.

Far Eastern Economic Review (1996) 'Between God and Mammon', 9 May: 58–60.

Far Eastern Economic Review (1996) 'High and dry: Asahi's deft moves win over Japan's beer drinkers', 3 October: 98–9.

Far Eastern Economic Review (1996) 'Rock solid', 5 December: 50–2.

Far Eastern Economic Review (1996) 'Children of plenty', 5 December: 54–5.

Far Eastern Economic Review (1997) 'Hot-seat experience', 31 July: 17–20.

Fields, G. (1983) *From Bonsai to Levi's*, New York: Macmillan.

Financial Times (1997) 'The price is right in Japan', 4 February: 1.

Financial Times (1997) 'The very model of a modern Moslem state', 26–27 April: 10.

Fishbein, M. (1967) 'Attitude and the prediction of behavior'. In Fishbein, M. (ed.) *Readings in Attitude Theory and Measurement*, New York: John Wiley, pp. 477–92.

Foa, V. and Foa, E. (1974) *Societal Structures of the Mind*, Springfield, IL: Charles C. Thomas.

Focus Japan (1994) 'Interbrand – it's all in the name', May: 7.

Forbes (1993) 'Sweet Chinese sirens', 20 December: 78–9.

Forestier, K. (1994) 'Researchers pick the consumer mind', *China Business Review*, 4 August: 3.

Fortune (1994) 'TV is exploding all over Asia', 10 January: 24–8.

Guillaume, A. (1956) *Islam*, London: Penguin.

Hall, E. (1976) *The Hidden Dimension*, New York: Anchor Press-Doubleday.

Hendry, J. (1990) 'Lovely gifts… beautifully wrapped', *Japan Digest*, **1**(1): 13.

Ho, S.C. and Sin, Y.M. (1986) 'Comparative advertising in Hong Kong: issues and problems', *Hong Kong Journal of Business Management*, **4**: 71–88.

Hofstede, G. (1984) 'Cultural dimensions in management and planning', *Asia Pacific Journal of Management*, **1**(2): 81–99.

Hofstede, G. (1984) *Culture's Consequences: International Differences in Work-related Values*, Beverly Hills, CA: Sage.

Hofstede, G. (1991) *Cultures and Organizations*, London: McGraw-Hill.

Hong, J. (1994) 'The resurrection of advertising in China', *Asian Survey*, **34**(4): 326–42.

Hotaka, K. (1997) 'The two consumers: what's happening to Japanese marketing in the 90s?', *Journal of Japanese Trade and Industry*, **16**(1): 12–17.

Hsu, F.L.K. (1971) 'Psychosocial homeostasis and *jen*: conceptual tools for advancing psychological anthropology', *American Anthropologist*, **73**: 23–44.

Huang, J. and Jaw, Y.L. (1991) 'Consumer marketing in Taiwan: changing environment and implication', *Singapore Marketing Review*, **5**: 53–63.

Huntington, S. (1996) 'The West: unique, not universal', *Foreign Affairs*, **75**(6): 28–46.

Hwang, K.H. (1987) 'Face and favor: the Chinese power game', *American Journal of Sociology*, **92**(4): 944–74.

International Herald Tribune (1995) 'To buy an antiseptic pen in Japan, launder the money', 28 July: 10.

International Herald Tribune (1996) 'Karaoke goes higher tech', 13 March: 2.

International Herald Tribune (1997) 'A demanding toy chicken takes over Japan', 25–26 January: 13.

International Management (1987) 'Crazy for European luxury', December: 24–8.

Jarvie, I.C. and Agassi, J. (1969) *Hong Kong: A Society in Transition*, London: Routledge & Kegan Paul.

Johansson, J.K. (1986) 'Japanese consumers: what foreign marketers should know', *International Marketing Review*, **3**(2): 37–43.

Johansson, J.K. (1989) 'Determinants and effects of the use of "made in" labels', *International Marketing Review* (UK), **6**(1): 47–58.

Johansson, J.K. and Nonaka, I. (1996) *Relentless: The Japanese Way of Marketing*, New York: Harper Business.

Johns, A.H. (1984) 'Islam in the Malay world', in Israeli, R. and Johns, A.H. (eds) *Islam in Asia:* Vol. II: *Southeast and East Asia*, Jerusalem: Magnes Press, pp. 115–61.

Johnson, F.A. (1993) *Dependency and Japanese Socialization*, New York: New York University Press.

Jones, K. and Ohbora, T. (1990) 'Managing the heretical company', *The McKinsey Quarterly*, **3**: 20–45.

Katz, D. (1960) 'The functional approach to the study of attitudes', *Public Opinion Quarterly*, **24**: 163–204.

Kaufman, C. and Lane, P. (1992) 'Crisscrossing the cultural time gap', *Cultural Dimensions of International Marketing*, **1**: 30–49.

Kindel, T.I. (1983) 'A partial theory of Chinese consumer behavior: marketing strategy implications', *Hong Kong Journal of Business Management*, **1**: 93–109.

Kipling, R. (1981) 'The man who was', in *Life's Handicap*. First pub. 1891, now a Penguin classic.

Kotler, P. (1994) *Marketing Management*, 8th edn, Englewood Cliffs, NJ: Prentice-Hall.

Kotler, P. and Armstrong, G. (1996) *Principles of Marketing*, 7th edn, Englewood Cliffs, NJ: Prentice-Hall.

Kotler, P., Ang, S.H., Leong, S.M. and Tan, C.T. (1996) *Marketing Management: An Asian Perspective*, Singapore: Prentice-Hall.

Kroeber, A.L. and Parsons, T. (1958) 'The concept of culture and social system', *American Sociological Review*, **23**: 582–3.

Kushner, J.M. (1982), 'Market research in a non-Western context: the Asian example', *Journal of Market Research Society*, **24**(2): 116–22.

Lai, T.C. (1960) *Selected Chinese Sayings*, Hong Kong: Wing Tai Cheung.

Laidler, N. and Quelch, J.A. (1993) *Mary Kay Cosmetics: Asian Market Entry*, Boston: Harvard Business School.

Lasserre, P. and Courbon, P. (1994) 'Carrefour in Asia (A)', Fontainebleau: INSEAD-EAC.

Lasserre, P. and Schütte, H. (1995) *Strategies for Asia Pacific*, Basingstoke: Macmillan.

Lebra, T.S. (1976) *Japanese Patterns of Behavior*, Honolulu: University of Hawaii Press.

Lee, C. (1990) 'Modifying an American consumer behavior model for consumers in Confucian culture: the case of Fishbein behavioral intention model', *Journal of International Consumer Marketing*, **3**(1): 27–50.

Lee, C. and Green, R.T. (1991) 'Cross-cultural examination of the Fishbein behavioural intentions model', *Journal of International Business Studies*, **22**(2): 289–305.

Levy, G.R. (1996) *Consumer Marketing in China: Chasing Billions, Catching Millions*, Hong Kong: Economist Intelligence Unit.

Lin, C.A. (1993) 'Cultural differences in message strategies: a comparison between American and Japanese TV commercials', *Journal of Advertising Research*, **33**(4): 40–8.

Linton, R. (1945) *The Cultural Background of Personality*, New York: Appleton-Century-Crofts.

McCracken, G. (1986) 'Culture and consumption: a theoretical account of the structure and movement of the cultural meaning of consumer goods', *Journal of Consumer Research*, **13**(1): 71–84.

McDonald, G.M. and Roberts, C.J. (1990) 'The brand-naming enigma in the Asia-Pacific context', *European Journal of Marketing*, **24**(8): 6–19.

Malayang, V. (1988) 'The distribution industry in Asian NIEs and ASEAN countries and the effects of the entry of Japanese retailers', *Management Japan*, **21**(2): 15–28.

Malhotra, N.K., Agarwal, J. and Peterson, M. (1996) 'Methodological issues in cross-cultural marketing research', *International Marketing Review*, **13**(5): 7–43.

Manrai, L. and Manrai, A. (1995) 'Effects of cultural context, gender, and acculturation on perception of work versus social/leisure time usage', *Journal of Business Research*, **32**(2): 115–28.

Markin, J. Jr (1974) *Consumer Behaviour: A Cognitive Orientation*, New York: Macmillan.

Maslow, A.H. (1970) *Motivation and Personality*, 3rd edn, New York: Harper & Row.

Mueller, B. (1987) 'Reflections of culture: an analysis of Japanese and American advertising appeals', *Journal of Advertising Research*, **27**(3): 51–9.

Mutalib, H. (1990) 'Islamic revivalism in ASEAN states', *Asian Survey*, **30**(9): 877–91.

Nakane, C. (1970) *Japanese Society*, Berkeley: University of California Press.

Naumann, E., Jackson, D.W. Jr and Wolfe, W.G. (1994) 'Examining the practices of United States and Japanese market research firms', *California Management Review*, Summer: 49–69.

New York Times (1995) 'China's known brands are most often Japanese', 16 February: 6.

Nishina, S. (1990) 'Japanese consumers: introducing foreign products/brands into the Japanese market', *Journal of Advertising Research*, **30**(2): 35–45.

NLI Research (1994) 'Families in Japan's company-centered society: survey of salarymen and families', **72**: 3–31.

Onkvisit, S. and Shaw, J. (1985) 'A view of marketing and advertising practices in Asia and its meaning for marketing managers', *Journal of Consumer Marketing*, **2**(2): 5–17.

Overmyer, D. (1986) *Religions of China*, New York: Harper & Row.

Palia, A. and Keown, C. (1983) 'Combatting parallel importing: views of US exporters to the Asian countries', *Industrial Marketing Management*, **12**: 113–23.

Passin, H. (1977) *Japanese and the Japanese*, Tokyo: Kinsheido.

Probert, J. and Lasserre, P. (1997) *The Asian Business Context: A Follow-up Survey*, Euro-Asian Centre Research Series No. 44, Fontainebleau: INSEAD-EAC.

Psychology Today (1976) 'How cultures collide', July: 66–74.

Reader, I. (1991) *Religion in Contemporary Japan*, Honolulu: University of Hawaii Press.

Redding, S.G. (1982) 'Cultural effects on the marketing process in Southeast Asia', *Journal of the Market Research Society*, **24**(2): 98–114.

Restall, C. and Gordon, W. (1993) 'Brands – the missing link; understanding the emotional relationship', *Marketing and Research Today*, **21**(2): 59–67.

Roberto, E.L. (1987) *Applied Marketing Research*, Manila: Ateneo de Manila University Press.

Robinson, C. (1996) 'Asian culture: the marketing consequences', *Journal of the Marketing Society*, **38**(1): 55–62.

Rogers, E.M. (1962) *Diffusion of Innovations*, New York: Free Press.

Rook, D.W. (1987) 'The buying impulse,' *Journal of Consumer Research*, **14**(2):189–99.

Sakaiya, T. (1993) *What is Japan?*, Tokyo: Kodansha.

Scarry, J. (1996) 'Putting children first', *China Business Review*, May–June: 30–5.

Schiffman, L.G. and Kanuk, L.L. (1994) *Consumer Behavior*, 5th edn, Englewood Cliffs, NJ: Prentice-Hall.

Schmitt, B. (1997) 'Who is the Chinese consumer? Segmentation in the People's Republic of China', *European Management Journal*, **15**(2): 191–4.

Schmitt, B.H. and Pan, Y. (1994) 'Managing corporate and brand identities in the Asia-Pacific region', *California Management Review*, **36**(4): 32–48.

Schütte, H. (1974) *Marketing in Indonesia*, Jakarta: Intermasa Publishing.

Schütte, H. (1993) *Competing and Cooperating with Japanese Firms*, Working Paper No. 21, Fontainebleau: INSEAD-EAC.

Schütte, H. and Ching, P. (1996) 'Consumer Behaviour in China – an Exploratory Study', Working Paper No. 38, Fontainebleau: INSEAD-EAC.

Schütte, H. and Ishida, E. (1990) 'Club Med Japan', Fontainebleau: INSEAD-EAC.

Schütte, H. and Probert, J. (1996) 'Cartier Japan', Fontainebleau: INSEAD-EAC.

Schütte, H. and Probert, J. (1997) 'Goal! Japan Scores in Soccer', Fontainebleau: INSEAD-EAC.

Seguela, J. (1994) *Pub Story: l'Histoire Mondiale de la Publicité en 65 Campagnes*, Paris: Hoebeke.

Shaw, S.M. and Woetzel, J.R. (1992) 'A fresh look at China', *McKinsey Quarterly* (3): 37–51.

Sherry, J.F. and Camargo, E.G. (1987) 'May your life be marvellous: English language labelling and the semiotics of Japanese promotion', *Journal of Consumer Research*, **14**(2): 174–88.

Sheth, J.N., and Sethi, S.P. (1977) 'A theory of cross-cultural buyer behaviour', in Woodise, A.G., Sheth, J.N. and Bennett, P.D. (eds) *Consumer and Industrial Buyer Behaviour*, New York: North-Holland.

Shultz, C.J., Pecotich, A. and Le, K. (1994) 'Changes in marketing activity and consumption in the Socialist Republic of Vietnam', *Research in Consumer Behavior: Consumption in Marketizing Economies*, Vol. 7, Greenwich, CT: JAI Press, pp. 225–57.

Simon, H. and Kucher, E. (1992) 'The European pricing bomb: and how to cope with it', *European Mangement Journal*, **10**(2): 136–44.

Solomon, M.R. (1996) *Consumer Behavior*, Englewood Cliffs, NJ: Prentice-Hall.

SRG News (1992) 'Women rise to the top', January: 1.

Steele, H.C. (1990) 'Marketing research in China: The Hong Kong connection', *Marketing and Research Today*, August: 155–65.

Tai, S.H.C. and Tam, J.L.M. (1996) 'A comparative study of Chinese consumers in Asian markets – a lifestyle analysis', *Journal of International Consumer Marketing*, **9**(1): 25–42.

Tan, C.H. (1991) 'Marketing in China: special emphasis on advertising', *Singapore Marketing Review*, **5**: 64–74.

Tobin, J.J. (1992) *Re-made in Japan*, New Haven, CT: Yale University Press.

Tokyo Business (1994) 'Improving your business in Korea', February: 38–41.

Tominaga, K. (1996) 'The spirit of capitalism: West vs. East – the immaturity of modernization in Asia', paper presented at the International Symposium 'Community and Values in Asia and Western Society', Tokyo: International House.

Tradescope (1997) 'Third brandname boom coming?', **17**(3): 12–13.

Trompenaars, F. (1993) *Riding the Waves of Culture*, London: Economist Books.

Tseng, C.S. (1996) 'Marketing in China: relevance of the Western model', unpublished paper, Fontainebleau: INSEAD.

Unger, L. and Kernan, J. (1983) 'On the meaning of leisure: an investigation of some determinants of the subjective experience', *Journal of Consumer Research*, **9**(4): 381–91.

Usunier, J. (1996) *Marketing Across Cultures*, Hertfordshire: Prentice-Hall.

Van Raaij, W.F. (1978) 'Cross-cultural methodology as a case of construct validity'. In Hunt, M.K. (ed.) *Advances in Consumer Research,* V, Ann Arbor: Association for Consumer Research.

Watsuji, T. (1961) *Climate and Culture: A Philosophical Study*, Tokyo: Hokuseido Press.

Woodise, A.G., Sheth, J.N. and Bennett, P.D. (eds) *Consumer and Industrial Buyer Behaviour*, New York: North Holland.

Yan, R. (1994) 'To reach China consumers, adapt to *guo qing*', *Harvard Business Review*, **72**(5): 66–74.

Yang, C.F., Ho, S.C. and Yau, O.H.M. (1989) 'A conception of Chinese consumer behavior', in Yang, C.F., Ho, S.C. and Yau, O.H.M. (eds) *Hong Kong Marketing Management: A Case Analysis Approach*, Hong Kong: Commercial Press, pp. 317–42.

Yang, K.S. (1986) *The Psychology of the Chinese People*, Hong Kong: Oxford University Press.

Yang, L.S. (1957) 'The concept of *pao* as a basis for relations in China', in Fairbank, J.K. (ed.) *Chinese Thought and Institutions*, Chicago: University of Chicago Press, pp. 291–309.

Yau, O.H.M. (1988) 'Chinese cultural values: their dimensions and marketing applications', *European Journal of Marketing*, **22**(5): 44–57.

Yau, O.H.M. (1994) *Consumer Behaviour in China*, London: Routledge.

Zakaria, F. (1994) 'Culture is destiny: a conversation with Lee Kuan Yew', *Foreign Affairs*, **73**(2): 109–26.

Zhang, Y. and Neelankavil, J.P. (1997) 'The influence of culture on advertising effectiveness in China and the USA', *European Journal of Marketing*, **31**(2): 134–49.

Zimmerman, M. (1985) *Dealing with the Japanese*, London: George Allen & Unwin.

Name index

Subject index